MUHAMMAD ALI

Muhammad Ali was not only a champion athlete, but a cultural icon. While his skill as a boxer made him famous, his strong personality and his identity as a black man in a country in the midst of the struggle for civil rights made him an enduring symbol. From his youth in segregated Louisville, Kentucky, to his victory in the 1960 Olympics, to the controversy that surrounded his conversion to Islam and refusal of the draft during the Vietnam War, Ali's life was closely linked to the major social and political struggles of the 1960s and 1970s. The story of his struggles, failures, and triumphs sheds light on issues of race, class, religion, dissent, and the role of sports in American society that affected all Americans.

In this lively, concise biography, Barbara L. Tischler introduces students to Ali's life in social and political context, and explores his enduring significance as a symbol of resistance. *Muhammad Ali: A Man of Many Voices* offers the perfect introduction to this extraordinary American and his times.

Barbara L. Tischler is the Head of the Speyer Legacy School in New York City.

ROUTLEDGE HISTORICAL AMERICANS

SERIES EDITOR: PAUL FINKELMAN

Routledge Historical Americans is a series of short, vibrant biographies that illuminate the lives of Americans who have had an impact on the world. Each book includes a short overview of the person's life and puts that person into historical context through essential primary documents, written both by the subjects and about them. A series website supports the books, containing extra images and documents, links to further research, and where possible, multi-media sources on the subjects. Perfect for including in any course on American History, the books in the Routledge Historical Americans series show the impact everyday people can have on the course of history.

Woody Guthrie: Writing America's Songs
Ronald D. Cohen

Frederick Douglass: Reformer and Statesman
L. Diane Barnes

Thurgood Marshall: Race, Rights, and the Struggle for a More Perfect Union
Charles L. Zelden

Harry S. Truman: The Coming of the Cold War
Nicole L. Anslover

John Winthrop: Founding the City upon a Hill
Michael Parker

John F. Kennedy: The Spirit of Cold War Liberalism
Jason K. Duncan

Bill Clinton: Building a Bridge to the New Millennium
David H. Bennett

Ronald Reagan: Champion of Conservative America
James H. Broussard

Laura Ingalls Wilder: American Writer on the Prairie
Sallie Ketcham

Benjamin Franklin: American Founder, Atlantic Citizen
Nathan R. Kozuskanich

Brigham Young: Sovereign in America
David Vaughn Mason

MUHAMMAD ALI
A MAN OF MANY VOICES

BARBARA L. TISCHLER

Routledge
Taylor & Francis Group

NEW YORK AND LONDON

http://www.routledge.com/cw/historicalamericans

First published 2016
by Routledge
711 Third Avenue, New York, NY 10017

And by Routledge
2 Park Square, Milton Park, Abingdon, Oxon OX14 4RN

Routledge is an imprint of the Taylor & Francis Group, an informa business

© 2016 Taylor & Francis

Library of Congress Cataloging-in-Publication Data
A catalog record for this book has been requested.

ISBN: 978-1-138-02305-5 (hbk)
ISBN: 978-1-138-02306-2 (pbk)
ISBN: 978-1-315-77668-2 (ebk)

Typeset in Minion and Scala Sans
by Apex CoVantage, LLC

Printed and bound in the United States of America by Publishers Graphics, LLC on sustainably sourced paper.

CONTENTS

ACKNOWLEDGMENTS

Writing is a solitary craft, whether on a strict schedule or in the occasional "spare" moments of one's life. But creating a book is a decidedly collaborative effort, and I am indebted to a number of people who helped to bring *Muhammad Ali: A Man of Many Voices* to fruition.

Series editor Professor Paul Finkelman first suggested this project in the fall of 2012. Although it took me another six months to think that I could actually write this book and another eighteen months after that to meet the goal of producing an acceptable manuscript, Paul was encouraging, helpfully critical, and energetic in his engagement with my ideas. I am grateful for the enthusiasm with which he approached my work. Professor Ellen Schrecker read the manuscript and provided valuable advice about the political context of the 1950s and 1960s as well as comments on how this book could be useful to students. Genevieve Aoki and the production staff at Taylor & Francis helped to turn a manuscript into a book. Genevieve's guidance throughout the project was especially helpful. Kyler Culver, the librarian and New York's Buckley School provided insight into the workings of a variety of data bases that helped advance my research.

My best critics are the members of my family. In conversations, few propositions are accepted without question. As a result, an idea becomes more nuanced and interesting. My sons, Ben and Dan, read early drafts and helped me to clarify and intensify my portrayal of the Greatest of All Time. Steve Tischler, the greatest editor ever and love of my life, read the book as much as I did and freely offered his expertise on the importance of sports to the American story. We did not always agree, but we laughed a lot, and the book is better for his love and care for me and the project.

Introduction Muhammad Ali's Many Voices

This book was written for students who wish to learn more about a great athlete and his impact on his sport and his country. The name "Muhammad Ali" is recognized throughout the world, and it's important to present aspects of his life that continue to make him an object of conversation and controversy. The literature on the Greatest of All Time is extensive, ranging from fight reports and blogs to creative essays on the meaning of Ali in American society and analyses of Ali's rhetoric of peace in the violent context of both boxing and war. He has been characterized as an upstart, a champion, a religious fanatic, a traitor, a washed-up heavyweight, a survivor, and a humanitarian. At various times in his life, Ali has spoken in a language and a style that revealed his commitment to his identity of that moment. In each instance, his voice has informed us about life as a young black man with ambition beyond anyone else's comprehension; as a winner in the ring who spoke his mind about his accomplishments; a member of the reviled and feared Nation of Islam; a conscientious objector who was willing to risk jail and the loss of income for his convictions; a former champion who could not bring himself to leave the ring; a man living with the symptoms of a debilitating disease; and a man who found ways to use his celebrity to help others. Muhammad Ali remains a champion and a man of many voices.

Throughout his life and career, Muhammad Ali, who was born Cassius Marcellus Clay, Jr., has spoken in many voices, each of which has revealed his character at different points in his life—a young fighter who was tough in the ring but was afraid of air travel; a brash new heavyweight champion ready to take on all challengers and critics; a Muslim; a draft resister; and the elder statesman of boxing. Ali will be remembered for stunning victories and painful defeats in the ring; vilification and vindication for his stand against the Vietnam War; and mockery and eventual acceptance of his religious conversion and the change of his name.

At each stage of his career, Ali was largely responsible for his image, and the Louisville Lip will likely be remembered as much for his outlandish claims, his terrible poetry, and his predictions of victory that frequently came true, as for his prowess in the ring that in many ways transformed the sport. The claims of the skinny kid from Louisville with the oversized name that he would one day be the heavyweight champion of the world were easy to ignore at the time because they seemed so outlandish. But he made that dream a reality and made himself impossible to ignore. Joyce Carol Oates called Ali an "image bearer for an age,"[1] describing the champ in the 1970s as a symbol of transition in America. Boxing changed partly as a result of his unconventional style. At the same time, many Americans came to challenge the wisdom of the traditional civil rights movement and the Cold War imperatives of fighting an unwinnable war in Vietnam. Muhammad Ali raised his voice in ways that previous fighters had never done. He spoke in the voices of his time, starting from his appearance at the Rome Olympics in 1960 to his work as a humanitarian in the twenty-first century.

Muhammad Ali was a unique presence in the ring. Men have engaged in hand-to-hand combat for the entertainment of audiences since the contests of ancient Greece and Rome. Like the ancient fighters, today's boxers frequently come from the ranks of society's poorest and least educated people. Modern boxing matches are fought for money, which gives the fighters a degree of social status derived from hefty purses, but historically these men have not been respected. Rather, they have been regarded merely as a source of entertainment for paying customers. In the twentieth century, the black boxer was particularly reviled outside the ring, no matter what his pugilistic accomplishments. Jack Johnson, nicknamed the "Galveston Giant," was the first African-American heavyweight champion. Nevertheless, he faced the racial discrimination so common in his time, and he was even charged with violating the Mann Act (a federal statute against transporting women across state lines for immoral purposes) because he consorted with white women. Johnson violated social taboos and suffered the consequences.

Other black boxers in the twentieth century achieved success because they conformed to the stereotype of the humble, self-effacing athlete/entertainer. Joe Louis, known for being "slow of foot but redeemingly fast of hands," presented to the world as "the plain, simple, unobtrusive Brown Bomber . . . with his crushing left jab and hook." Louis was regarded as "probably the best heavyweight fighter of all time." His defeat of Max Schmeling, the darling of Adolf Hitler, in 1938 (a year after losing to Schmeling in Yankee Stadium) further endeared Louis to the American people. Part of Louis's appeal stemmed from his demeanor outside the ring. During his long reign as heavyweight champion from 1937 to 1949, Louis was regarded as clean and honest, helping to elevate boxing from its reputation as a haven for gamblers, members of organized crime, and men of considerable ill-repute. The champ dedicated his life in and outside the ring to fulfilling the wishes of others. He was a champion and he was also the archetype of the patriotic black American. Louis served as a sergeant in the United States Army during World War II, traveling more than 21,000 miles to perform ninety-six exhibition matches for two million members of the military in the European theater of war.[2] Louis burnished his image when he declared that the United States would win World War II "because we're on God's side." A few writers referred to Louis as an "Uncle Tom," but sportswriter Jimmy Cannon expressed a more mainstream view, writing that Louis was "a credit to his race — the human race."[3]

The image of heavyweight champion Charles "Sonny" Liston was the antithesis of the accommodating, polite young black man. He was a criminal who had been arrested no fewer than nineteen times and who served time for armed robbery. His ties to organized crime figures who had the power to control the outcome of his fights were described by ESPN writer Mike Puma: "In 1952, after serving two years in prison, he was paroled to a team of boxing handlers with ties to John Vitale, a St. Louis underworld figure. Six years later, Frankie Carbo and Blinky Palermo, top Mafia figures in the Northeast, became the majority owner of Liston's contract."[4] Carbo later faced charges of conspiracy and promoting unlicensed fights. Under the aegis of the Carbo/Palermo partnership, Liston fought twelve times. In 1960, Liston, the convicted felon and illiterate boxer, offered testimony to a Senate subcommittee that was investigating the relationship of the criminal underworld to boxing.

Sonny Liston fulfilled some of the negative stereotypes of black boxers in the 1950s and early 1960s. He was barely articulate, a brute in the ring, and not the nicest person in the sport. His life and even his death confirmed the worst impressions of black men who made their living punching each other for the entertainment of audiences eager to see blood.

In contrast, Ali was a boxer who seemed to have opinions about everything and who was able to make those opinions matter beyond the ring. Like Johnson and Liston, Ali was the heavyweight champion at a time when the title carried great prestige and status in the sports world. But Ali transcended the traditional image of the boxer as a brutish slugger to speak in his own voice that made an impression on reporters, other athletes, and the world at large. And, unlike champions before him, he asserted control over his voice and his career.

Muhammad Ali was truly different from the heavyweight champions who preceded him. He was his own man whose image changed with the times and his circumstances. He was a natural entertainer who strove throughout his career to have a measure of control over his life. His various personalities, presented to a public eager to hear what outrageous thing he would say next or what feat of speed and dexterity in the ring he would perform, marked him as a free spirit not common in the world of boxing. Over a long career, he spoke with many voices, each of which was uniquely his.

The life and career of Muhammad Ali represents a turning point in boxing, a point after which the sport was more exciting and in which the hero in the ring earned a larger purse. In the wake of Ali's long-shot victory over heavyweight champion Sonny Liston, baseball star Jackie Robinson praised the young challenger who had clearly impressed him as more than a boxer. Writing in *The Amsterdam News*, Robinson first acknowledged that the new champ had "exploded the myth" of Sonny Liston. Then he exhorted readers to:

> Say all you will about Cassius and his great flow of language, his towering ego, his unorthodox manner of projecting himself. You must still admit that he put the deeds behind the words and came through victorious. Clay did more than win. He achieved the feat of out-smarting a man who had not only captured the title, but who had built a tremendous reputation for being able to scare his opponents almost literally, to death.

Robinson recognized Ali's contribution beyond the ring, even as early as 1964: "Despite the loudness—and sometimes crudeness—of Clay, he has brought excitement back to boxing."[5] To many, Ali was a clown, a braggart, and a fraud who talked too much, said too much, and danced around the ring rather than facing his opponents with a heavy hand. Sports writers dismissed his skill, crediting his victories to luck and his pre-and post-fight rants to immaturity or even mental deficiency. And many dismissed his religious conversion as implausible, or certainly as evidence that he had been duped by a dangerous black separatist cult. But there was a method to Ali's apparent madness, as, from the very beginning of his career, he made his reputation with words as well as punches. Ali understood the racial and class implications of his clowning persona. He has been quoted in many places as having wondered:

> Where do you think I'd be next week if I didn't know how to shout and holler and make the public take notice? I'd be poor and I'd probably be down in my home town saying "yes suh" and "nu suh" and knowing my place. Instead, I'm one of the highest paid athletes in the world. Think about that. A southern colored has made one million dollars.[6]

Ali's self-awareness and his ability to succeed in the business of boxing as well as in the ring helped to challenge the image of black athletes as having few positive attributes except for a "naturally" superior talent on the field or in the ring.

Unlike some of his predecessors in the ring who were exploited financially and ended their lives in poverty, Muhammad Ali understood that his talent could yield long-term financial benefits. He knew that he fought for money and that audiences would pay a premium to see him fight. That many would pay to see him lose early in his career gave him all the more satisfaction because he rarely lost—he won the battles that others doubted he would even survive. He changed the image of the heavyweight boxer from that of a Joe Louis-style master of the single knockout punch to a jive-talking master of the rope-a-dope who could wear out his opponent by keeping him busy trying to catch up with a faster and more energetic foe.

Ali's words were a powerful influence on others. Musician B.B. King recalled his own reaction to Ali's stand against the Vietnam War: "By [Ali] standing up as he did, it gave many of us much more courage than we had; it gave us much more hope than we ever had before."[7] At about the same time, when Ali was under suspension by boxing authorities and unable to earn a living as a fighter, he became an idol on some college campuses and in the broader civil rights community. According to Congress Member John Lewis, who was then the chair of the Student Non-Violent Coordinating Committee (SNCC), Ali's assertion that "No Vietnamese ever called me a Nigger" was a source of inspiration for members of the movement who faced violence every day in many regions of the United States and were very aware of the connection between the battles they fought for rights and dignity at home and the struggle of the Vietnamese people of color for independence from American influence.[8]

The champ's decision to resist the draft and to speak out against the war in Vietnam continues to draw criticism. Today, Ali speaks quietly, if at all, but his words from the past can still spark passionate debate. In November of 2005, Ali joined singer Aretha Franklin, golfer Jack Nicklaus, Federal Reserve Chairman Alan Greenspan, and comedienne Carol Burnett at the White House to receive the Presidential Medal of Freedom, the country's highest civilian honor. President George W. Bush wondered how the "Greatest of All Time" had "stayed so pretty" after so many years. He concluded that, "It probably had to do with his beautiful soul." The event, lauding Ali's position as an elder statesman of sports, reflected a spirit of respect and a sense that the champ's past actions and what many regarded as his verbal "excesses" reflected his sincere convictions that had been validated by the court of historical opinion.

Not everyone was willing to forgive Ali for refusing to fight in Vietnam, as Joe Davis, president of the Veterans of Foreign Wars (VFW), reported that he had received two complaints from his members that Ali did not deserve the award. But Davis reported that the VFW itself had "moved on" and did not have a public position on Ali's award. In a much more forgiving spirit, Davis commented that Ali had refused to serve "for religious principles, and he paid the price . . . And what he did in his later life, he was an excellent representative of the United States of America."[9] In response to the award, *USA Today* published an angry letter from a veteran who wrote:

> I can't believe your [newspaper] had the nerve to publish the picture of Bush hanging the Medal of Freedom around Ali's neck. That's a disgrace to veterans all over, especially Vietnam vets. You have the freedom to write what you like not because of Ali but because of all those crosses in Arlington National Cemetery.[10]

These comments notwithstanding, the sporting press and, indeed, most American sports fans, have been willing to allow their image of Muhammad Ali to change with the times. Just as the champ spoke with many voices throughout his career, his audiences proved receptive to his messages in their own time.

NOTES

1 Joyce Carol Oates, "Muhammad Ali: The Greatest," ESPN, *Sports Century* (New York: Hyperion, 1999), http://www.usfca.edu/jco/muhammadali/.

2 Joe Louis Obituary, http://www.arlingtoncemetery.net/joelouis.htm.

3 Larry Schwartz, "Brown Bomber was a Hero to All," https://espn.go.com/sportscentury/features/00016109.html.

4 Mike Puma, "Liston Was in Trouble In and Out of the Ring," http://espn.go.com/classic/biography/s/Liston_Sonny.html.

5 Jackie Robinson, "Cassius Did More than Just Win," *Amsterdam News* (March 14, 1964).

6 See David Remnick, *King of the World* (New York: Vintage, 1998), p. 124 and Amir Saeed, "What's in a Name? Muhammad Ali and the Politics of Cultural Identity," *Culture, Sport, and Society* Vol. 5, Issue 3 (Autumn, 2003), p. 55.

7 Ellen W. Gorsevski and Michael L. Butterworth, "Muhammad Ali's Fighting Words: The Paradox of Violence in Nonviolent Rhetoric," *Quarterly Journal of Speech* Vol. 97, No. 1 (February, 2011), p. 50.

8 Ibid., p. 57.

9 "Bush Presents Ali with Presidential Medal of Freedom," *Associated Press* (November 14, 2005), http://sports.espn.go.com/sports/boxing/news/story?id=2219166.

10 Bill Lange, "Ali Still Drawing Fire for Refusing to Serve," *USA Today* (November 22, 2005). Cited in Gorsevsky and Butterworth, "Muhammad Ali's Fighting Words," p. 58.

PART **I**

MUHAMMAD ALI

CHAPTER 1

From Gold Gloves to a Gold Medal

Cassius Marcellus Clay, Jr. was born in Louisville, Kentucky on January 17, 1942. He was an African-American whose birth likely attracted no more attention than any other in this mid-sized segregated city in the Upper South. His was an elegant name for a small boy: Cassius Clay Senior named his son not only after himself, but also after a white Kentucky abolitionist who leaned more toward the pronouncements of New Englander William Lloyd Garrison than the "Great Compromiser" and son of Kentucky, Henry Clay. Young Cassius carried the weight of Kentucky history in his name from birth. He would soon make boxing history as the Greatest of All Time, Muhammad Ali.

The famous Kentuckian for whom Cassius Clay was named was a well-known abolitionist, lawyer, newspaper publisher, and bowie knife fighter. Born on the Clermont plantation near Richmond, Kentucky on October 19, 1810, Cassius Marcellus Clay flirted with the ministry in his studies at Kentucky's Transylvania College but abandoned the life of the cloth for secular studies. While studying at Yale University, Clay was inspired by the anti-slavery oratory of William Lloyd Garrison. He earned a degree from Yale in 1832 and returned to Transylvania College to complete his legal studies, soon establishing himself in central Kentucky as a prominent "emancipationist." In the 1830s and 1840s, Clay was a member of the Kentucky General Assembly representing Madison County. True to his anti-slavery principles but in opposition to the prevailing wisdom in his part of the state, Clay freed his own slaves in 1844.

In the mid-nineteenth century, opposing the peculiar institution, even in the Upper South, could be dangerous. In 1845 Clay began to publish *The True American*, an abolitionist newspaper in Lexington, Kentucky. He posted guards at the paper's office, but this did not prevent the seizure of his printing press by his opponents. From 1845 to 1846, Clay was forced to publish *The True American* in Cincinnati, across the Ohio River. He continued to distribute the paper throughout Kentucky, where slavery was not only tolerated but was the engine of the plantation economy. In the antebellum period, the Ohio River was a symbolic dividing line between South and North, slavery and freedom. Alexis De Tocqueville noted that difference in 1831:

> Ohio is perhaps the State of the Union in which it is easiest to see, in a striking way and close up, the effects of slavery and of liberty on the social state of a people. The State of Ohio is separated from Kentucky just by one river; on either side of it the soil is equally fertile, and the situation equally favorable, and yet everything is different.
>
> Here a population devoured by feverish activity, trying every means to make its fortune; the population seems poor to look at, for they work with their hands, but that work is the source of riches. [Speaking of Kentucky] There is a people which makes others work for it and shows little compassion, a people without energy, mettle or the spirit of enterprise. On one side of the stream, work is honored and leads to all else, on the other it is despised as the mark of servitude. Those who are forced to work to live cross over into Ohio where they can make money without disgrace.[1]

One hundred and thirty years later, the young boxer Cassius Clay would find that his hometown of Louisville on the south bank of the Ohio River embodied many of those same forces and attitudes that could hold him back, as an athlete and as a young black man. He would have to cross that river and transcend the barriers of his youth to become "The Greatest."

The nineteenth-century Clay was forthright in his condemnation of slavery, but he was also loyal to his state. He served honorably as a captain of a Kentucky militia company in the Mexican War, but he saw slavery as a national problem. In 1860, the *New York Times* described Clay as:

> a man who speaks out upon Slavery with as much frankness as any Northern Free-Soiler. He condemns it morally, and economically, and politically—declares it to be a curse and a crime, and avows his desire to see it abolished.[2]

This perspective was reflected in his early support for the national Republican Party in the years leading up to the Civil War. Clay met and befriended Abraham Lincoln and served as the United States ambassador to Russia in 1861–62 and again from 1863 to 1869. He strongly supported the purchase of Alaska from Russia in 1867. He was a man of national vision and ethical action from a state committed to its own definition of sovereignty and the peculiar institution.

Cassius Marcellus Clay supported the education of African-Americans in the founding of Berea College in 1855. In that year, he donated cash and land to Rev. John G. Fee, who began construction on Kentucky's first college to educate black and white students at the same time in the same location. Throughout his life, Clay continued to support the cause of racial equality in the Upper South and was a prime mover in the creation of Kentucky's modern Constitution in 1890. On the occasion of his death, his funeral procession passed through streets lined with African-Americans who paid their respects to the "Abraham Lincoln of Kentucky."[3]

Marveling at the fact that Clay was such an active stump speaker on behalf of the abolitionist cause who had nevertheless escaped the tar and feathers faced by others who dared to speak on behalf of the slave, the *New York Times* declared that Clay escaped molestation and death because he was willing to fight in support of his beliefs:

> he has twice defended his right to free speech, pistol in hand, has killed and wounded those who sought to put him down, and has himself been left for dead on the field. Moreover, he openly avows that he will still resist any attempt to gag him, or disturb him by force, and he mounts the rostrum all ready for the fray.[4]

Writing in the St. Louis *Globe-Democrat* long after the Civil War from Clay's hometown of Richmond, Kentucky, journalist Frank G. Carpenter observed that General Clay's life had been one

> of constant fighting. Kentucky has always been a hot-blooded State. Here a word is always followed by a blow, and an insult has to be wiped out in death. Life is of less account here than in the North, and it was of still less value in the days of Gen. Clay's youth, nearly two generations ago. It is sixty years now since he delivered the Washington Centennial oration at Yale College, in which he espoused the cause of the negro and became the most hated man in Kentucky among the slaveholders. All his life he has had to fight for his ideas, and the stories of his personal encounters reads like a romance.[5]

General Clay's reputation was based not only on his outspoken anti-slavery position, but also on his reputation as one of the best bowie knife fighters of his day. The nineteenth-century Cassius Marcellus Clay was his day's version of the "the greatest."

Young Cassius Clay was proud to be identified with the great Kentucky abolitionist—so proud in fact that he incorrectly claimed he was related to him. Indeed, early in his career, Clay expressed some pride in his white heritage. Of the relationship between his family and the original Cassius Marcellus Clay, the young boxer said:

> My own grandfather was brought up on the old man's land, he never [was] a slave. My grandfather was with the old man, but not in a slave capacity, no sir![6]

Later in his life, Muhammad Ali would denounce his "slave name" Cassius Clay as representing the oppression of black people, much to the disappointment of his father and his family in Louisville. It is true that the name "Clay" might have come from slavery, but this was true of the names of many African-American families, both North and South. Nevertheless, in his career, Ali proudly claimed (either mistakenly or conveniently) to be the descendant of the Kentucky slave owner, abolitionist, and bowie knife fighter.

There was more than one white ancestor in the young boxer's lineage. In addition to the claim by Ali's aunt, Mary Clay Turner, that "Henry Clay was Cassius's great-great-grandfather, and that's no legend," the Clay family on the maternal Grady side included a white great-grandfather, Abe Grady of Ennis, Ireland, who came to the United States shortly after the Civil War. Grady married a black woman, the daughter of Lewis and Amanda J. (Mandy) Walker, who hailed from nearby Todd County, Kentucky. The couple gave birth to John Lewis Grady, whose daughter, Odessa Lee Grady, was Ali's mother.

There is irony here in the white lineage in the man who became known as "the greatest" black man as well as heavyweight champion. When the young champion converted to Islam and changed his name to Muhammad Ali, he asked, "Why should I keep my white slave master's name visible and my black ancestors invisible, unhonored?"[7] Reflecting on the white blood in his family, Ali decried the fact that his white blood "came from the slave masters, from raping." He declared that "White blood harms us, it hurts us. When we was darker, we was stronger. We was purer."[8] But those sentiments were years and many fights away from the life of the boy who grew up in working-class, black Louisville.

Eventually, Ali would soften his attitude toward his racial heritage. In September of 2009, at the age of sixty-seven and suffering from Parkinson's Syndrome, Ali visited Ennis, the home of his ancestors in Western Ireland. More than 10,000 spectators witnessed a concert and the unveiling of a plaque in Ali's honor. Signs in store windows sported messages like "Welcome Home Ali O'Grady."[9] The champion had come full circle in acknowledging his diverse ancestry.

The young Clay's family also included his other maternal great-grandfather, Tom Morehead, who was the son of a white man and a slave named Dinah. Morehead served during the Civil War in Company B of the 122nd infantry regiment of the United States Colored Troops. His company, which consisted of volunteers from Louisville and surrounding counties, fought in Portsmouth, Virginia from December of 1864 to February of 1865, and later at the final battles at Petersburg, and Richmond, Virginia between February and the end of the war in April of 1865.[10]

Family, specifically his father, mother, and brother in Louisville, was a central and essential element in the growth and development of the young Muhammad Ali. Cassius Clay, Sr. (November 11, 1912–February 8, 1990) earned his living as a sign painter, but he was also a religious muralist. The elder Clay occasionally took his sons, Cassius and Rudolph, on jobs with him, teaching them "how to paint pretty good."

> Before he started fighting, Muhammad could lay out a sign. Draw letters, do the spacing, mix the paint, and fill it in right . . . I was an artist, not just a sign painter. I was born painting. And if it wasn't for the way things were at the time, a lot more people would have known what I could do.[11]

Clay's mother, Odessa Lee (Grady) Clay (February 12, 1917–August 20, 1994), was a domestic servant whose own upbringing was influenced by "the way things were." She barely knew her father and was raised by her mother and aunt. In spite of hard times and little education, Mr. and Mrs. Clay possessed skills that made it possible for them to earn a respectable living. Cassius Clay, Sr. was proud of the fact that he provided for his family. He told Thomas Hauser that Cassius and his brother, Rudolph

> didn't come out of no ghetto. I raised them on the best street I could: 3302 Grand Avenue in the west end of Louisville. I made sure they were around good people; not people who would bring them into trouble. And I taught them values—always confront the things you fear, try to be the best at whatever you do. That's what my daddy taught me, and those are things that have to be taught. You don't learn those things by accident.[12]

The Clay family lived in relative comfort compared to the poorest people, black and white, in Louisville and surrounding Jefferson County. Clay's parents owned their own home in the West End neighborhood populated almost exclusively by working-class black families.[13] By all accounts, Cassius and Rudolph were well cared for. In 2012, in recognition of Muhammad Ali's 70th birthday, the City of Louisville placed a historic marker at the Clay house. The marker said, in part, "Here is where young Clay's values were instilled, transforming him into a three-time heavyweight champion and world renowned humanitarian."[14]

The relatively secure financial circumstances of the Clay family notwithstanding, the range of action and ambition for a black teenager in segregated Louisville after World War II was severely limited. Neighborhoods were defined by race, and public facilities and schools separated white and "colored" citizens. Soldiers coming home from service in a segregated Army fighting fascism in World War II were understandably disappointed to discover how little had changed in their time away. This was the world into which Ali was born. Few people would have assumed that young Cassius would advance beyond his West End neighborhood, much less become a world-renowned athlete. Clay was born into a world in which black professional athletes like Joe Lewis and Jesse Owens were more the exception than the rule. He was five years old before Jackie Robinson made his first major league appearance. Professional football had been integrated the year before, when Jackie Robinson's UCLA teammate, Kenny Washington, began playing for the Los Angeles Rams of the National Football League in 1946. Blacks would begin playing in the National Basketball Association in 1950.

Racism in Louisville was real, if not always obvious. The city exhibited less of the overt racism of cities in the deeper South, and Louisville's citizens, white and black, knew and kept to their "places," maintaining a veneer of Southern civility that was seldom visibly pierced by racial conflict. In this regard, the northern Kentucky city deserved the label of a "nice nasty town" that historian William Chafe applied to Greensboro, North Carolina, a city with a similar demographic profile.[15] Middle-class black citizens could be comfortable in their communities, they could serve that community as teachers, ministers, barbers, or morticians, but they still bore the disability of their color. Writing about Ali's early years, Gregory Allen Howard observed the delicate balance that both black and white citizens maintained by "keeping things cool" and having as little meaningful contact as possible:

> If you were black, or rather *colored*, and stayed *in your place*—both physically and psychically—then your life could be okay. The white dominating society was not going out of their way to inflict intentional suffering and anxiety on their coloreds. In the Louisville of Cassius Clay's youth, the racism was passive.[16]

Rahman Ali (born Rudolph Clay), Muhammad's younger brother, confirmed that Louisville was not the worst place to live, but there was an undercurrent of discrimination and threatened violence that could be avoided only by "staying in one's place":

> Louisville was segregated, but it was a quiet city, very peaceful and very clean. There wasn't much crime; no drugs; very little drinking or prostitution. Things were different from the way they are now. Growing up, the only problems Muhammad and I had with whites were if we were walking in a certain part of town. If we were in the wrong place, white boys would come up to the car and say, "Hey, nigger, what are you doing here?" I never got into any fights. No one attacked me. It wasn't like the Deep South, but people would call us nigger and tell us to get out if they thought we were someplace we didn't belong.[17]

The Clay brothers stayed out of trouble in Louisville, but they were aware of the violence perpetrated against African-Americans in the deep South and the emerging struggles against segregation. On August 25, 1955, Emmett Till, a fourteen-year-old boy from Chicago, was murdered near Money, Mississippi for stepping out of his "place" by speaking to Carolyn Bryant, the twenty-one-year-old wife of Roy Bryant, who owned Bryant's Grocery and Meat Market where Till and his cousins had gone to purchase snacks.[18] The young man's actions violated the southern "code" that prohibited African-Americans from speaking to white people without permission. Till's brutal beating and torture was front-page news in both the African-American and the mainstream press, and the Clay family followed the story with interest. Ali recalled:

> I stood on the corner with a gang of boys, looking at pictures of him in the black newspapers and magazines. In one, he was laughing and happy. In the other, his head was swollen and bashed in, his eyes bulging out of their sockets and his mouth twisted and broken . . . My father talked about it at night and dramatized the crime.[19]

Even as an Olympic champion in 1960, Clay continued to be mindful of the presence of a color line in Louisville. Sports journalist Dick Schaap recalled visiting Clay to write a feature article about him for the *Saturday Evening Post*. The two men spent several days together. One day, as they were driving through the streets of town,

> we were stopped for a traffic light and there was a very pretty girl standing on the corner. A white girl. I turned to Cassius, which was his name then, and said, "Boy, she's pretty." And he grabbed me, and said, "You're crazy man. You can get electrocuted for that; a Jew looking at a white girl in Kentucky."[20]

When Cassius Clay drove the streets of segregated Louisville with his brother, when he and his family and friends followed the murder and funeral of Emmett Till, and when he became aware of struggles for freedom in places like Montgomery and Birmingham, Alabama, he could not have anticipated that there would come a time when he would no longer have to "stay in his place." But soon enough, the skinny Louisville boy would become a citizen of the world as "The Greatest," Muhammad Ali.

This was the "nice nasty" society into which Cassius and Odessa Clay brought their children. Mrs. Clay found refuge in the Baptist Church, and her faith remained strong throughout her life. Even though he was raised a Methodist, Cassius Sr. allowed and even appreciated the fact that his boys were raised in a strong church-going Baptist tradition. Odessa was a source of inspiration and strength to her sons, even though they later followed a different spiritual path. After his conversion, Ali described his mother's profound influence on him:

> I've changed my religion and some of my beliefs since then, but her God is still God; I just call him by a different name. And my mother, I'll tell you what I've

told people for a long time. She's a sweet, fat, wonderful woman, who loves to cook, eat, make clothes, and be with family. She doesn't drink, smoke, meddle in other people's business, or bother anyone, and there's no one who's been better to me my whole life.[21]

But there were strains in the marriage. Cassius Clay, Sr., the sign painter who created religious murals for Louisville's black churches and who once said that a crucifixion scene he had painted would "make a stone weep," had a dark side. He was described variously as a

Jive talker (rapper without a stage); bar room singer; heavy drinker; jokester (always at someone else's expense); a street corner Socrates; womanizer; narcissist. And most of all frustrated grand artist.[22]

The elder Clay often turned to drink, and he was known to have threatened his wife as a way to deal with his anger and frustration at not being recognized as the great artist he was sure that he was. The FBI reported that in 1966 that Clay had been arrested for reckless driving, disorderly conduct, and assault and battery. Mrs. Clay called the police for protection from her husband on at least three occasions. Clay's problems did not abate as he grew older and his son became more famous. Between 1975 and his death in 1990, the elder Clay was arrested five times for drunk driving, according to Louisville Police Department records.[23]

Ali maintained an intense loyalty to his family, in spite of the troubles at home. According to writer Jack Olsen:

"There was a lot of trouble, bad trouble, between his father and mother," one of Cassius Clay's early backers recalls, "but Cassius would bite his tongue before he'd mention it. He had too much pride. When he was fighting prelims on salary, he suddenly told Angelo Dundee that he had to have money to go home right away, all the way back to Louisville from Miami. He'd gotten word that his mother and father were gonna split up, and he was gonna go back and stop it. But Angelo was the only person he told, because Angelo wasn't gonna let him leave without knowing the reason. It's a very attractive quality in Cassius, not talking about his personal troubles. He'd talk about his ambitions and dreams, but not his problems. Those were kept inside as a matter of family pride."[24]

Both parents remained proud of their son throughout his boxing career, with all of its triumphs and tribulations, both in and outside the ring. Ali's mother died after suffering a stroke, in 1994, four years after the death of his father.

A strong yet challenged family, survival instincts honed in his segregated community, and remarkable speed and natural ability would eventually help young Cassius Clay to become an accomplished, admired, and even feared fighter. But it was the accident of a stolen bicycle that brought him together with people who would teach him to fight and help him start a career. After visiting the Louisville Home Show in the Columbia Auditorium and wandering through the exhibits and eating free popcorn and other treats offered by the exhibitors, the twelve-year-old Cassius discovered that his new Schwinn bicycle had been stolen. Angry and frightened, the boy was directed to the gym in the basement to tell his tale of woe to police officer Joe Martin, who happened to be a boxing coach and local television personality. On hearing Cassius's declaration that he was going to "whup" the person who stole his bike, Martin told the boy, "Well, you better learn how to fight before you start challenging people that you're gonna whup."[25]

Cassius Clay's entry into Joe Martin's Columbia Gym was a turning point in his young life. The gym was part of a community center at the corner of Fourth and York Streets in Louisville that included facilities for table tennis, bowling, and billiards as well as a boxing ring. Clay was one of many young boys who spent hours after school in supervised recreation rather than on the streets. He recalled much later that he was searching for a purpose to his life, a way to negate what some African-Americans in Louisville saw as standard wisdom that it was better to be white. He could not have known then that he would become special in the eyes of the world, but he believed, as he later recounted, that, "Some people have special resources inside, and when God blesses you to have more than others, you have a responsibility to use it right."[26] When he entered Martin's gym searching for revenge against the bicycle thief, Clay remembered that

> The sights and sounds and the smell of the boxing gym excited me so much that I almost forgot about the bike . . . There were about 10 boxers in the gym, some hitting the speed bag, some in the ring, sparring, some jumping rope. I stood there, smelling the sweat and rubbing alcohol, and a feeling of awe came over me. One slim boy shadowboxing in the ring was throwing punches almost too fast for my eyes to follow.

> When I got to the gym, I was so eager, I jumped into the ring with some older boxer and began throwing wild punches. In a minute my nose started bleeding. My mouth was hurt. My head was dizzy. Finally someone pulled me out of the ring.[27]

Clay immediately signed on to work with Martin to learn the fundamentals of boxing. He also learned life lessons from the white police officer who was willing to take a chance on helping the disappointed and angry young man become a disciplined fighter.

According to Martin, who had operated an amateur gym to take young fighters off the streets and help them develop into responsible young men since 1938, there was very little evidence in 1954 that the skinny boy who was alternately crying and threatening retribution against a bicycle thief would become "the greatest," not only in his own mind but in the minds of an adoring public. In his first days in Martin's gym,

> he looked no better or worse than the majority. If boxers were paid bonuses on their potential like ball players are, I don't know if he would have received one. He was just ordinary, and I doubt whether any scout would have thought much of him in his first year . . . He stood out because, I guess, he had more determination than most boys, and he had the speed to get him someplace. He was a kid willing to make the sacrifices necessary to achieve something worthwhile in sports. I realized it was almost impossible to discourage him. He was easily the hardest worker of any kid I ever taught.[28]

Ali remembered the circumstances a bit differently. While acknowledging that Martin had given him his start in boxing, Clay recalled that "Martin knew a little. He could show me how to place my feet and how to throw a right cross. But he knew little else."[29] Clay continued to work with Martin while, at the same time, he learned the art of boxing from Fred Stoner, an African-American trainer on the other side of town whose gym at the Grace Community Center was open at night after Martin's closed. From Stoner, Clay learned the speedy and graceful technique that would carry him into a professional career.

People who knew Cassius Clay knew that, from a very young age, he bragged that he would one day be the heavyweight champion of the world. Hard work, intense focus, and supreme self-confidence made it possible for the skinny twelve-year-old boy to realize his athletic dream. In addition to training with Martin and Stoner, young Cassius worked out on his own, often running several miles before reporting to Louisville Central High School. Shirlee Smith, a childhood friend, remembered that he often chased the school bus:

> He would jog and of course we'd pass him up. Then we'd stop at every corner to pick somebody up and he'd pass us up. And he'd laugh and wave at us all the way to school . . . It didn't faze him in the least.[30]

Childhood friend Yates Thomas remembered that, even as a high school student, Clay took good care of himself. He would bring a breakfast of two eggs and a quart of milk to school each morning:

> He would break the eggs into the milk and shake it up . . . He'd say, "Now I'm ready to go to school. I'm the baaaaadest man in Looville." All he thought of was fight-fight-fight. We used to go to a teenage place at night, and he'd stay till 10 o'clock, even on a Saturday night, and then he'd say, "I'll see ya. I'm

goin home to bed." He didn't smoke. He'd say, "Ain't gonna put that stuff in my lungs."[31]

As he became more aware of his physical gifts and the need to work hard to prepare for a career as a professional boxer, Cassius Clay stopped eating pork, arguing that it raised his blood pressure. Similarly, he rejected soda and alcohol as bad for his growth and development.[32] Another friend from Louisville, Lawrence Montgomery, remembered that Cassius expressed great confidence that he would earn the title of heavyweight champion of the world:

> He told me then that he was going to be the heavyweight champion of the world, and I didn't believe him. I told him, "Man, you better get that out of your mind." But he succeeded. He followed through.[33]

From the beginning of his career, Clay was known for his speed and fancy footwork in the ring as well as his glib tongue outside the ropes. People who saw him agreed that his boxing style was characterized by speed and athleticism more than by a heavy hand that was certain to deliver a knockout:

> Muhammad Ali boxed like no one else. He was fast. So fast that he didn't duck punches like most other boxers; instead, he just leaned back away from them. He also didn't put his hands up to protect his face; he kept them down by his hips.[34]

This approach to boxing, idiosyncratic as it was, nevertheless proved useful to the young fighter. People who saw him remembered him. Perhaps it is even more accurate to say they could not forget him. Establishing a connection with Police Officer Joe Martin marked the start of Ali's boxing career. He trained in Martin's gym, and he fought his first rounds on "Tomorrow's Champions," Martin's weekly local television program, only six weeks after starting his training. He won a 2–1 split decision in a three-round bout against Ronnie O'Keefe. Another Louisville native, Jimmy Ellis, who held the heavyweight title years later during Muhammad Ali's "exile" from professional boxing, knew Cassius Clay as a teenager. He observed that the kid from the west end of town

> took his boxing very seriously. Even then he did a lot of talking, telling guys they couldn't beat him, saying he was gonna knock everyone out. But he learned about what went on in the ring, because he was working at it constantly and had the desire to fight. I mean, he was a fighter. Even when he was young, he had a fighting heart. I saw him get knocked down and get up to knock the other guys out. He could be in a hole, getting beat, and still come back to win.[35]

Martin's wife, Christine, remembered that Cassius carried his serious approach into aspects of his personal life. Unlike many of the young fighters in Martin's gym, he did not smoke, drink, eat pork, or pursue young women. She recalled that on trips,

> most of the boys were out looking around to see what they could get into, whistling at pretty girls. But Cassius didn't believe in that. He carried his Bible everywhere he went, and while the other boys were out looking around, he was sitting reading his Bible.[36]

From Martin's Columbia Gym, a next logical step was entry into local, state, and then national Golden Gloves tournaments. Started in 1928 by Arch Ward, then the sports editor of the *Chicago Tribune*, the mission of the Golden Gloves organization is to

> provide an activity and safe environment that promotes and enhances the physical and emotional well being and social development of young athletes; develops individual athletic skills, work ethic, discipline, sportsmanship, self-respect, and pride; and provides entertainment to citizens of the community.[37]

For the first three years, Golden Gloves champions all came from Chicago. In 1931, the 175-pound and heavyweight champions came from neighboring Gary, Indiana. The next year, Golden Gloves winners hailed from Joliet, Illinois and Davenport, Iowa. Within a few more years, the winning boxers were coming from Golden Gloves chapters all over the Midwest and, eventually, all over the country. In 1957, the fifteen-year-old Cassius Clay competed in the Golden Gloves quarter finals in Chicago. He was defeated on February 26, 1957 by Kent Green but was awarded a trophy for being the "most aggressive fighter in his division." Golden Gloves coach Chuck Bodak recalled that the young fighter made an impression wherever he went. He recalled that Clay looked like

> a young colt, very spindly legged and wiry. Framework was just about all he had, but even then there was an aura about him. People would stop and look and not know what they were looking at, but they were looking at him. He lost that first year to a kid named Kent Green, who was an older, seasoned amateur from Chicago. But Cassius had talent; he made an impression. And each year after that, the improvement was obvious. The more he matured, the sharper he got. I mean, you'd have had to be blind not to see how good this kid was. I told his mother once, "Cassius must be from outer space, because I've never seen anyone like him in my life."[38]

Bob Surkein, another Golden Gloves coach, remembered that Clay had "reflexes like no one had ever seen." Even as an amateur fighter, Clay had "the same reflexes and skills he had later on. Normally, you saw an amateur fighter jump out of harm's way. Cassius would stand there, move his head two inches, turn his body another six inches. I said to myself, it can't be, but after watching him in the ring many times, I knew this kid had it."[39] In 1959, young Cassius Clay was the national Golden Gloves champion in the 175-pound weight class. By 1960, Clay was the Golden Gloves heavyweight champion.

The year 1959 also saw a setback in Clay's competitive career. He traveled to the Pan American Amateur Boxing Trials in Madison, Wisconsin. Throughout the 1940s and 1950s, boxing was a popular sport in Madison, and fans could see the future of the sport in events like the Pan American trials at the University of Wisconsin Field House for as little as $1.00. Although Clay was described as a "hot-headed cocky teenager" by Madison coach and tournament official Joe Walsh, the 178-pound high school student's reputation was established more by his 34-fight win streak than by the verbal bravado that would soon characterize every appearance, whether in the ring or in front of microphones and cameras. Clay worked his way through the preliminary rounds, defeating all the competition. His victory over Leroy Bogar in the semifinal bout was a technical knockout, called because of the ferocity of Clay's assault. In the finals of the event, Clay faced Amos Johnson, a twenty-five-year-old Marine veteran. Clay was favored to win, but Johnson's experience in the ring and a punishing left hand gave Clay a difficult time, and he lost his first fight by a 2–1 decision. Clay attended the Pan American Games in Chicago as an alternate, but he did not fight. The loss inspired him to train even harder when he returned home. Back in Madison, local boxing writer Randy Coughlin wrote, "When Clay gets better on defense, brother he will be hard to beat."[40]

The next few years were filled with hard work and a string of local victories, as Clay developed his fast footwork and lightning punches. He also competed on a larger regional and national stage. In addition to two national Golden Gloves titles and six Kentucky Golden Gloves championships, Clay won Amateur Athletic Union national light heavyweight titles in Toledo, Ohio in April of 1959 and again in April of 1960. He was on his way.

The 1960 Olympic trials were held in the San Francisco Cow Palace from May 19–21. Clay's first opponent in the 178-pound light heavyweight division was former marine Henry Hooper. The fight appeared relatively static until the third round, when Clay landed a right that knocked his opponent out. He had won in this first level of the competition. Step two was a fight against Fred Lewis, who entered the Olympic trials as the champion of the United States Air Force. He was older than Clay but was no match for the hand speed and quick footwork that Clay displayed. But, according to Jack

Fiske, writing in the *San Francisco Chronicle*, those qualities stood in the way of universal approval for the young Louisville fighter:

> The crowd booed cocky Cassius Clay's clear cut decision . . . The fans were displeased because of the eighteen-year-old high school student's clowning tactics against the wild swinging Lewis. The loser, from Phoenix, packed plenty of power and was willing enough but was no match for Clay's ramrod left jabs and right smashes to the head.[41]

Clay was ready for the final qualifying match. Again, he faced a member of the armed forces, Allen Hudson of Long Island, New York, who represented the United States Army. At one point in the fight, Clay was hit by his opponent's elbow, a blow that the referee ruled a knockdown. Clay was so agitated by the ruling that he came back and scored a brutal knockout victory. He was headed to the Olympics in Rome.

The 1960 Olympics marked a number of symbolic turning points for the Americans. For the first time, the 292 athletes (241 men and 51 women) marched under the new 50-star American flag that reflected Alaska's and Hawaii's statehood, and their athletic exploits were broadcast on the new medium of television for the first time. CBS paid $394,000 for the rights to exclusive Olympic footage. This is a far cry from the amounts that are paid for broadcasting major sporting events today, but it was a tremendous sum at the time. The Cold War was never too far from the surface, in spite of the efforts to project an image of the Olympics as non-political athletic competition. Nationalist China was forced to compete as Formosa, and the People's Republic of China did not exist as far as the Olympics were concerned. The battle for medals continued to be waged by the United States and the Soviet Union, with the USSR scoring 103 medals and the United States 71. The nearest competing country was Italy in third place with 36 total medals. The Soviet victory in the medal race notwithstanding, the real stories for Americans were the basketball team led by Jerry West and Oscar Robertson, the victories and personal triumphs of sprinter Wilma Rudolph, and the light heavyweight boxing gold medal won by Cassius Marcellus Clay of Louisville, Kentucky.

Before traveling to Rome for the Olympics, Clay and the other American athletes gathered in New York to make the flight together. Dick Schaap remembers him as a young man,

> fresh out of high school in Louisville, Kentucky, and he had lost only one amateur bout in two years, a decision to southpaw named Amos Johnson. He was supposed to be one of the two best pro prospects on the boxing team, he and Wilbert McClure, a light-heavyweight, a college student from Toledo, Ohio.

For this young athlete from a medium-sized southern city on his way to Olympic glory, a night in New York City must have seemed exciting. Clay was probably most excited when Schaap took a few of the members of the Olympic boxing team to Harlem to meet Sugar Ray Robinson. As they traveled uptown, Clay regaled his teammates with pronouncements that he would win in Rome, return home to a successful professional career, and become the champion of the world. According to Schaap, Clay had "no doubts, no fears, no second thoughts, not an ounce of false humility . . . He was so outrageously bold he was funny. We all laughed at him, and he didn't mind the laughter, but rode with it, using it to feed his ego, to nourish his self-image." Clay got to meet his idol that day. Sugar Ray autographed a photograph and gave it to the young boxer, wishing him luck in the Olympics. "That Sugar Ray, he's something," Clay said, "Someday *I'm* going to own two Cadillacs-and a Ford for just getting around in."[42]

Clay overcame his fear of flying to journey to Rome for the 1960 Olympic Games. According to his old mentor, Joe Martin,

> We [had] had a rough flight going to California for the trials so when it came [time] to go to Rome he said he wasn't gonna fly and that he wouldn't go . . . I finally took him out to Central Park here in Louisville and we had a long talk for a couple or three hours, and I calmed him down and convinced him if he wanted to be the heavyweight champion of the world, then he had to go to Rome and win the Olympics.[43]

The young man who calmed his fear of the air by making predictions of who among his teammates would win medals in Rome was a member of a United States boxing team that included nine other fighters, three of whom also came home with medals. The American boxing team's total was three gold medals and one bronze medal.

To win the gold medal, Cassius Clay had to make his way through three levels of competition before the final bout. In his first fight, he defeated Belgian Yvon Becot in the second round, when the referee stopped the fight. In the quarter finals, he triumphed over Gennadiy Shatkov from the USSR by a unanimous decision. The Soviet boxer was smaller than Clay and almost as quick, but he proved unable to land effective punches. Australian boxer Tony Madigan was Clay's opponent in the semi-final round, and the result was another unanimous decision. In the final round, Clay had to face Zbigniew Pietrzyskowski of Poland just after teammate Eddie Crook's victory over Tadeusz Walasek for a gold medal in the 175-pound weight category. The crowd apparently disapproved of the decision awarding Crook the victory, but the boos only made the young American fight harder. The battle was not easy, according to British journalist John Cottrell:

> In the first round, it seemed that Clay would be badly mauled. He was confused by his opponent's southpaw style, took some heavy punishment, and once showed his inexperience by closing his eyes in the face of a barrage of blows.

Clay managed to keep out of trouble in the second round, and in the last minute he abandoned his show-off style with the fancy footwork and dropped hands, and stood his ground to throw four hard rights to the head. Even so, he was still behind on points at this stage. "I knew," he explained afterwards, "that I had to take the third round big to win."

Clay did finish big. In that final round he suddenly found his top form, moving in and out with expert judgment, punching crisply and with perfect timing. This sharper, better coordinated Clay stormed back with a torrent of combination punching which left Pietrzykowski dazed. He no longer relied too much on his left jab, but made equal use of his right to penetrate the southpaw's guard. Ripping into the stamina-lacking Pole, he drew blood and came preciously close to scoring a knockout. At the final bell, Pietrzykowski was slumped helplessly against the ropes. There was no doubting the verdict. All the judges made Clay the points winner.[44]

Pietrzykowski himself seemed to know that after the first round, his opponent would outlast him in the ring that day. He realized that Clay had scored a mental as well as a physical victory over him by the second round, and he may even have had a sense that the young man from the American South brought something special to the competition that would transcend the Olympic Games. He recalled that, during the fight

I had to work at a very fast pace to avoid his punches. This was good for the first round. Clay was missing a lot of punches. But in the second round, I realized I was losing my strength, and that it would be difficult for me to survive three rounds. I had to think about defense, and that hampered thoughts of victory. It left me with nothing else but to try to survive three rounds and not be knocked out. I would have done anything then to beat him. But later, I began to cherish his victories.[45]

On September 5, 1960, Cassius Marcellus Clay, Jr. of Louisville, Kentucky became the Olympic light heavyweight champion by a unanimous decision. He had overcome his fear of flying to get to the games in Rome, and he fought for himself and for his country. After the games, he regaled reporters and fans with one of his first poems:

To make America the greatest is my goal
So I beat the Russian and the Pole
And for the USA won a medal of gold.
The Greeks said, "You're better than the Cassius of Old."

We like your name, we like your game,
So make Rome your home if you will.
I said I appreciate your kind hospitality,
But the USA is my country still,
'Cause they're waiting to welcome me in Louisville.[46]

Called the "unofficial mayor of the Olympic Village" for his outgoing nature, Clay quickly became a familiar figure at the games. Reporters noted his travels from "one national area to another, spreading greetings and snapping pictures with his box camera."

> He took hundreds of photographs—of Russians, Chinese, Italians, Ethiopians, of everyone who came within camera range. Reporters from Europe and Asia and Africa tried to provoke him into discussions of racial problems in the United States . . . Cassius just smiled and danced and flicked a few jabs in the air and said, "Oh, we got problems, man, but we're working 'em out. It's still the bestest country in the world."

With these remarks, he showed himself to be an "innocent, an unsophisticated good-will ambassador, filled with kind words for everyone."[47]

Young Cassius was so proud of his gold medal that he ate with it, slept with it, and never took it off, according to fellow gold medalist, Wilma Rudolph. Both athletes were hailed as black heroes and American heroes as the athletes returned from Rome. Louisville was ready to welcome home "the champ." His father painted the steps to the porch in red, white, and blue stripes, and the town came out to greet his motorcade.

But gold medal triumph notwithstanding, little had changed in race relations in Louisville, and Cassius Marcellus Clay was still an uppity black kid who puffed himself up with his brash talk. One story has it that he was denied service at a local restaurant, another that he was harassed by motorcyclists sporting Confederate flags on their bikes who demanded that he turn over his prized medal. In both tales, Clay is said to have thrown his Olympic medal into the Ohio River. It is not clear whether he engaged in this symbolic protest or simply lost track of his medal. In 1996, he received a replacement when he appeared at the Olympics in Atlanta. Whatever the fate of his medal, Clay was confronting the contrast between this athletic success and his status as an ambassador for his country and his second-class citizenship at home. Clay himself took the high road when it came to discussing his feelings about race relations in America. Approached by a Russian reporter after his Olympic victory, he was asked how he felt about being a winner in Rome who could not "eat with the white folks because you're a colored boy." He answered the "commie cat" that the United States was the best country in the world, that competent people were working on solving the problem of race relations in America, and that, "It may be hard to get something to eat sometimes, but anyhow I ain't fighting alligators and living in a mud hut." Clay told *Sports Illustrated* writer Huston Horn: "Poor old Commie, he went dragging off without nothing to write the Russians." Later in his career, Clay emerged as an outspoken opponent of racism, but in the early 1960s he said and did little that conveyed any personal feelings that might embarrass his family, his Louisville supporters, or his country.[48]

While racism remained a profound reality in Louisville, there were prominent businessmen and civic leaders who recognized Clay's talent and accomplishments and also saw a way to profit from his continuing success. The first of these was Billy Reynolds, the vice-president of Reynolds Metals Co. He had known Clay for about two years and was prepared to offer him a ten-year contract. However, largely because of friction between Cassius Clay, Sr. and Joe Martin, who would have been Clay's advisor in the deal, the Reynolds deal never materialized. Instead, shortly after his return from Rome, Clay signed an agreement with the Louisville Sponsorship Group, which paid him $10,000 as a signing bonus and a guarantee of $4,000 for the following two years and $6,000 for each additional year through 1967. This amount, $24,000 over five years, would be worth nearly $185,000 today.[49] This would hardly be an impressive figure for many of today's super-athletes, but it was a huge amount of money for a young man from Louisville in the early 1960s. The Group, comprised of ten local businessmen and one New Yorker, most of whom had already earned their first million, also paid all of Clay's training and travel expenses, salaries for his trainer and sparring partners, and rent for a house in Miami Beach, as well as receiving 50 percent of the receipts earned from his fights. Clay's "adoption" by local Louisville boosters and men who understood business was a departure from many promotional deals in boxing that had brought the sport perilously close to organized crime. Three years after Clay's Louisville Sponsorship Group deal, *Sports Illustrated* described Clay's supporters as a positive influence in a boxing world that had long been marred by corruption, fixed fights, and mob connections. The group's interest in the young boxer was as much financial as athletic, and they seemed to be relatively immune to boxing's perennial evils:

> [T]hey are so innocent of any background in professional boxing that when you say "uppercut" they think first of their income taxes. Yet they are giving boxing a fresh look. They have provided Clay an ideal, all-expenses-paid training program, they offer him the benefit of all their experience and business acumen, and they surround him with a substantial moral and ethical environment, a rare commodity in professional boxing. And since they are independently wealthy Clay is assured that he will never end up exploited and broke through any fault of theirs. By setting such an example the syndicate is encouraging other businessmen elsewhere to get behind boxing the way they have been behind baseball and professional football for years.[50]

These were the men who can be seen as starting Cassius Clay on his way as a professional boxer.

The syndicate's primary organizer was Bill Faversham, Jr., who had some amateur experience as a boxer at both Groton and Harvard. He was easily able to convince other prominent Louisville businessmen to invest in Clay's future. Huston Horn described the men who put up the money to launch Clay's career:

> Faversham, a vice-president of Louisville's Brown-Forman distillery (Old Forester, Jack Daniels) and a big, bustling man of breezy temperament, sold the syndicate idea to such other Louisville friends as W. L. Lyons Brown, a onetime boxer at the Naval Academy and now *the* Brown of Brown-Forman; William Cutchins, the president of Brown-Williamson Tobacco Co. (Raleighs, Viceroys); and Vertner D. Smith Jr., the chairman of a liquor distributing company.[51]

Faversham believed that in Cassius Clay he had found

> a good local boy with a clean background from start to finish. With the proper help and encouragement, he could bring credit to himself and his home town. There are plenty of wolves who would leap at the chance to get their paws on Cassius, to exploit him and then to drop him. We think we can bring him along slowly, get him good fights and make him the champion he wants to be.[52]

The Louisville Sponsorship Group played a major role in arranging Clay's first nineteen fights, in which he compiled an undefeated record before taking on Sonny Liston for the Heavyweight Championship title. Soon, Clay would decide to go his own way. Having created his own image and defied the odds to beat Liston in the ring, he would emerge as a more outspoken critic of racism in America. By 1964, Cassius Clay was changing, as was his country. We would soon see a new version of "the greatest." He would be the champ, and his name would be Muhammad Ali.

Notes

1 Alexis de Tocqueville, *Journal Entry* from his visit to Ohio (December 2, 1831), http://www.tocqueville.org/oh.htm.

2 "Cassius M. Clay in Kentucky," *New York Times* (January 17, 1860), http://www.nytimes.com/1860/01/17/news/cassius-m-clay-in-kentucky.

3 http://madisonhistoryky.org/Cassius_Clay.php.

4 Ibid.

5 Frank G. Carpenter, "A Kentucky Gladiator: General Cassius M. Clay Talks of His Duels and Fights," *St. Louis Globe-Democrat*, published in the Sacramento *Record-Union* (November 14, 1891), http://bowieknifefightsfighters.blogspot.com/2011/11/03cassius-marcellus-clay.

6 *Louisville Defender* (September 1, 1960), in Thomas R. Hietala, "Muhammad Ali and the Age of Bare-Knuckle Politics," in Elliott J. Gorn, ed., *Muhammad Ali: The People's Champ* (Urbana and Chicago: University of Illinois Press, 1997), p. 122. Troy R. Kinunen, *Cassius Clay* (August 21, 2006), http://www.mearsonline.com/index.php?mact=News,cntnt01,print,0&cntnt01articleid=169&cntnt01showtemplate=false.

7   Dick Eastman, "Muhammad Ali's Irish Heritage," http://www.irishculturalsociety.com/essays andmisc/muhammadali.html.

8   Jack Olsen, "Growing Up Scared in Louisville," *Sports Illustrated* (April 18, 1966), http:// sportsillustrated.cnn.com/vault/article/magazine/MAG1078435/1/index.htm.

9   David Wilkes, "Welcome Back to Ireland, Muhammad O'Ali: Boxing Legend Thrills 10,000 With Visit to Home of his Irish Great Grandfather," *Mail Online* (September 2, 2009), http:// www.dailymail.co.uk/news/article-1210524/Muhammad-Ali-freeman-ancestral-home-Ireland.html.

10 http://www.nps.gov/civilwar/search-regiments-detail.htm?regiment_id=UUS0122RI00C.

11 Thomas Hauser, *Muhammad Ali: His Life and Times* (New York: Simon & Schuster, 1991), p. 16.

12 Ibid., p. 15.

13 In 2012, Nevada developer Jared Weiss purchased the Ali family home for $70,000, hoping to turn it into a historic site, although by 2014, he had not yet raised sufficient funds to begin the renovation project.

14 Joseph Lord, "Muhammad Ali's Boyhood Home Gets Historical Marker," *Louisville Courier-Journal* (May 9, 2012) and Sheldon S. Shafer, "Owner of Boyhood Home Doubts Schedule," *Louisville Courier-Journal* (October 21, 2014).

15 William H. Chafe, *Civilities and Civil Rights: Greensboro, North Caroline and the Black Struggle for Freedom* (New York: Oxford University Press, 1980), p. 18.

16 Gregory Allen Howard, "The Power of Dreams . . . In Louisville," http://www.gregoryallen howard.com/powerofdreams.html.

17 Hauser, *Muhammad Ali: His Life and Times*, p. 17.

18 PBS, "The American Experience," The Murder of Emmett Till, http://www.pbs.org/wgbh/ amex/till/timeline/timeline2.html.

19 Hietala, "Muhammad Ali and the Age of Bare-Knuckle Politics," p. 119.

20 Dick Schaap in Thomas Hauser, *The Lost Legacy of Muhammad Ali* (Toronto: Sport Classic Books, 2005), p. 134.

21 Hauser, *Muhammad Ali: His Life and Times*, pp. 18–19.

22 Howard, "The Power of Dreams . . . In Louisville."

23 William Nack, "Young Cassius Clay," *Sports Illustrated* (January 13, 1992), http://sports illustrated.cnn.com/vault/article/magazine/MAG1003337/index.htm.

24 Olsen, "Growing Up Scared in Louisville."

25 Jack Olsen, *Black is Best* (New York: Putnam, 1967), p. 74.

26 Hauser, *Muhammad Ali: His Life and Times*, p. 18.

27 Ira Berkow, Obituary, "Joe Elsby Martin, 80, Muhammad Ali's First Boxing Teacher," *New York Times* (September 17, 1996), http://www.nytimes.com/1996/09/17/sports/joe-elsby-martin-80-muhammad-ali-s-first-boxing-teacher.html. Also in Muhammad Ali with Richard Durham, *The Greatest: My Own Story* (New York: Random House), 1975.

28 Ali with Durham, *The Greatest: My Own Story*, p. 19.

29 Joe Martin Obituary, http://www.independent.co.uk/news/people/obituaryjoe-martin-136 4717.html.

30 Bruce Schreiner, "Muhammad Ali's Childhood Friends Reflect On His Early Days," *Huffington Post* (January 10, 2012), http://www.huffingtonpost.com/2012/01/10/muhammad-ali-early-days_n_1197044.html.

31 Ibid.

32 Nack, "Young Cassius Clay."

33 Schreiner, "Muhammad Ali's Friends Reflect on His Early Days."

34 http://Muhammad-ali-biography.blogspot.com.

35 Hauser, *Muhammad Ali: His Life and Times*, pp. 19, 20.

36 "Boxing was Allah's Way of Getting Me Fame to do Something Bigger," *Emirates 24/7* (September 18, 2009), http://www.emirates247.com/eb247/sports/other/boxing-was-allah-s-way-of-getting-me-fame-to-do-something-bigger-2009–09–18–1.18655.

37 Golden Gloves of America Official Website, http://goldengloves.com.welcome.

38 Hauser, *Muhammad Ali: His Life and Times*, pp. 20–1.

39 Troy R. Kinunen, *Cassius Clay* (August 21, 2006), http://www.mearsonline.com/index.php? mact=News,cntnt01,print,0&cntnt01articleid=169&cntnt01showtemplate=false.

40 Ibid., and Nick Daniels, "A Legend in the Making: Cassius Clay's Madison Bouts," *The Badger Herald* (April 24, 2014), http://badgerherald.com/sports/2014/04/24/a-legend-in-the-making/#. U5GW7C_aiQo.

41 Cited in David Maraniss, *Rome 1960: The Olympics that Changed the World* (New York: Simon & Schuster, 2008), p. 198.

42 Dick Schaap, "From Louisville to the Nation of Islam: My Ups and Downs With Ali" (originally published in *Sport* magazine in 1971), http://thestacks.deadspin.com/from-louisville-to-the-nation-of-islam-my-ups-and-down-1428081378.

43 "50 Stunning Olympic Moments, No. 17: Cassius Clay Wins Gold in 1960," http://www.theguardian.com/sport/london-2013-olympics-blog/2012.

44 Ibid.

45 Hauser, *The Lost Legacy of Muhammad Ali*, p. 133.

46 Dave Zirin, *What's My Name, Fool? Sports and Resistance in the United States* (Chicago: Haymarket Books, 2005), p. 58 reprints the first half of the poem. The entire text appears in Hauser, *Muhammad Ali: His Life and Times*, p. 30.

47 Schaap, "From Louisville to the Nation of Islam."

48 Huston Horn, "Who Made Me—is Me," *Sports Illustrated* (September 25, 1961), http://www.si.com/more-sports/2010/06/11/muhammad-alistories.

49 "Dollar Times," http://www.dollartimes.com/inflation/inflation.php?amount=24000&year=1962.

50 Huston Horn, "The Eleven Men Behind Cassius Clay," http://si.com/vault/article/magazine/MAG1074600/index.htm.

51 Horn, "Who Made Me—is Me."

52 Ibid.

CHAPTER 2

BECOMING "THE GREATEST"

Winning the gold in Rome was only a first step for Cassius Marcellus Clay: he had his sights set on the Heavyweight Championship of the World. He also was determined to earn respect for his skills as a fighter, even if he had to create a larger-than-life personality to project his greatness to the world. From his earliest days of training at Joe Martin's Columbia Gym, he regaled anyone who would listen with prognostications of his eventual dominance in the ring. It must have sounded odd for the skinny kid who worked out by having his brother throw stones at him to increase his foot speed as he dodged the missiles to claim that he would even develop into a heavyweight, much less the world champion. Each day as he made his early (4:00 a.m.) morning run on the streets of Louisville, he greeted neighbor John Powell, who worked in the local liquor store. Powell remembered Clay's demanding training routine and his brash confidence:

> I'd be sitting on the counter . . . and I could see his shadow coming around the corner from Grand Avenue. Clay was on his way to Chicksaw Park. Cold, dark winter mornings. You could see that shadow coming. Then here he comes, running by, with those old big army brogans. He'd be the onliest person in the early morning. And I'd walk outside, and he'd stop and shadowbox. He once said to me: "Someday you'll own this liquor store and I'll be heavyweight champion of the world." Both of those came true too.[1]

To earn the heavyweight title, Clay would have to prove his worth in the ranks of professional fighters. He could already count 100 wins in 108 amateur fights, but his National Amateur Athletic Union and Gold Gloves titles (in 1959 and again in 1960), even his Olympic gold medal, were insufficient in the eyes of many boxing experts to establish Clay as a professional fighter.

To become a champion, Clay would have to earn the credentials in the ring to contend for the heavyweight title, and, given the difficulty of gaining recognition and respect from the boxing press, he would have to create his own reputation and hype with his mouth as well as his fists.

Prior to the Rome games, *Sports Illustrated* had praised Clay as the US boxing team's most likely medal winner, but the sports voice of record in the United States did so with only mild enthusiasm, concentrating more on athletes in more popular Olympic sports such as track and field. This was not surprising, as public enthusiasm ran high for runners and swimmers, and, for many, it was sprinter Wilma Rudolph, not fighter Cassius Clay, who was the darling of the Rome Olympics. Even after Clay's victory, London's *Guardian* noted the Olympic victory but provided no details of the light heavyweight fight. The *New York Times* provided a perfunctory description of Clay's victory over silver medalist Pietrzkowski but focused on the career of the silver medalist almost as much as it described Clay's exploits in the ring. The next day, *Times* sports columnist Arthur Daley reported on the gold medal won by Clay's roommate Willie "Skeeter" McClure and described the light heavyweight battle with a historical reference:

> Cassius Marcellus Clay of Louisville followed the script of another Cassius and bloodied his Caesar, even though this Caesar bore the rather inappropriate [*sic*] name of Zbigniew Pietrzykowski. No Roman was he, but Polish light-heavyweight.[2]

Months later, Daley would join the chorus of writers who praised Clay's talents in the ring, but it took a while for the sporting press as a whole to accept Cassius Clay as a champion.

Soon after his Olympic victory Cassius Clay came to New York and was met by *Newsweek*'s Assistant Sports Editor, Dick Schaap, who remembered that

> Cassius was an imposing sight, and not only for his developing light-heavyweight's build, 180 pounds spread like silk over a six-foot-two frame. He was wearing his blue American Olympic blazer, with USA embroidered upon it, and dangling around his neck was his gold Olympic medal, with PUGILATO engraved in it. For 48 hours, ever since some Olympic dignitary had draped the medal on him, Cassius had kept it on, awake and asleep. "First time in my life I ever slept on my back," he said. "Had to, or that medal would have cut my chest."

Clay enjoyed being recognized on his Manhattan jaunt, Schaap said, which included a visit to Times Square, where, "at a penny arcade, Cassius had a bogus newspaper headline printed: CASSIUS SIGNS FOR PATTERSON FIGHT" (Floyd Patterson was the reigning heavyweight champion). The faux headline might have been an example of Clay's wishful thinking, but he knew it would play well in his old Louisville neighborhood. "'Back home,' he said, 'they'll think it's real. They won't know the difference.' He took three copies of the paper, jammed them into his pocket, and we moved on, to Jack Dempsey's restaurant." The evening featured two New York "firsts" for the young fighter: he tried cheesecake for the first time and experienced a single drop of whiskey poured into a glass of Coca-Cola. When Clay had the chance to spend time with a young woman, Schaap reported that the fighter shied away from the experience, saying, "Man, I'm in training. I can't fool around with no girls." The evening ended with the champ sharing his photographs of the Rome Olympics with the *Newsweek* reporter.[3] After his one-night conquest of New York City, young Cassius Clay, the Olympic star from Louisville who was thrilled to be recognized on the streets of the city, was certain that he was ready to enter the ranks of professional fighters and claim the heavyweight title in the not-too-distant future.

As his professional career began, Clay knew he needed to impress the right people with his boxing style and his ability to sustain his energy throughout an extended fight. Most boxing writers found his style to be unorthodox, if not foolhardy. Writing in *Sports Illustrated* in September of 1961, Huston Horn argued that Clay's success was more a matter of luck and financial backing than boxing talent. Unlike the ring heroes of the 1950s, Clay fought with his hands down, making use of his lightning speed to stay out of reach of his opponents. He was not known for throwing a single knockout punch. Rather, he used his fast feet to outmaneuver an opponent until he wore him out and finally landed the blow that would end the fight. Horn observed that Clay "is still just a boxer, still just an unsophisticated Olympic gold medalist . . . who has turned professional and hasn't run out of luck. How very fine a fighter he is remains to be seen." Horn also observed that Clay was "still a boy with some growing up to do and still a boxer with some learning to do."[4]

Soon, Clay would gain recognition as well as criticism for his poetry and his antics in front of the television cameras. TV was a new medium in Clay's youth, and he was quick to see the potential for using the small screen to project his larger-than-life personality. Writing in 1998, D. Keith Mano acknowledged that Clay was adept at projecting his image and demonstrating that he could back up at least some of his outrageous claims: "He knew how important TV was for the diffusion of hype. And, of course, it didn't hurt that Ali had magical reflexes, deep courage, ring wisdom, a perfect physique, and the prettiest face since Errol Flynn played Gentleman Jim."[5]

Some sportswriters criticized Clay's style in the ring because it seemed to be evasive rather than aggressive. He violated many of the basic tenets of boxing form, and he engaged in a bob and weave strategy that produced feints and jabs rather than knockout blows. In 1962, A.J. Liebling wrote in *The New Yorker* that Clay had

> a skittering style, like a pebble over water. He was good to watch, but he seemed to make only glancing contact. It is true the Pole finished the three-round bout helpless and out on his feet, but I thought he had just run out of puff chasing Clay, who had then cut him to pieces. A boxer who uses his legs as much as Clay used his in Rome risks deceleration in a longer bout.[6]

Clay knew he was a newcomer who challenged traditional boxing wisdom, and he knew he needed the support in his corner that would take him beyond the horizons of the Columbia Gym or Fred Stoner's community center. As early as 1957, three years before his Olympic victory and his entry into the professional fight game, Clay had introduced himself to trainer Angelo Dundee, who happened to be in Louisville with Willie Pastrano, a fighter he was training at the time who would eventually hold the light heavyweight title from 1963 to 1965. Dundee was no ordinary trainer. He and his brother, Chris, ran the famous Fifth Street Gym in Miami, and Angelo was known as an outstanding corner man and coach. He had earned his reputation as the corner man for Carmen Basilio, when he won the world welterweight title in 1955 with a knockout of Tony DeMarco in the twelfth round. Dundee was known for his patience and his ability to bring out the best qualities in his fighters. A long career partnership lay ahead for Clay and Dundee, but in 1957 the trainer had barely heard of the person on the phone who introduced himself as Cassius Marcellus Clay.

On that important afternoon in Louisville, the young fighter called Dundee and talked his way into a conversation with the older professional that lasted several hours. At first, Dundee thought Cassius Clay was outrageous, perhaps even a bit crazy. But he came to see that the young man was a serious student of boxing. That afternoon, the two had what Dundee called

> some of the finest conversation I've ever had with a human being . . . He wanted to know how I trained my fighters, what they do, when to eat, when not to eat. [He was] a very, very in-depth young man . . . That was the beginning of a friendship that I nurture to this day because he's one of my best friends. Cassius Marcellus Clay was the nicest thing that ever happened to my life and I think the nicest thing that ever happened to boxing.[7]

The two men met again in 1959, when Dundee and Pastrano were in Louisville again for a fight against Alonzo Johnson. Dundee remembered that

> Cassius came to the gym and asked if he could spar with Willie. I don't like pros sparring with amateurs; it's a good way to get someone hurt. But Willie was willing, and I figured why not let them go a round? Cassius was seventeen. Willie

was a professional on his way to winning the light-heavyweight championship of the world. And I gotta tell you, Cassius won that round.

Clay became accustomed to winning. These two meetings represented more than the introduction of a young fighter to one of boxing's foremost trainers. Even though Clay's first trainers in his professional career were his old Louisville mentor Fred Stoner and the light heavyweight legend, Archie Moore, his career, both as Cassius Marcellus Clay and Muhammad Ali, is most clearly identified with Angelo Dundee.[8]

Known as the "Old Mongoose," Moore survived injuries and illnesses to box for nearly two decades before he had a chance to win the Light Heavyweight Championship in December of 1952. He held that crown until his retirement in May of 1962. Moore grew up in a segregated fight game, competing in the all-black "Chittlin Circuit" before achieving success and recognition by mainstream boxing organizations and fans. In his day, Moore had his own unorthodox style that helped him to score 131 knockouts in his long career. He also practiced his own brand of banter that was intended to divert the attention of his opponents:

> He wore long shorts decades before today's NBA players made them fashionable. Instead of fighting with fists raised at his opponents, Moore often would cross his arms and form his famed "armadillo curtain," a precursor to Muhammad Ali's 1970s "rope-a-dope." Moore would feign nonchalance and then blister an opponent with a punishing right jab. He also talked a good game—even during his fights. He once told a soon-to-be-vanquished opponent, "You're looking great. Keep up what you're doing. You're the next champion."[9]

Toward the end of his career in November of 1960, Moore welcomed Clay to his San Diego gym at the request of members of the Louisville Sponsorship Group. The two clashed immediately over both style and boxing substance, as Clay resented the older fighter's attempt to modify his presence in the ring. It was a generational conflict, with the trainer insisting that Clay needed time to learn how to box, and the brash young man declaring that he was ready to take on any competition. Clay also refused to help with chores, including washing dishes and sweeping the kitchen, declaring, "I don't sweep the kitchen for my mother, so why I got to sweep the kitchen for Archie Moore?" Moore told a member of the Louisville Group that it was time for Cassius to go home. "My wife is crazy about him, my kids are crazy about him and I'm crazy about him, but he just won't do what I tell him to do. He thinks I'm trying to change his style, but all I'm trying to do is add to it." There was consensus on the phone that Clay "needed a spanking."[10] As a result of their differences and what Angelo Dundee called "a clash of personalities," Clay and Moore parted ways. By the time the two faced each other in the ring on November 15, 1962, Clay had established himself as a Dundee fighter. In December of 1960, Dundee got a call from Bill Faversham of the Louisville Investors Group and settled on terms that allowed Clay to begin his new training routine with Dundee in Miami by Christmas of 1960.[11]

Clay's dancing in the ring, his tendency to jab at an opponent's face rather than pound his body with massive blows, and the long reach that enabled him to play with an opponent while remaining out of reach of a counterattack, not to mention his obvious lack of respect for established fighters and boxing conventions, annoyed other fighters as well as members of the press. Early in 1961, just after he signed on with Angelo Dundee, Clay sparred for a few minutes with a former champion, Ingemar Johansson, at the Fifth Street Gym, and the results were far from pretty for the annoyed Swede. After a few minutes of bobbing, weaving, and taunting, Clay was clearly getting to the champ, who told trainer Angelo Dundee, "Get him the fuck away from here, and never, ever put him back in here again. I can't touch him. Nobody is going to touch the guy."[12] Ali's unconventional behavior and boxing style, while not totally new among fighters with big egos, represented a challenge to boxing's hierarchy as well as the strictures of race that required young black men to pay deference to white people. This young fighter deferred to no one. A few years later, trainer Dundee acknowledged Clay's brilliance and stubborn nature. He noted that he had taught the fighter a few things, but only through indirection and suggestion rather than straightforward critique and advice:

> "He thinks he's done everything himself," Angelo says, "and that's fine with me, and if you look at it his way he's right. All I did was suggest. You can't handle him the way you do the usual fighter. You don't regiment him. He had enough of that. You just have to use indirection. He never used to have the left jab he has now. A daily nicking at his pride did it. He'll be the last guy in the world to admit that anybody did it but him, but that doesn't bother me. He didn't have a left uppercut. He's got one now. He was throwing a left jab, but it was a slap. It had no authority. He would keep his left knee up. Now you'll see when he throws a left jab his left knee is bent. Gives him leverage, distance: he *reaches* you. But you have to show him things slowly. Up until a few fights ago he never hit a speed bag. It took me that long to teach him this was good for his reflexes, his rhythm."[13]

Few other trainers would have had the patience to put up with Clay's antics. Dundee understood how to work with Clay and, by 1964, his fighter was the heavyweight champion of the world.

As a fighter, Clay gave little credit or attribution to anyone for his style or his success in the ring. Even in his early years as a student of the sport, he chafed at instruction from Joe Martin, preferring to develop his own strategy in Fred Stoner's gym, and he resisted Archie Moore's efforts to teach him basic technique or change his freewheeling style. Even his longtime friend and trainer, Angelo Dundee, understood that there were limits to what he could teach Clay. In contrast, as a self-promoter, Cassius Clay paid homage to the braggadocio and outsized personality of the professional wrestler, George Wagner, known to the public as "Gorgeous George." In June of 1961, both men were in Las Vegas, Clay to fight the Hawaiian Duke Sabedong and George to take on "Classy" Fred Blassie, who would soon develop his own version of "I am the greatest" self-promotion. The Gorgeous One was already a sports legend—an extreme showman in the flamboyant world of professional wrestling. Before his emergence in the ring in the 1940s, Peter Carlson observed that:

> sports stars were heroes—never villains or "heels," in wrestling parlance. They were tough, modest and short-winded, like Lou Gehrig or Joe Louis. Gorgeous was a diva in every gesture and syllable. Other grapplers wore plain, dark trunks, black shoes and ratty old robes; George wore pink satin, silver lame, lace and ermine. He pulled up to arenas in purple Packards and big Cadillacs. "Pomp and Circumstance" blared over P.A. systems as he strode to the ring, and before he deigned to place his dainty white-shod feet on the mat, his "valet" Jefferies, a Jeeves-ish character in tails, would use a spray gun to mist the floor with perfume. Jefferies would then remove the gold-plated pins holding the Gorgeous curls in place, and the wrestler would toss them to women in the audience. (Scuffles were common. During the match George would kidney-punch and eye-gouge, then hide behind the ref. Incensed, the audience . . . rained jeers down on him.) "You're ignorant peasants," George informed them. "Beneath contempt."[14]

In 1961, George was nearing the end of his career, and Cassius was just getting started. Their promoters thought that a joint radio interview would provide helpful publicity for both men. The interview was anything but calm. When asked to comment on his opponent, with Clay listening carefully, Gorgeous George shouted:

> I am the greatest . . . I cannot be defeated! All my so-called opponents are afraid of me, and they're right to be afraid—because I am the king. I'm warning everybody right now: if this bum I'm fighting messes up the pretty waves in my hair, I'm going to kill him. I'll tear off his arm! And if that uneducated punk somehow manages to beat me, I'll crawl across the ring and cut off all my beautiful hair—and then I'll take the next jet to Russia! But that won't happen, because I am the greatest! . . . I am the Gorgeous One. Not only am I the best wrestler, the most highly skilled, with the greatest technique, but I'm also the most beautiful wrestler who ever lived! That's why all these curs, these ignorant brutes, don't want to take me on—they're afraid of my brilliant style of wrestling. And they know the fans only want to gaze on my manly beauty.

Witnessing this performance, it was as if Clay could see his future self. He went to watch the match between the Gorgeous One and Blassie, which the referees called a draw. But who cared? The fans, those who loved him and those who hated him, had come to see George's *style*, and 15,000 of them were not disappointed. After the Blassie match, Clay went into the dressing room, where the Gorgeous One told him that

> Boxing, wrestling—it's all a show. You gotta get the crowd to react. You saw that crowd out there. Most of 'em hated me and the rest of 'em wanted to kiss me. The important thing is, they all paid their money, and the place was full . . . You've got your good looks and you've got a good mouth on you. Talk about how pretty you are. Tell them how great you are, and a lot of people will pay to see somebody shut your big mouth. So keep on bragging, keep on sassing, and always be outrageous![15]

Over the next two years, until the wrestler's untimely death in December of 1963, Clay sought George's advice on how to create his own image of invincibility. It would be an understatement to say that Cassius Clay took Gorgeous George's advice to heart.

The lessons learned from Gorgeous George resonated with Clay because he already possessed an outgoing personality and a desire to be at the center of attention. From his days as a scrappy kid in school, he would occasionally start a schoolyard fight, just to attract attention. Reflecting on his motivation to be at the center of the ring, Clay told Alex Haley in *Playboy* magazine that professional fight fans were not so different from the boys and girls who thought he was "nuts" for running behind the school bus every morning:

> When I started fighting serious, I found out that grown people, the fight fans, acted just like those school kids. Almost from my first fights, I'd bigmouth to anybody who would listen about what I was going to do to whoever I was going to fight, and people would go out of their way to come and see, hoping I would get beat. When I wasn't no more than a kid fighter, they would put me on bills because I was a drawing card, because I run my mouth so much. Other kids could battle and get all bloody and lose or win and didn't hardly nobody care, it seemed like, except maybe their families and their buddies. But the minute I would come in sight, the people would start to hollering "Bash in his nose!" or "Button his fat lip!" or something like that. You would have thought I was some well-known pro ten years older than I was. But I didn't care what they said, long as they kept coming to see me fight. They paid their money, they was entitled to a little fun.[16]

Between Clay's Olympic victory on September 5, 1960 and his triumph over Sonny Liston that gave him the world heavyweight title on February 25, 1964, the young man who would become "The Greatest of All

Time" defeated nineteen opponents in venues ranging from the Kentucky State Fairgrounds to Wembley Stadium in London and New York's Madison Square Garden. These battles served a number of important purposes: they allowed him to develop his craft and his style in the ring; they provided more frequent opportunities for boxing writers to cover his work and come to accept that style; and they allowed Clay to create his own hype as the "Louisville Lip." The rhymed couplets of "Gaseous Cassius" attracted attention, and that attention made Clay a household name in the early 1960s.

Clay's first professional fight took place on October 29, 1960, only seven weeks after his gold medal Olympic performance. He won every one of the scheduled six rounds against Fayetteville, West Virginia police chief Tunney Hunsaker. According to the *Louisville Courier Journal*, in spite of the fact that "The dancing fast-moving Clay bloodied Hunsaker's nose in the third round with a flood of blows and it was in the fourth that he opened a cut over his eye," the fighters were relatively evenly matched. In the fight, whose gate was donated to the Kosair Crippled Children's Hospital, Clay's speed and agility were matched by Hunsaker's experience. Indeed, the older fighter thought he had actually won the first and final rounds.[17] Clay was new to the professional game. He impressed Hunsaker as a

> nice young man. In no way brash: The day of the fight I ran into him in a downtown department store and he started to clown around with a basketball and a baseball bat, but nothing outrageous. He didn't do that "I am the greatest" routine until he became better known.

Even as Hunsaker praised Clay's modesty and ingenuous behavior at the time, he felt that he had given the younger man a good fight. He declared that Clay "wasn't the toughest fighter I ever had, but he was certainly the best fighter I ever fought. He could hit you from any position and you just couldn't knock him off balance." He also declared that Clay was "awfully good for an 18-year-old and as fast as a middleweight." As for Clay, he said that the six-round fight did not wear him out at all (the blood on his boxing trunks was Hunsaker's, the result of a severely bloodied nose) and that he felt "ready to go 10 rounds any time."[18] At this early stage of his career, Clay was developing the skills he would need to compete as a professional.

George King managed Clay in his first professional fight. King, also a Louisville native, had learned the art of boxing at Fred Stoner's Grace Gym and had a brief boxing career of his own that was ended by an eye injury. His managing career was equally short with regard to Cassius Clay. Two months after the Hunsaker battle, Clay began working with Angelo Dundee. Training at Miami's Fifth Street Gym, he defeated Herb Siler (December 27, 1960),

Tony Esperti (January 17, 1961, his nineteenth birthday), and Jim Robinson (February 7, 1961) in rapid succession. Robinson, who was brought in by Chris Dundee as a last-minute substitute for Willie Gullatt, felt that he had fared better against Clay than the referee declared. Robinson compared Clay negatively to boxing's "Brown Bomber," Joe Louis. Louis had been one of America's most famous fighters in the 1930s and 1940s, and he was the world heavyweight champion from 1937 to 1949. Louis's (and Robinson's) style in the ring featured powerful knockout blows more than the dancing style that Clay brought to the fight game. Robinson remembered that, in the first round of his fight with Clay, the younger man

> bloodied my nose, but I was a smart fighter. I had been fighting before he was born. But he caught me with a heavy right hand and I went down. I sat on my knees and took a nine count before getting up. The referee looked at my nose and stopped the fight. Clay had fast hands but he never had one great punch. He couldn't have lived with Joe Louis.[19]

Perhaps such comparisons were inevitable, but the man who was coming to know Clay best saw things differently. Angelo Dundee noted that early on:

> a lot of people criticized Ali [as he would later be known] for not being able to take a punch. That's why he danced around the ring, they thought. Those guys didn't know what they were talking about. Ask any fighter and he'll tell you, you don't get hit because it's fun. You get hit because sometimes you can't avoid it, and if you can avoid it, more power to you. Another thing they said was, "All Cassius had was a jab." Well, he had a lot more than that, but remember, a jab is a punch in the face.[20]

Only two weeks after his fight with Robinson, Clay took on Donnie Fleeman, who was described by Angelo Dundee as a "Texas kid—pretty tough." In his post-fight interview, Clay said he had been "scared to death" before he got into the ring:

> Fighting a pro who has had 45 fights is quite different than what I faced before. This fellow had been 24 rounds with Roy Harris and beat Ezzard Charles [two established fighters; Charles held the Heavyweight title between 1949 and 1951]. Now that I whipped him, I guess I'm a little greater than average.[21]

Clay was not yet the braggart whose predictions almost always came true, but he was starting to express himself about his plans for his opponents, occasionally in rhyme. As his manager introduced him to increasingly strong opponents in the ring, he was gaining strength and confidence. It would soon be time to tell the world.

On April 19, 1961, Clay fought LaMar Clark, a fighter from Utah who was "knocking everybody out," according to Angelo Dundee. For the first time, Clay made a public prediction of the outcome—a knockout in the second round, and that's precisely what happened at 1:27. Less than two months later, Clay fought Duke Sabedong in Las Vegas. Before the fight, Clay told Dundee that "the big guy from Hawaii will go in four," as Sabedong remembered. This prediction proved to be a bit optimistic, but Clay did defeat the 6′7″ Sabedong in a unanimous decision after ten rounds. After that, the fight predictions became more frequent, they were frequently expressed in rhymed couplets, and, often, they proved to be true.

On July 22, 1961, Clay returned to the Kentucky State Fairground in Louisville to fight Alonzo Johnson in his first nationally televised bout. This fight was important because of the television coverage and Johnson's impressive 19–7 professional record. Before the fight, Clay revealed his plan to win the heavyweight championship. In an exchange that revealed Clay's growing confidence, he was asked if he feared getting knocked out by Johnson, to which he replied, "If a man intends to buy a Lincoln Continental next month, does he worry about the cost of a Ford to get him around in the meantime? Floyd Patterson is the Lincoln and Johnson is the Ford that will help me drive down to the showroom." Trash talk emanated from both corners. Johnson's trainer, Bob Baker, replied:

> Let him talk, let him talk, Clay looks like an amateur, still is an amateur. Alonzo has been ranked sixth in the heavyweight division. He's got nothing to worry about. Clay sparred with Alonzo down in Florida this spring and he's got the idea that he had Alonzo going. Well, the truth is Alonzo was toying with him, didn't want to hurt the kid, you know. Oh, they say Clay is great, but I don't see it that way.

In a moment of self-awareness, Clay said, "I got to win tonight. I talk too much to lose."[22] And win he did, even though he did not put forth much of an effort until the final rounds. The Associated Press reported that "Clay, indifferent in the early rounds, finally went to work in the ninth and tenth and had his opponent hanging on at the end before approximately 6,000 fans. The victory ran Clay's record to 8–0."[23] It was a unanimous decision, with Johnson nursing a swollen eye at the end of the evening.

Clay returned to Louisville on October 7, 1961 to fight the Argentinian Alex Miteff. He scored a technical knockout in the sixth round of the scheduled ten-round bout. Once again, the fight was a battle of boxing styles, with Miteff representing the old style brutal boxer and Clay showing his fancy footwork in the ring, declaring before the fight, "I expect Miteff to be strong, to hit hard, but hitting hard don't mean a thing if you can't find nothing to hit." Before the third round, Dundee told Clay to get serious about boxing. Gilbert Rogin reported the course of the fight in the sixth and final round in *Sports Illustrated*:

> Miteff seemed to get more loutish as the fight progressed, occasionally letting his arms fall by his side, daring Clay to hit him, at other times making curious faces. Through the fourth and fifth rounds the pattern remained the same: Alex hooking for the body, and Clay either tying him up or fencing him off with rapid, appallingly accurate sequences of blows to his bruised face. It was still a relatively close fight, and Miteff was very much in it, indeed often the aggressor, when the end suddenly came in the middle of the sixth round. Cassius had started a combination with a fairly tentative left jab, a measuring jab, no more, which didn't move Alex's head. He followed it with a short right hand of great sweetness that hit Alex on the chin, and Alex went down slowly. He stumbled up at perhaps four or five and seemed able to continue the fight, but he was truly out on his feet . . . Referee Don Asbury stopped the fight as it was incontestably apparent that Miteff was in no shape to go on.

In the Miteff fight, Clay received some genuine praise, as Rogin went on to say the fight was a "notable victory for Clay, proving his ability to endure as well as dish out, and Dundee was well pleased with his prodigy."[24]

The next eight months saw a series of fights that featured only a few notable moments but drew increasing attention to the young fighter. The Louisville Sponsorship Group, Clay's official management at the time, declined to have him fight Ingemar Johansson on November 29, 1961, substituting Willi Besamanoff, a German fighter who lost in the seventh round. Then came a surprise. In a fight in New York's Madison Square Garden, Clay was knocked down in the first round by Sonny Banks before 2,000 fans. More surprised than hurt, Clay went on to beat Banks in the fourth round, saying,

> That was my first time knocked down as a professional. I had to get up to take care of things after that because it was rather embarrassing, me on the floor. As you know, I think that I'm the greatest and I'm not supposed to be on the floor, so I had to get up and put him out, in four as I predicted.[25]

Eighteen days later at the Miami Convention Center, Clay dispensed with Don Warner in the fourth round for his twelfth straight victory in front of 4,012 fans. Less than four months after that, on April 24, 1962, George Logan threw in the towel in the fourth round. More than 7,000 fans saw the fight in the Los Angeles Sports Arena. On May 19, a cut eye in the second round momentarily stopped Clay's fight with Billy Daniels. In this event, held at the St. Nicholas Arena in New York, Clay's predicted fifth round victory was delayed until the referee stopped the fight for good in the seventh. Back in

Los Angeles two months later, Clay knocked out Alejandro Lavorante in the fifth round on July 20, 1962.

The fight that followed in Los Angeles on November 15, 1962 was a showdown against Archie Moore. Clay had declared, "Don't block the aisle and don't block the door. You will all go home after round four." This was a big time fight held in Los Angeles, and Clay was a 3–1 favorite to defeat Moore, who was twenty-six years his senior. Gilbert Rogin wrote in *Sports Illustrated* that

> Due largely to Clay's active mouth and sandbox manners, the fight drew 16,200 paying $182,599.76, a California indoor record. From the beginning it was evident Moore had no chance. Archie came out in a severe crouch, arms, as customary, a stout gate-crossing in front of his face. He clumped in pursuit of Clay but only rarely did he have an opportunity to punch. Clay stood off, always just out of range, stately, composed, serenely firing a dazzling variety of swift hooks, jabs, and uppercuts at Archie's graying head. Clay's were not, of course, singularly powerful blows, but they added up.[26]

With descriptions like "stately" and "composed," along with big time publicity and a large gate, Clay was beginning to be taken seriously. He was listening to his trainer more frequently and fighting with speed and precision. Clay's sponsors were moving him toward a heavyweight title fight at a measured pace with a professional record of 16–0.

In 1963, Clay fought three times, against Charlie Powell on January 24, Doug Jones on March 13, and Henry Cooper on June 18. In the first battle, Clay scored a knockout in the third round, but he had to go the distance against Jones in a Madison Square Garden fight that was broadcast on closed-circuit television. Clay was a 3–1 favorite, and he predicted a knockout in four rounds. The actual scoring ranged from 5–4 to 8–1 by the referee and judges, and Clay acknowledged that his opponent was "tougher than I thought he was."[27]

With his victory over Powell, it was clear that Clay and heavyweight champion Sonny Liston were keeping an eye on each other's performance in the ring. Clay said, "I understand Liston is watching. When I get back to Miami, I'll take care of the bum. He'll fall in eight. I won't mess around next time." To which the champ replied, "Clay showed me that I'll get locked up for murder if we're ever matched." In the March 1963 issue of *Ebony* magazine, Clay made clear his intention to beat Liston and "save" boxing in an extended succession of rhymed couplets:

> This is the story about a man
> With iron fists and a beautiful tan.
> He talks a lot and boasts indeed
> Of a powerful punch and blinding speed.

The boxing game was slowly dying
And fight promoters were bitterly crying
For someone, somewhere to come along
With a better and a different tone.

Patterson was dull, quiet, and sad
And Sonny Liston was just as bad.
Along came a kid named Cassius Clay
Who said, "I will take Liston's title away."

His athletic prowess cannot be denied
In a very short time it has spread far and wide.
There's an impression you get watching him fight
He plays cat and mouse and then turns out the light.

This colorful fighter is something to see
And heavyweight champ I know he will be.

The battle was on. Almost.[28]

On June 18, 1963, with a professional record of 18–0, Clay traveled to London's Wembley Stadium to fight Henry Cooper, and the public relations war began. Clay understood that he would increase the gate for his fight if he could rouse public opinion, and it didn't matter if that opinion was stirred in his favor or in opposition to his presence in England. *Sports Illustrated* stated it succinctly: "Cassius in England applied the economic theory that he found so workable in the U.S.: to sweeten the gate you must first sour the people." He made it clear that fighting Henry Cooper was but the most recent challenge in his long quest to become the heavyweight champion: "I'm only here," he told local reporters, "marking time before I annihilate that ugly bear, Liston." A few weeks before the fight, public opinion favored Cooper, who was popularly known at home as "Our 'Enery." By the time Clay finished his barrage of insults at both Cooper and Liston and his constant assertions that he was fighting only for the money, members of the press were becoming weary of Clay's "rudeness, his immodesty, and his big mouth." But Clay kept talking and people kept buying tickets. Cooper remained the sentimental favorite in England, but "the smart money was all behind Cassius Clay."[29]

The fight itself saw a win for Clay, but the bout was not without controversy. In the fourth round, Cooper landed a left hook that knocked Clay to the canvas. Immediately, Dundee and others in Clay's corner discovered that the fighter's glove was slightly torn. Henry Cooper told the London *Daily Mail*:

I thought that was it. He was in a lot of trouble, his pupils had gone inside his head. Then Ali went back to his corner with his trainer, Angelo Dundee. He said he had torn one of his gloves. That gave him a minute to recover, which, for a fit person, is time enough.[30]

In spite of the suspicion that Dundee had caused a deliberate and unnecessary delay in the fight to Clay's advantage, the extra few seconds hardly made a difference, as Clay went out for the fifth round with the same split glove. Cooper remembered that, "with the second or third punch he caught me in the eye and it started to gush blood. If he had wrapped sandpaper around his gloves, he couldn't have done better with an eye like mine."[31] Tommy Little, the fight referee, elected to stop the battle because of the severity of the cuts over Cooper's left eye. According to the *Daily Mail*, "there was no one in the crowd of more than 40,000 who would have wanted him to continue."[32] Henry Cooper remained a crowd favorite in England, while Clay returned home a victor determined to take on that "ugly bear," Sonny Liston.

Charles "Sonny" Liston was the reigning heavyweight champion, having defeated Floyd Patterson by a knockout in the first round on September 25, 1962. He was known as a hard puncher and a professional fighter with mob ties and a criminal record of his own. Born around 1929 or 1930 to a sharecropping family in a poor region of Arkansas, Liston was part of a family of twenty-five children of whom he was the youngest son and second youngest child. By 1950, he had moved to St. Louis to live with his mother and joined a robbery gang. It was in jail for a brutal robbery that Liston first stepped into a boxing ring at the suggestion of Father Alois Stevens, who served as the athletic director at the Missouri State Penitentiary. The priest introduced him to fight promoters who helped Liston to earn parole in October of 1952. He entered the Golden Gloves tournament, winning in local, regional, and national competitions. In June of 1953, he knocked out West German champion Hermann Schreibauer in 2:16 of the first round to become the Golden Gloves world heavyweight title holder. In an ascent that was even faster than that of Cassius Clay, Liston signed a professional contract in September of 1953. In his first fight during that same month, he knocked out Don Smith, again in the first round. Known for his extended reach and powerful left hand, he was often called the "Big Bear."

Writing years later, trainer Angelo Dundee shared his impression of Liston, saying, "It was almost as if some geneticist had bred him for the sole purpose of beating up others."[33]

Boxing did not keep Liston out of trouble with the law. He was arrested for various infractions and major crimes in St. Louis fourteen times between 1953 and 1958, when he moved to Philadelphia. And if he was not in trouble with the law, Liston was just in trouble. He had signed on to be managed by Frankie Carbo and Blinky Palermo,

two notorious mobsters who controlled big time boxing throughout the 1950s and 1960s. Both California and Pennsylvania suspended Liston's boxing license, and Liston himself had to appear before a Senate subcommittee investigating organized crime's influence in professional boxing.

At the time, organized crime was a major force in the profession, and there were frequent rumors that fights were fixed. Gambling was rampant, and the sport was considered by many to be disreputable at best. "Boxing", as Paddy Flood, an associate of promoter Don King, told a Congressional committee, "is the most treacherous, dirtiest, vicious, cheatingest game in the world . . . That's the nature of the business. It's a terrible business."[34] Sonny Liston came of age in the sport at a particularly low point. According to historian Randy Roberts, during the late 1950s and early 1960s boxing had earned the label as the "red-light district" of professional sports. While many sportswriters bemoaned boxing's ill repute, some critics saw the sport as simply boring. Joe Louis and Rocky Marciano had been towering figures in the sport who could command huge gates and fan loyalty, but those who ascended to the heavyweight throne after Marciano's retirement in 1956 did not inspire much public enthusiasm. Floyd Patterson fought few challenging contenders and maintained his championship until he was felled by Ingemar Johansson on June 26, 1959. Patterson won his title back a year later.[35] Boxing was perceived to be both corrupt and lackluster.

It is likely that Liston signed a contract with known mob figures because no one else would back him. After a series of fights that he won mostly by knockouts, Liston found new management and started his own campaign in the media and to whoever would listen to force Floyd Patterson, the reigning heavyweight champion, to fight him. He even accused Patterson of being afraid to take him on, preferring instead only white fighters. In response, civil rights leaders opposed the bout on the grounds that Liston was not an acceptable challenger for Patterson because of his connection to organized crime. Objections notwithstanding, the two fighters met in Chicago's Comiskey Park on September 25, 1962. The fight lasted only 2:05 seconds. After less than one round, Sonny Liston became the heavyweight champion. The results were similar in the re-match on July 22, 1963 at the Las Vegas Convention Center.[36]

The first fight was not pretty, and some disgruntled fans were sure that Patterson had been influenced by mob forces to let Liston knock him out. *Sports Illustrated* writer Gilbert Rogin disagreed, although he saw little beauty in the ring that night:

> Never have so many paid so much to see so little as the more than 600,000 people who shelled out an estimated $4 million, either live in Chicago or via television in 260 theaters, to dimly perceive Sonny Liston's astonishing one-round knockout of Floyd Patterson. At first, the fans regarded the pathetic outcome

in truculent silence; then, baffled and disgruntled, they spilled into saloons and living rooms complaining like mutinous lascars. There was a near unanimity of opinion, some of it by people who should have known better. The fight was fixed to set up a lucrative return match, they said. Patterson went into the ring a quivering coward, they said. Patterson was a bum made of glass. One theory, no more bizarre than the others, had it that the mob ordered Patterson to lose and promised him a one-sided High Noon if he didn't.

Rogin understood the power of Liston's punches, and he characterized the final punch in the first round as hitting Patterson's cheek "like a diesel rig going downhill, no brakes."

Sports Illustrated grudgingly acknowledged that Liston, the bad man with the long rap sheet and prison record, was the heavyweight champion. Rogin noted that Liston was not a perfect champion and that he might be de-throned one day, but he was the champion nonetheless:

> Sonny Liston would appear to rank with the better heavyweight champions. He has deficiencies in boxing skill, and a Jack Johnson or a Joe Louis—also big, strong men, but with greater skill—might have beaten him in their prime. But this is futile speculation. Liston is far and away the class now and there appears to be no one around to challenge his supremacy. Young Cassius Clay might give him a fair tussle in a few years, for here is a swift and dazzling boxer and a strong hitter, too. He might be able to fight Sonny the way everyone thought Floyd would. But at the moment, Cassius is far from ready.[37]

Of course, Cassius Clay thought he *was* ready, even in 1962, just two years into his professional career. But Angelo Dundee and the members of the Louisville Sponsorship Group kept the young fighter on a measured path that led to nineteen victories and no defeats in preparation for the championship fight. When Liston beat Patterson a second time on July 22, 1963, Cassius Clay stepped up his promotional campaign that featured regaling reporters with his many attributes and baiting, if not stalking, Sonny Liston, challenging him to a title match. The fake newspaper on which he had printed news of his victory over Patterson back in 1960 was yellowed and tattered. Clay had his sights on taking the heavyweight title away from the new champ, Sonny Liston.

Clay trained for his battle with Liston, but he also engaged in a one-man grab for media attention. It was during this period that the slogans "I am the greatest" and "Float like a butterfly, sting like a bee," the latter first shouted by Clay's ubiquitous cheerleader, Drew Budini Brown, hit the airwaves and newspapers all over the country. In spite of the growing respect that Clay was getting from sportswriters, Liston was favored to win by odds of seven to one. But Tex Maule wrote in Sports Illustrated that Liston was about to meet his match, even though the older fighter possessed more "ring craftsmanship, punching power and an ability to take a smart clip on the jaw with no loss of equanimity or senses." Liston was the more experienced fighter, but Clay was also a good fighter, "better than his constant bragging would lead one to believe." There were a few, but hardly a majority, of writers in the mainstream press who concluded that the brash Louisville Lip would "make a battle of it."[38]

Miami Herald sportswriter Edwin Pope was part of a generation of journalists who still admired Joe Louis as a model fighter and citizen but who slowly came to admire Cassius Clay's skill in the ring. Unlike some of the older boxing pundits, Pope could see Clay's potential for future glory, even if he chafed at his bravado. Pope observed that many of the writers in Miami to cover the fight

> felt that Cassius Clay would be champion eventually but they certainly didn't give him a chance against Liston. You have to remember that a lot of the writers of that time were older. Or they certainly seemed older to us then than they do now: Red Smith, Jimmy Cannon, Al Buck, Lester Bromberg, a lot of, ah, good writers, good, ah, writers of great reputation from New York and they, having been around Joe Louis, I think they resented Cassius Clay's, ah, his loudness, his brashness because Joe Louis set a standard that, ah, unfortunately for a lot of other fighters to come after him, ah, they, these other fighters were judged by, a standard of decency, gentlemanliness, ah, he always conducted himself in, in a way that made people love him.

Pope himself "had no doubt whatever that Sonny Liston would absolutely demolish Cassius Clay."

> At one time I believed Liston was a 20 to 1 favorite. Liston was a very, very tough egg. Ah, he did time in Jefferson City, Missouri for, ah, for really bashing some heads in. And he fought the same way as he acted on the street. He was merciless. He wasn't the fastest guy in the world but he had a left jab that would just hit you like anybody else's left hook. And the very idea of this spindly kid from Louisville, just out of the Olympics going in there with Liston, he'd had so many fights, in and out of the ring, and having a chance was impossible for anybody to digest.[39]

Of course, Clay's trainer, Angelo Dundee, knew all about Liston's past and his skills. He offered a more analytical assessment of Clay's chances in Miami. On the eve of the fight, he told *Sports Illustrated* writer Tex Maule that

> Clay has a style Liston has never seen before. He is much faster than Liston. He has the faculty of getting under Liston's skin and he will not be browbeaten by him. Cassius respects the champion, but really, deep down inside himself, Clay thinks he is unbeatable. And he can hit Sonny with every punch he has. Sonny isn't hard to hit. We can beat Liston with quantity and consistency. We can hit

him with uppercuts. Left and right. Cassius is the only heavyweight in the world with a good left uppercut, and Liston can be hit easy with uppercuts . . . If you built a prototype of what kind of fighter can whip Liston, you couldn't improve on Clay. He hits hard, he moves, he has every punch in the book. We can knock Liston out in the 11th or 12th round by wearing him down with the quantity of punches. If Cassius will do what he is told.[40]

Dundee's comments reveal that, for those who knew Clay and looked beyond the hype that the boxer himself had generated in the weeks leading up to the bout, there was a young man with genuine talent and a passion to win. Dundee and his fighter had studied films of Liston's prior fights, and they learned that if Clay could keep moving in the ring and stay just beyond Liston's reach, they could tire the champ, who was not accustomed to battling for more than ten rounds. Dundee figured that Clay could win by frustrating the hard punching Liston because "A frustrated fighter loses the snap out of his punches."[41] Clay had his own plan of attack and his own idea of how to win, both in and outside the ring.

In early 1964, as he followed in the footsteps of Gorgeous George, appearing more like a professional wrestler than a highly skilled boxer, Clay's rhetoric and his antics were shocking to many and amusing to some. He was brash, exuberant, a free spirit. Those who wanted to see him as a con man had to admit that he backed up his words with punches. As the title bout with Liston approached, it was tempting to see Clay as a child whose ability could not possibly match his confidence. In a 1963 Columbia recording, Clay shouted to the world Sonny Liston was

nothing. The man can't talk. The man can't fight. The man needs talking lessons. And since he's gonna fight me, he needs falling lessons. I'll hit Liston with so many punches from so many angles he'll think he's surrounded. I don't want to be champion of the world, I'm gonna be champion of the whole universe. After I whup Sonny Liston, I'm gonna whup those little green men from Jupiter and Mars. And looking at them won't scare me none because they can't be no uglier than Sony Liston.[42]

It's clear that Clay felt that those who followed the fight game could be influenced by hype as well as by brute force. He found Liston deficient in the very aspect of boxing at which he was starting to excel—self-promotion.

Cassius Marcellus Clay had become adept at the art of self-promotion through rhyme and short quips. In 1964, Alex Haley asked him when he had begun reciting poetry. He replied that what he and others called simple trash talk originated early in his career: "Somewhere away back in them early fights in Louisville, even before I went to the Olympics, I started thinking about the poetry. I told a newspaperman before a fight, 'This guy must be done / I'll stop him in one.' It got in the newspaper, but it didn't catch on then." Eventually, his poetry did "catch on," and reporters waited eagerly for the next quip, even as they criticized Clay's style, both in and outside the ring. Clay said his poetry really struck home starting with his fight with Archie Moore. Clay claimed that his talk really got to Moore who said, "He's not going to get me in four" in response to the claim that Clay would win the fight in the fourth round. Clay remembered that, "When he *did* go down in four, just like I said, and the papers made so much of it, I knew I had stumbled on something good." Haley followed up with the provocative reminder that many people considered Clay's "poetry" to be "horrible," to which the fighter replied:

> I bet my poetry gets printed and quoted more than any that's turned out by the poem writers that them critics like. I don't pay no attention to no kind of critics about nothing. If they knew as much as they claim to about what they're criticizing, they ought to be doing that instead of just standing on the side lines using their mouth.[43]

Clay's determination to control his own hype and create his own image marked a change in the relationship between sportswriters and fighters. Not content to become a creature of the media or to accept a journalist's moniker such as the "Great White Hope" or the "Brown Bomber," Clay asserted that he was nothing short of "The Greatest." Today, the term G.O.A.T., Greatest of All Time, to describe Cassius Clay/Muhammad Ali is commonplace, but in 1964, it was not at all typical for a fighter to develop his own persona. Edwin Pope provided some insights into the special relationship between writers and fighters and the extent to which Cassius Clay challenged that relationship and took control of his dealings with the press:

> Traditionally writers and fighters have always gotten along together. Writing, fighting has been a really, a treasure-trove of material for writers, all the way from Jack London to Ernest Hemingway to Jimmy Cannon to Red Smith. Writers love fighters and fighters loved writers. Always a great relationship. Joe Louis would do anything, sit still for anything you wanted to do, sit down and talk to you all day. Anything you wanted was fine that, that most fighters could help you with. And suddenly, in Cassius Clay, before he become Muhammad Ali and after, you had a fighter that, I don't know whether manipulate is a right word or not, but you had a fighter that wouldn't do what you exactly, what you wanted him to do. He wasn't always at your beck and call. It was very disconcerting to a lot of the older writers. I think they resented this. Ah, I don't think they saw a new wave coming, a new generation, any, any great sociological change but they weren't comfortable with Cassius Clay before Ali or after he became Muhammad Ali. He was a real unknown quantity for them, as well as everybody else.[44]

The process of developing pre-fight hype for Cassius Clay had its quirky moments. On February 18, less than a week before the bout, the Beatles were scheduled to meet Sonny Liston, but the champ did not appear. Instead, the Fab Four found themselves in Angelo Dundee's dingy Fifth Street Gym. Noted sports commentator Robert Lipsyte remembered that the Beatles felt they had been duped by photographer Harry Benson, who "dumped them in the training camp of Liston's next victim, Cassius Clay, who John Lennon called 'that big mouth who's going to lose.'" Just as John, Paul, George, and Ringo were about to leave in frustration, Clay burst in and bellowed, "Hello Beatles. We oughta do some roadshows together. We'll get rich." The pictures from that photo shoot show the five men clowning, with Clay pretending to knock out all four Beatles. George Harrison described the event as "all part of being a Beatle, really; just getting lugged around and thrust into rooms full of press men taking pictures and asking questions. Muhammad Ali was quite cute . . . There is a famous picture of him holding two of us under each arm." As they smiled and clowned for Benson, "Paul and George traded some good-natured insults with Cassius, he said, 'You ain't as dumb as you look!' John deadpanned: 'No, but you are.'" Soon, the fun was over. The Beatles felt they had been made to look silly. They left the gym and never saw Ali again. A week after the fight, the Beatles sang for a second time on *The Ed Sullivan Show* in New York. Sullivan commented about the fight on the air: "I saw the Liston-Clay fight. This was a stinker of all time. I swear the Beatles could beat the two of 'em! No kidding!"[45]

As the day of the fight approached, the larger questions remained: once he got into the ring, would Clay do what he was told, would he be able to compete against a more traditional fighter known for brutalizing his opponents, and would his unorthodox style carry him through a long fight to beat the "ugly bear," Sonny Liston? Boxing writers wondered if his antics were calculated primarily to drum up interest in the fight or call attention to himself. Of course, they accomplished both goals. As for Liston, it would be impossible to think that the reigning champion paid no attention to Clay's theatrics and displays of enthusiasm at his press conferences. A week before the fight, Angelo Dundee observed that, "This boy is getting under his skin. It bugs Liston, all these things he does." In response, Liston's sparring partner, Leotis Martin, declared that the champion was "not mad at people the way he used to be. He doesn't try to kill us every day." Liston himself said that Clay needed "a lesson in manners. Maybe I can help him by beating his brains out."[46] Clay's rejoinder was a poem in which he predicted victory:

> So don't bet against me, I'm a man of my word.
> He is the greatest! Yes!
> I am the man this poem's about,

I'll be champ of the world, there isn't a doubt.
Here I predict Mr. Liston's dismemberment,
I'll hit him so hard; he'll wonder where October and November went.
When I say two, there's never a third,
Standin against me is completely absurd.
When Cassius says a mouse can outrun a horse,
Don't ask how; put your money where your mouse is!

I AM THE GREATEST![47]

Speaking with Alex Haley after his defeat of Liston, Clay acknowledged that most writers thought of him as a clown whose record did not justify a shot at the Heavyweight Championship fight. To Clay, in hindsight, his hype was a combination of good luck and pure genius:

> The press, everybody—I didn't want nobody thinking nothing except that I was a joke. Listen here, do you realize that of all them ring "experts" on the newspapers, wasn't hardly one that wasn't as carried away with Liston's reputation as Liston was himself? You know what everybody was writing? Saying I had been winning my fights, calling the rounds, because I was fighting "nothing" fighters. Like I told you already, even with people like Moore and Powell and Jones and Cooper, the papers found some excuse; it never was that maybe I could fight. And when it come to Liston, they was all saying it was the end of the line for me. I might even get killed in there; he was going to put his big fist in my big mouth so far they was going to have to get doctors to pull it out, stuff like that. You couldn't read nothing else. That's how come, later on, I made them reporters tell me I was the greatest. They had been so busy looking at Liston's record with Patterson that didn't nobody stop to think about how it was making Liston just about a setup for me.[48]

Soon, the debate would be settled in the ring, but in the days leading up to the battle in Miami, a problem emerged that threatened to derail the financial foundation on which the championship bout rested: Clay's membership in the Nation of Islam. Although he had not yet announced his new religion or his new name, Clay's conversion was well-known among his close circle. If the public learned about Clay's new religious affiliation, promoters feared that the gate would suffer. Most Americans knew nothing of the Nation of Islam but the anti-white rhetoric of Malcolm X and Elijah Muhammad. Sportswriter Lou Eisen explained the problem:

> White people hated Malcolm X and the Nation of Islam for their hatred of white people. The public at large would assume that Ali, because he had converted to Islam, shared similar views about white people to that of Malcolm X. The perception could very well kill the entire promotion.

This was a serious situation. Fight promoter Chris Dundee, brother of trainer Angelo, declared, "Before it was perfect. I had a bad guy [convicted felon Liston] and a good guy [Olympic gold medalist Clay]. Now I have two bad guys facing each other. This will kill the gate." When faced with the choice of keeping quiet about his religious beliefs or losing the opportunity to fight Liston, Ali told Bill McDonald, the fight's major financial backer, that he would not deny his religion. It was trainer Angelo Dundee who thought of a compromise. If Clay could wait until after the fight to reveal his new religion and his new name, the fight would go on as scheduled, everyone would make money, and Clay could than make whatever announcement he chose. The compromise was acceptable to all parties, who could now get back to the business of boxing.[49]

The 1964 Heavyweight Championship fight between Liston and Clay was a case study in conflicting images. Clay was brash, outspoken, loud, and annoying. Clay also had the advantage of sponsorship by Louisville businessmen rather than the Mafia, who reportedly bankrolled Liston. The muscle that could be called upon to break legs or knock out opponents was not an attractive image in early 1960s America. As civil rights workers demanded equality and presented a righteous face to a country that was slowly beginning to respond to their claims for justice, *Look* magazine called Liston "the Negro untouchable, the angry dark-skinned man condemned by the white man to spend his life in the economic and social sewers of his country" in an article with the provocative article titled, "Sonny Liston: King of the Beasts."[50] If Clay was a clown to be tolerated, Liston was a dangerous man. In a few years, the tables would be turned, as Clay became Muhammad Ali and Liston was dead, but, on the eve of the title fight, Clay was the outsider challenging the boxing establishment and its control of bodies like Liston's.

The confusion as to who was the real Negro hero or black villain was evident in the press coverage of the championship fight. According to Peter Guralnick, Liston was described in the press as the "devil incarnate." Many black writers and public figures refused to accept Liston as a representative of their cause, even as they were becoming less comfortable with Clay's antics and rumors that he was moving close to the Nation of Islam. Singer Sam Cooke, himself a troubled talent, spoke on Liston's behalf, saying, "Sonny Liston isn't the worst person in the . . . world and should not be treated like he's the world's first public figure to have a record of being in trouble." Guralnick noted that the mainstream white press, "faced with Clay's baffling mixture of unpardonable braggadocio and inappropriate religious preference" was "forced almost by default to pick Liston as its choice." A few days before the fight, Arthur Daley of the *New York Times* announced that, "An aura of artificiality surrounds Tuesday's heavyweight championship fight . . . On that evening, the loud mouth from Louisville is likely to have a lot of vainglorious boasts jammed down his throat by a ham-like fist." Black sports commentators also felt pushed to support Liston, as they saw Clay as an embarrassing presence both in and outside the ring.[51]

Before the fight, Clay was called a freak, a heavyweight who fought like a bantamweight, and a man who clearly had no sense because he was willing to get into the ring with an obviously stronger fighter. Forty-three of the forty-six sports writers who made predictions about the fight agreed that, even though Clay was the bigger talker, Liston would prevail in the ring. At the morning weigh-in, Clay shouted and raced toward Liston as if to attack him. The doctor who presided over the event declared that Clay's pulse rate had reached a dangerous 120 beats per minute and that he was "nervous and scared to death." There were unsubstantiated rumors that Clay would not show up for the bout or that, if he did appear, he would run away during the National Anthem. This was all part of the hype, which included a lot of shouting and baiting of "The Bear" by the upstart challenger, and Clay was fined $2,500 by Ed Lassman of the World Boxing Association for his antics at the weigh-in.

On February 25, 1964, the two men finally faced each other in the ring. They were almost evenly matched. At 6 feet 3 inches tall and 210 pounds, Clay was a bit taller than Liston, who was two inches shorter and only seven pounds heavier than the challenger. As the two fighters faced each other, Clay shouted, "I've got you now, chump." The crowd at Miami's Convention Hall was disappointing. Only about half of the 16,000 seats had been sold, and closed-circuit television revenue was not expected to make up the financial deficit.[52] The crowd, including literary luminaries Norman Mailer and Truman Capote, along with the boxing writers who predicted disaster for Clay, saw instead a battle that resembled ballet as much as boxing. Clay attacked Liston with a frenzy in the first round, winning handily. The second round seemed like more of a grind, with Liston pounding away at the younger fighter but with less ferocity and effectiveness than he had displayed in his earlier brutal victories. In the third round, Clay connected with a blow that cut Liston under his left eye. Liston came back in the fourth round, which seemed to be a repetition of the second. Toward the end of the fourth round, some liniment or lubricant from Liston's gloves temporarily blinded Clay, who was able to avoid his adversary until his eyes could clear.

A single "punch" in the fifth round was the source of controversy that remains unresolved to this day. According to writer Nick Tosches, "Clay reached out his left arm, rested his gloved fist against Sonny's nose, as if to keep the beast at bay; and, though Sonny's reach was greater, he never struck or swatted that arm away." Liston reeled, but was not knocked out or down. Had there been a punch? Was Liston "faking" an injury? In the sixth round, Clay got to Liston, and the fight was even in terms of points. But "the big ugly bear" stayed on his stool and did not come out of his corner for the seventh round, claiming numbness in his shoulder. "Eat your words!" shouted Clay at the doubting press.

Liston's shoulder injury was controversial. His manager claimed that the initial injury had taken place during training, causing him to skip sparring sessions on February 3, 4, 5, and 14. When he was asked after the fight why the Liston camp had not postponed the bout, manager Jack Nilon told reporters, "We thought we could get away with it." Liston declared before round seven, "I just can't go back." Sportswriter Robert Lipsyte wrote in the *New York Times* that the crowd was

> cheering and booing, which is something like laughing and crying. Because it was the wildest thing they had ever seen. It didn't make sense. For weeks, Clay had played the fool and been tagged at will by unworthy sparring partners. This morning, at the weigh-in, he had acted bizarre and disturbed . . . And tonight, he had been cool and fast and without fear.

Lipsyte concluded that, "Poetry and youth and joy had triumphed over the 8–1 odds."[53]

Liston's injury was real, but had he thrown the fight? Nick Tosches described the scene at Missouri's Jefferson City Penitentiary, Liston's "alma mater," "In the halls and cellblocks . . . the blare of radios was suddenly overtaken by howls of anger. The son of a bitch had thrown the fucking heavyweight championship of the motherfucking world." Angelo Dundee saw the results in a different light:

> Some fans thought that Liston had thrown the first fight in order to get a big payday in the return bout—that he would now show his power and stop Ali. There were more speculations and more half-baked theories than there were after President John F. Kennedy's assassination the previous year. But any fan who thought that didn't understand what it meant to be a champion. No champion would ever willingly throw away his title—especially the heavyweight title; that's where the money is. Now it would be harder for Liston to win it back because Ali was not about to give it away.[54]

While the conspiracy theorists may not have been correct, reporters and the public later learned that, even before the Heavyweight Championship fight, Liston's sponsors, Inter-Continental Promotions Inc., had signed a contract with the Louisville Sponsorship Group for the promotional rights to Clay's first fight as the champion, should he win. Inter-Continental Promotions, of which Liston owned a 22.5 percent share, would choose the opponent for the re-match, but it was a foregone conclusion that if Liston lost in 1964, he would be first in line to fight Clay. The money involved was staggering ($50,000) for a fight with a young fighter who everyone agreed was certain to lose in the first title match. Nevertheless, in vague language designed to circumvent the World Boxing Association's rule against fight contracts with re-match agreements, the contract suggested the possibility of a second fight should Liston lose.

When the two fighters did agree on a re-match shortly after the first fight, the World Boxing Association (WBA) voted to strip Clay's title from him and to remove Liston's name from its rankings, but this was a hollow gesture, as the New York State Athletic Commission, and *Ring* magazine continued to recognize Clay, now Muhammad Ali, as the world heavyweight champion. *TIME* magazine offered its own interpretation of the WBA's actions in March of 1965:

> The W.B.A. is anti-Black Muslim, anti-return-bout contracts and antinoise. It also controls what there is of boxing in 39 states (notable exceptions: California and New York). So last September it declared the heavyweight title vacant, and last week in Chicago it staged a new "world championship" fight between two harmless creatures named Ernie Terrell and Eddie Machen.

Hardly a major media event or a particularly exciting fight, *TIME* declared that the most interesting fight of the evening took place when two spectators argued over their seats and threw a few punches. Terrell won the bout in the ring, declaring, "I am the champ. The W.B.A. says so." But Ali, who answered Terrell's shouts with his own assertion that he was the "king of kings," was in no hurry to take on the WBA title holder.[55] He had more important business to tend to in his scheduled re-match with Sonny Liston. Eventually, WBA Chairman Ed Lassman allowed the champ to re-claim his title on the condition that he moderate his pre-fight rants, a demand to which Ali paid no attention.

Was the timing of the contract, which dated from October of 1963, four months before the fight, along with Liston's shoulder injury that took him out of the fight, just a coincidence for the promoters? It certainly was not a lucky set of circumstances for Liston, who may or may not have been suffering from bursitis of the shoulder for some time before the fight. After he lost the title, Liston continued to have legal difficulties. Almost immediately after the fight, the Internal Revenue Service filed a lien of $868,000 against Liston's earnings. Sportswriter Arthur Daley said that Liston's performance in the fight "showed unmistakably that he was the biggest hoax since the Cardiff Giant," Jimmy Cannon called him "as dumb as a scarecrow on a stick," and *Ring* magazine called him "by nature a lazy man." The State Attorney in Florida, Richard Gerstein, investigated the possibility of fraud with respect to Liston's shoulder injury, and the Colorado State Boxing Commission suspended him. The Gerstein investigation revealed no fraud, but the investigators determined that Liston had requested a postponement of the fight because of his sore arm, a request that was ignored by the Miami Beach Boxing Commission. To make matters worse for Liston, Senator Philip Hart of Michigan turned the attention of his Subcommittee on Antitrust and Monopoly to the fight as an example of corruption. While they did not find evidence of wrongdoing, the senators did not approve of the corrosive and corrupt climate in which professional boxing thrived through the exploitation of its fighters. New York Senator Kenneth Keating declared that the Liston–Clay fight, and what he termed "the antics that both preceded and followed it," brought professional boxing "into widespread public disrepute."[56]

At the same time, Liston's promoters made a new deal with the Louisville Sponsoring Group to promote Ali's next fight, should he beat Liston a second time. Liston's own promoters were betting on him to lose.[57] In his re-match with Clay on May 25, 1965, Liston was no longer the bruising killer he had once been. Clay, now Muhammad Ali, knocked him out at 2:12 of the first round with a much-disputed call by the referee to end the fight. Liston never regained the championship title, and he died of a presumed heroin overdose on December 30, 1970. On February 25, 1964, the Heavyweight Championship crown had changed hands. As Robert Lipsyte reported, "Incredibly, the loud-mouthed bragging, insulting youngster had been telling the truth all along."[58] The Louisville Lip had made his predictions come true.

Notes

1 "50 Stunning Olympic Moments No 17: Cassius Clay Wins Gold in 1960," *Guardian*, http://www.theguardian.com/sport/london-2012-olympics-blog/2012/mar/07/stunning-olympic-moments-cassius-clay.

2 Arthur Daley, "The Gladiators," *New York Times* (September 5, 1960).

3 Dick Schaap, "From Louisville to the Nation of Islam: My Ups and Downs with Ali," *Sport Magazine* (1971), http://thestacks.deadspin.com/from-louisville-to-the-nation-of-islam-my-ups-and-down-1428081378.

4 Huston Horn, "Who Made Me is Me!" *Sports Illustrated* (September 25, 1961), http://www.cnnsi.com/vault/article/magazine/MAG1073035/index.htm.

5 D. Keith Mano, "Still the Greatest," *National Review* Vol. 50, Issue 21 (November 9, 1998).

6 A.J. Libeling, "Reporter at Large," *The New Yorker* (March 2, 1962), in Thomas Hauser, *Muhammad Ali: His Life and Times* (New York: Simon & Schuster, 1991), pp. 41–2.

7 "Eyes on the Prize II Interviews: Angelo Dundee" (March 28, 1989), http://digital.wustl.edu/e/eii/eiiweb/dun5427.0117.040angelodundee.html.

8 Angelo Dundee to Thomas Hauser in *Muhammad Ali: His Life and Times*, p. 35.

9 Ron Flatter, "Moore Packed a Lethal Punch," ESPN Sportscentury Biography, http://espn.go.com/classic/biography/s/Moore_Archie.html.

10 Jack Olsen, "All Alone With the Future," *Sports Illustrated* (May 9, 1966), http://sportsillustrated.cnn.com/vault/article/magazine/MAG1078513/4/index.htm.

11 "Eyes on the Prize Interviews: Angelo Dundee."

12 Mikal Gilmore, "How Muhammad Ali Conquered Fear and Changed the World," *Men's Journal* (November, 2011), http://www.mensjournal.com/magazine/how-muhammad-ali-conquered-fear-and-changed-the-world-20130205.

13 Olsen, "All Alone With the Future."

14 John Capouya, "King Strut," *Sports Illustrated* (December 12, 2005), http://www.si.com/vault/article/magazine/MAG1114630/index.htm.

15 Peter Carlson, "Gorgeous George Tutors Cassius Clay," *American History* Vol. 46, Issue 5 (December, 2011), pp. 24–5.

16 Alex Haley, Interview with Cassius Clay, *Playboy* (October, 1964), http://www.alex-haley.com/alex_haley_cassius_clay_interview.htm.

17 "Muhammad Ali vs Tunney Hunsaker," *BoxRec Encyclopedia*, http://boxrec.com/media/index.php/Muhammad_Ali_vs._Tunney_Hunsaker.

18 Michael Brennan, "Ali and His Educators," *Sports Illustrated* (September 22, 1980), http://sportsillustrated.cnn.com/vault/article/magazine/MAG1148116/index.htm and "Muhammad Ali vs Tunney Hunsaker," *BoxRec Encyclopedia*, http://boxrec.com/media/index.php/Muhammad_Ali_vs._Tunney_Hunsaker.

19 Brennan, "Ali and His Educators."

20 Hauser, *Muhammad Ali: His Life and Times*, p. 42.

21 "Muhammad Ali vs Donnie Fleeman," *BoxRec Encyclopedia*, http://boxrec.com/media/index.php/Muhammad_Ali_vs._Donnie_Fleeman.

22 Huston Horn, "Fast Talk and a Slow Fight," *Sports Illustrated* (July 31, 1961), http://sportsillustrated.cnn.com/vault/article/magazine/MAG1072828/2/index.htm.

23 "Muhammad Ali vs Alonzo Johnson," *BoxRec Encyclopedia*, http://boxrec.com/media/index.php/Muhammad_Ali_vs._Alonzo_Johnson.

24 Gilbert Rogin, "Cautious Comes of Age," *Sports Illustrated* (October 16, 1961), http://sportsillustrated.cnn.com/vault/article/magazine/MAG1073086/1/index.htm.

25 "Muhammad Ali vs Sonny Banks," *BoxRec Encyclopedia*, http://boxrec.com/media/index.php/Muhammad_Ali_vs._Sonny_Banks.

26 Gilbert Rogin, "Campaign's End for an Ancient Warrior," *Sports Illustrated* (November 26, 1962), http://sportsillustrated.cnn.com/vault/article/magazine/MAG1074343/index.htm.

27 "Cassius Clay vs Doug Jones," *BoxRec Encyclopedia*, http://boxrec.com/media/index.php/Cassius_Clay_vs._Doug_Jones.

28 Ibid.; and Alex Poinsett, "A Look at Cassius Clay: Biggest Mouth in Boxing," *Ebony* Vol. 188, No. 5 (March, 1963), p. 35.

29 "C. Marcellus Clay Esq.," *Sports Illustrated* (June 10, 1963), http://sportsillustrated.cnn.com/vault/article/magazine/MAG1074856/index.htm.

30 "Henry Cooper vs Cassius Clay: The Punch that (Almost) Changed the World," *Daily Mail* (London), http://www.dailymail.co.uk/sport/othersports/article-1382819/Henry-Cooper-v-Cassius-Clay-The-punch-changed-world.html.

31 Brennan, "Ali and His Educators."

32 "Henry Cooper vs Cassius Clay," http://www.dailymail.co.uk/sport/othersports/article-1382819/Henry-Cooper-v-Cassius-Clay-The-punch-changed-world.html.

33 Angelo Dundee (with Bert Randolph Sugar), *My View from the Corner, A Life in Boxing* (New York: McGraw-Hill, 2008), p. 89.

34 Randy Roberts, *Joe Louis: Hard Times Man* (New Haven: Yale University Press, 2010), p. 21.

35 Randy Roberts, "The Politics and Economics of Televised Boxing," in Elliott J. Gorn, ed., *Muhammad Ali: The People's Champ* (Urbana and Chicago: University of Illinois Press, 1997), p. 35.

36 "Sonny Liston-From the Big House to the Big Time," http://sports.jrank.org/pages/2863/Liston-Sonny-From-Big-House-Big-Time.html.

37 Gilbert Rogin, "The Facts About the Big Fight," *Sports Illustrated* (October 8, 1962), http://sportsillustrated.cnn.com/vault/article/magazine/MAG1147918/2/index.htm.

38 Tex Maule, "Liston's Edge: A Lethal Left," *Sports Illustrated* (February 24, 1964), http://sportsillustrated.cnn.com/vault/article/magazine/MAG1075666/index.htm.

39 Edwin Pope Interview (June 19, 1989), *Eyes on the Prize II Interviews*. Washington University Gateway Texts, http://digital.wustl.edu/e/eii/eiiweb/pop5427.0310.131edwinpope.html.

40 Tex Maule, "Liston's Edge: A Lethal Left," *Sports Illustrated* (February 24, 1964).

41 Dundee, *My View from the Corner*, p. 90.

42 *The Greatest*, Columbia Records (1963) in Hauser, *Muhammad Ali: His Life and Times*, p. 58.

43 Alex Haley, Interview with Cassius Clay, *Playboy* (October, 1964).

44 Edwin Pope Interview.

45 Robert Lipsyte, "Winner by a Decision," *Smithsonian* (February, 2004), http://www.smithsonian mag.com/arts-culture/winner-by-a-decision-1, "The Beatles Meet Cassius Clay," http://www.beatlesbible.com/1964/02/18/beatles-meet-cassius-clay/, H2O Man, "Cassius X and The Beatles," http://www.democraticunderground.com/10024562213 and E.L. Judge, "The Beatles & Cassius Clay Meet in the Ring," http://wcbsfm.cbslocal.com/top-lists/the-beatles-cassius-clay-meet-in-the-ring/.

46 Tex Maule, "The Sting of the Louisville Lip," *Sports Illustrated* (February 17, 1964), http://sports illustrated.cnn.com/vault/article/magazine/MAG1075646/3/index.htm.

47 Muhammad Ali, "This is the Legend of Cassius Clay . . .," http://www.goodreads.com/quotes/326903-this-is-the-legend-of-cassius-clay-the-most-beautiful.

48 Alex Haley, Interview with Cassius Clay, *Playboy* (October, 1964), http://www.alex-haley.com/alex_haley_cassius_clay_interview.htm.

49 Lou Eisen, "The Redemption of Muhammad Ali," *Fight Network* (June 25, 2013), http://fightnetwork.com/news/39470:the-redemption-of-muhammad-ali/.

50 "Sonny Liston, King of the Beasts," *Look* (February 25, 1964) in Nick Tosches, *The Devil and Sonny Liston* (Boston: Little, Brown, 2000), p. 202.

51 Peter Guralnick, excerpt from *Dream Boogie: The Triumph of Sam Cooke*. "Great Encounters #22: Cassius Clay, Malcolm X, and Sam Cooke—the Clay/Sonny Liston fight, Miami, 1964," http://www.jerryjazzmusician.com/2005/10/great-encounters-22-cassius-clay-malcolm-x-and-sam-cooke-the-claysonny-liston-fight-miami-1964/.

52 One result of the poor attendance was a suit brought by Inter-Continental Promotions, Inc. against the fight's promoter, William MacDonald, for breach of contract. MacDonald paid Inter-Continental only a third of the contracted amount for the gate receipts. MacDonald argued that his contract with Inter-Continental was illegal, and therefore unenforceable, under Florida law. The United States District Court agreed with MacDonald, but the Fifth Circuit Court of Appeals reversed that decision and found for Inter-Continental, noting that the fight was legitimate. It was a pyrrhic victory because the fight had not yielded enough money to satisfy the terms of the contract. See Andres F. Quintana, "Muhammad Ali: The Greatest in Court," *Marquette Sports Law Review* Vol. 18, Issue 1 (Fall, 2007), p. 178.

53 Robert Lipsyte, "Clay Wins Title in Seventh-Round Upset As Liston is Halted by Shoulder Injury," *New York Times* (February 26, 1964), http://www.nytimes.com/books/98/10/25/specials/ali-upset.html.

54 Dundee, *My View from the Corner*, p. 110.

55 "Prizefighting for All the Cheese," *TIME* (March 12, 1965), http://content.time.com/time/subscriber/article/0,33009,839408,00.html.

56 "This Just In: Ali's Hernia Killed Liston!" (November 13, 1964) posted by Paul Gallender on Boxing.com (November 20, 2012), http://www.boxing.com/this_just_in_alis_hernia_killed_liston.html.

57 Ibid.

58 Robert Lipsyte, "Clay Wins Title in Seventh-Round Upset As Liston is Halted by Shoulder Injury," *New York Times* (February 26, 1964).

CHAPTER 3

"What's My Name?"

From the Sports Pages to the Front Page

Cassius Clay stunned the boxing world with his defeat of Sonny Liston on February 25, 1964, but he was not finished shocking the sports world and the general public. The day after the fight, he revealed that he had rejected his Baptist faith and become a member of the Nation of Islam. Many sportswriters had suspected for months that Clay was developing an allegiance to the Nation, based on the time he was spending with Minister Malcolm X and other members of the religious group. With Clay's new religious identity came a new name. He spent a short time calling himself Cassius X, a rejection of his Christian, "slave" name. In rejecting his birth name, he also rejected the legacy of the nineteenth-century Cassius Marcellus Clay of which he had once been proud. Soon after Clay's announcement, the Honorable Elijah Muhammad, leader of the Nation of Islam, bestowed on him the name Muhammad Ali. Muhammad means praiseworthy and Ali means most high. This communicated to the world the clear message that the newest recruit to the ranks of the Nation of Islam was a most honored man.

The Nation of Islam was part of a continuum of African-American self-help, cultural, political, and nationalist organizations that emerged in the nineteenth and early twentieth centuries. These groups provided both a positive identity and substantive help for the descendants of freed slaves in the United States. Institutions for the education of former slaves and their descendants such as Fisk University in Nashville, Tennessee in 1866; Howard University in Washington, DC in 1867; Hampton University, founded as the Hampton Institute in 1868 in Virginia; the Tuskegee Institute established by Booker T. Washington in Alabama in 1881; and other historically black colleges, served as a training ground for an emerging African-American middle class of teachers, preachers, and small business owners. Black self-help institutions such as the National Association for the Advancement of Colored

People (founded in 1909) were assisted by white reformers, whose goals included improvement for the African-American population. These organizations often walked a fine line between asserting individual and group independence, which might alienate white supporters, and promoting a safer position that called for Negro "uplift" without pushing for full legal and social rights in white society until later in the twentieth century.

Marcus Garvey's Universal Negro Improvement Association and African Communities League (UNIA-ACL) espoused a specifically black nationalist and pan-African position, arguing against integration as a solution to the economic and social problems of black American citizens and pushing instead for economic and social separation from mainstream white society and even a return to Africa to reclaim both land and heritage from European colonial powers. Garvey's parades and speeches inspired thousands in American cities to consider the possibility of redeeming Africa for Africans and African-Americans. Garvey's approach, which ignored ties that black Americans might have to this country in favor of a return to Africa and African cultures, was one strand of influence that contributed to the founding and success of the Nation of Islam. It is not surprising that Malcolm X's father was involved in Garvey's movement and that Cassius Clay, Sr. also appreciated the teachings and focus on independence of Garvey's organization.

All of these organizations, whether they advocated self-improvement and integration or African nationalism and separation from white society, shared a goal of helping generations of African-Americans to learn about their unique identity and a sense of racial pride. In 1913, Timothy Drew, who later called himself Prophet Noble Drew Ali, founded the Canaanite Temple, which was soon re-named the Moorish Science Temple, in Newark, New Jersey. Drew was born in North Carolina in 1886. His parents were former slaves who lived in a community of Cherokee Indians after Emancipation. Drew's personal creation story holds that he signed on as a merchant seaman at the age of sixteen, made his way to Egypt, and became the prophet Noble Drew Ali after a visit to the Pyramid of Cheops. He returned to the United States to found his temple on the basis of a dream in which he was instructed to establish a religion to uplift downtrodden American descendants of Africans.

Noble Drew Ali preached that all black Africans, including African-Americans, were descendants of Moors, who were Muslims from Morocco originally descended from Ham, one of the sons of Noah. He criticized black Americans for ignoring their Moorish heritage and accepting the "Negro" label, saying that if the Africans who were brought here had "honored their father and mother" and not "strayed after the strange gods of Europe," they would not have been enslaved.[1] Ali said that slavery and colonialism had taken away both religion and pride from black people and that their hope of spiritual redemption lay not in a return to Africa but in a variety of Islam propagated by Ali himself. He claimed that he had converted to Islam on a pilgrimage to Morocco and had been called to propagate the faith as he interpreted it to blacks in America.

Noble Drew Ali claimed that the path to spiritual redemption for Moors or "Asiatics" (he rejected the terms "Negro" and "Black") could be found in the Holy Koran, a text he said had been "divinely prepared by the Prophet Noble Drew Ali, by the guiding hand of his father, God Allah." In this respect, his Koran was similar to the original Qur'an, in which Muhammad is said to have taken down directly the words of Allah. Noble Drew Ali's text retained some of Islam's basic tenets, although it is a unique document. Ali's followers were attracted to the simplicity and clarity of the message that their ancestors had possessed a noble identity that had been stolen from them by the white institution of slavery. Their attraction to this variant of Islam, which Ali was careful to call Islamism, seemed to make sense because of the presence of Muslims in West Africa and the close identification of Christianity with slavery and oppressive discrimination in the United States.

Noble Drew Ali's organization grew rapidly in black neighborhoods in Baltimore, Richmond, Cleveland, Lansing, Philadelphia, Milwaukee, Chicago, Pittsburgh, and Detroit. Ali moved his organization's headquarters to Chicago in 1923 and changed its name to the Moorish Holy Temple after a dispute with other members of the organization. When Ali moved, his opponents stayed in Newark and called themselves members of the "Holy Moabite Temple of Science." Despite the competition for adherents, Ali proved to be a successful recruiter, claiming 30,000 members by 1923. In a final name change, he re-named his organization the Moorish Science Temple of America in 1928.

Ali's creed, a belief in one God, was simple and accepting, even as his rules of conduct for adherents were complex and restrictive. Temple followers avoided smoking, drinking, gambling, and eating pork. The rapid growth of the Moorish Science Temple community, fueled in part by the mythical stories of the sect's founding, contributed to the development of factions vying for power and influence. Noble Drew Ali died in 1929 under mysterious circumstances after an encounter, which might have included a beating, with the Chicago police. After Ali's death, the Temple split into smaller groups, one of which developed into the Nation of Islam.[2]

Some of Ali's Chicago followers joined Wallace D. Fard in founding the Lost-Found Nation of Islam in Detroit in 1930, during the depths of the Depression. Like the Prophet Noble Drew Ali, Fard preached that Islam was the true religion of African Americans. Fard invented a version of Islam that embraced Black Nationalism and strict rules that provided structure in the lives of his followers. The new organization established temples and schools, a governance structure, and the Fruit of Islam, a paramilitary organization.

Fard himself was a mysterious character. Some sources say he came from Arabia, while some say he was a white man from New Zealand. In his early days in Detroit, he led a growing group of followers, revealing little about his own background or personal life. Historian Peter Goldman described Fard's origins:

> God, it is written, appeared to the black people of Detroit's Paradise Valley slums on July 4, 1930, in the person of a peddler of clothing and silks known variously as Wallace D. Fard, W. Fard, Muhammad, F. Muhammad Ali, or simply Mr. Fard.[3]

The man of many names was also a man of many occupations, some of them criminal. He had served time in San Quentin Prison for bootlegging and trafficking in morphine in 1926. Wallace D. Fard, who also called himself Master Fard Muhammad, claimed to be the reincarnation of Noble Drew Ali. With his experience as a door-to-door salesman in poor communities, this white/Arab/black leader with a suspect, or at least unknown, background easily assumed the leadership of the remnants of Ali's Temple. Fard's theology was unique, to say the least. He preached that Allah

> had evolved from a spinning atom some 76 million years ago. He was no "spook God" but a man, the Original Man, and all his descendants—all the Black people of the earth—were the Original People. They had lived in peace and harmony for eons, their future foreseen and "written" by a council of imams—brilliant, clairvoyant, scientists-priests who had mastered far more advanced technology than anything we have to this day. They had built the pyramids of Egypt with their superior "hydraulics," and their experiments in high explosives had raised the world's mountain ranges, separated the continents, and even brought about "the deportation of the moon" from its original location in the earth's single ocean.

This was fanciful at best. Fard also asserted that white people were devils, Jews were particularly devious and dangerous, and black people were descended from the Tribe of Shabazz. Originally white (a story Fard used to explain away his own Caucasian appearance), the Original People had moved to Africa, where their bodies became hardened and their skins darkened. Fard created an appealing theology and worldview that attracted people whose ancestors had been brutalized by slavery, colonial domination, and racism that placed white people at the top of a social ladder whose upward-leading rungs were not even accessible to most black people.[4]

Fard's departure from the Lost-Found Nation of Islam was as mysterious as his original appearance in Detroit. In the early 1930s, he chose Elijah Poole to lead his organization, at which point he disappeared. His anointed successor was one of the millions of black men whose early lives had been shaped by violence and racism in the deep South. Born in Sandesville, Georgia in 1897, he and his family moved to Detroit after World War I, but discrimination, a lack of education, and the effects of alcohol kept Poole as poor in the North as he had been in Georgia. He attached himself to Fard and the Temple of Islam and became a preacher. According to the official Nation of Islam History, Fard choose Poole, who began to call himself Elijah Muhammad, to serve as his Divine Representative

> in continuing this most difficult task of bringing truth and light to His lost and found people. For 3 1/2 years, he taught and trained the Honorable Elijah Muhammad night and day into the profound Secret Wisdom of the Reality of God, which included the hidden knowledge of the original people who were the first founders of civilization of our Planet and who had a full knowledge of the Universal Order of Things from the beginning of the Divine Creation.[5]

The Nation of Islam was now the province of the Honorable Elijah Muhammad, who claimed that African Americans were the Original People from the city of Mecca, that God was black, and that the white man was the Devil. With these ideas as guiding principles, Elijah Muhammad became the leader of the Detroit Temple in 1933, leaving that city in 1935 to set up Mosque No. 2 in Chicago, which served as the headquarters of the Nation of Islam for decades. Within a few years, Muhammad established Temple No. 3 in Milwaukee and then No. 4 in Washington, DC.

In 1941, at the age of forty-four, just a year shy of the upper limit on the draft age, Muhammad announced his public opposition to participation in a "white man's war." Later, he remembered that, when the World War II draft calls were announced, "I refused (NOT EVADED) on the grounds that, first, I was a Muslim and would not take part in war and especially not on the side of infidels." He was arrested in May of 1942 for failure to register with the Selective Service System and sedition for some of his public statements. Muhammad served three-and-a-half years of a five-year federal prison sentence. After his release in 1946, he returned to Chicago, where he faced the task of putting the Nation of Islam back together.[6] The organization grew significantly throughout the 1940s and 1950s, propounding an ideology of racial separation. By 1959, there were twenty-two Nation of Islam mosques in twelve states. As the mainstream non-violent civil rights movement preached integration, peace, and love, the Nation of Islam preached independence, self-reliance, separation from white society, and hatred of white people. By the 1960s, the rhetoric and theology of the Muslims was attractive to young black men, including the up-and-coming fighter, Cassius Marcellus Clay.

The Honorable Elijah Muhammad helped to transform the Nation of Islam into a social movement as well as a religion. His strict rules for his adherents included prayer five times a day, abstinence from alcohol, tobacco, pork, narcotics, and sports, no absences or vacations from work, and no more sleep than is necessary for good health. These rules are repeated again and again in publications from Elijah Muhammad's *Message to the Black Man in America*, first published in 1965, to articles and editorials in the Nation's newspaper, *Muhammad Speaks*, which began publication in October of 1961. In addition, the Nation founded temples in cities all over the United States, schools that taught subjects ranging from world history from a Muslim perspective to home economics for girls, restaurants that adhered to Muslim dietary restrictions, farms, and other local businesses. Codes of behavior were strict, as described by the wife of Hon. Elijah Muhammad in the 1990s:

> We are taught cleanliness inwardly and outwardly with the practice of good manners and respect to one and all. We are taught that the family is the backbone of society and that our children must be reared to reflect the highest morals and training to perfect our society. We are trained to eat and to prepare the best of foods for the longevity of life, without the use of alcohol, smoking and substance abuse which endangers the ethics of healthy living. We are taught to respect and protect our women who are the mothers of civilization.
>
> Our women are taught a dress code of modesty that will lead to the practice of high morality. We are trained to be an exemplary community expressing the highest spiritual goals for the reform of ourselves and others based on wisdom, knowledge and beauty.[7]

Members of the Fruit of Islam were easily recognizable in their white shirts and black bow ties, and women frequently dressed in long tunics and veils.

The success of the Nation of Islam attracted the attention of the mainstream media, which regarded the group's insistence on independence from white America as a threat to the righteous claims of the civil rights "beloved community" that attracted many black and white supporters and participants.

Only a few years after Cassius Clay listened to the reports of Emmett Till's murder and public funeral, the message of the Nation of Islam was all over the airwaves.

This religious group came to the broader American public's attention with the 1959 television documentary, "The Hate that Hate Produced," which featured CBS reporter Mike Wallace. The five-part series began with Wallace's description of what he called "Black racism," a growing call for black supremacy among a growing segment of African Americans.

> While city officials, state agencies, white liberals and sober-minded Negroes stand idly by, a group of Negro dissenters are taking to street corner step ladders,

church pulpits, sports arenas and ballroom platforms across the nation to preach the gospel of hate that would set off a federal investigation if it were to be preached by Southern whites. What are they saying?

Wallace called these dissenters "black supremacists" who preached hatred of white people to as many as a quarter of a million urban black people. In a popular morality play of sorts enacted hundreds of times, Nation of Islam speakers placed white America on "trial." Wallace broadcast the result of the trial, as recounted by the National Islam speaker:

> I charge the white man with being the greatest liar on earth. I charge the white man with being the greatest drunkard on earth . . . I charge the white man with being the greatest gambler on earth. I charge the white man, ladies and gentle-men of the jury, with being the greatest murderer on earth . . . I charge the white man with being the greatest adulterer on earth. I charge the white man with being the greatest robber on earth. I charge the white man with being the greatest troublemaker on earth. So therefore, ladies and gentlemen of the jury, I charge you to bring back a verdict of guilty as charged.

The penalty for all of these sins was death. The documentary made it clear to white America that there was a growing movement that preached a very different gospel from that of the church-related civil rights movement as modeled by Dr. King's Southern Christian Leadership Conference or orga-nizations like the Congress of Racial Equality or the NAACP, all of which supported non-violence.[8]

One of the primary ideological positions of the Nation of Islam was its opposition to Christianity. The Nation often equated Christianity with slavery and oppression, and this message appealed to some poor urban African-Americans whose lives in this world were not made any better by having faith in a better life in the next. Herbert Muhammad, son of Honor-able Elijah Muhammad, said that Cassius Clay was attracted to the Nation of Islam because he saw

> that this was a Black group, a Black man calling all White people devils, and then he say he went back home and he looked at the picture on his wall where he had Jesus and all of the twelve disciples of Jesus, The Last Supper, and he noticed everybody was White. And so, so then he started having a conflict in his self about what, what effect would this, would be on the White society if it was reversed, if these people was all Black and they had to live with a Black Jesus, and a Black, what we called disciples. What kind of effect would it be on their mind. And he came to the conclusion that this would definitely have a bad effect on any society using racism in divinity. So then he saw that this wasn't right, and he joined my father because that this little Black man was, was bold enough to tell the world that they was, all Whites was devils.[9]

Although Clay had been raised as a Baptist, he was drawn to the messages he heard on the street corners of Harlem and in the mosques of Chicago and Miami.

But it was not a foregone conclusion that the Nation of Islam would be interested in a young man who aspired to be boxing's heavyweight champion. In the early issues of *Muhammad Speaks*, the Nation of Islam's official publication, articles and editorials on sports were generally confined to profiles of black players in professional leagues, a few advertisements featuring black athletes, and denunciations of the deleterious effects of sports culture on the black family. The Honorable Elijah Muhammad decried professional sports as injurious to the spiritual health of black people, primarily because of the connection to gambling. On October 15, 1962, Muhammad connected sports and gambling, which he regarded as an evil visited on African Americans:

> Hundreds of millions of dollars change hands for the benefit of a few to the hurt of millions, and suffering from the lack of good education, with their last few pennies they help the already helped to try winning with these gambling "scientists" who have prepared a game of chance that the poor suckers have only one chance out of nine hundred to win. Therefore, the world of sports is causing tremendous evils.

Muhammad also asserted that "the poor so-called Negroes are the worst victims of this world of sport and play because they are trying to learn the white man's games of civilization."[10] Within a few years, the Nation of Islam (NOI) would have a new member who would place the culture of professional sports, if not the gambling that often accompanied athletic contests, at the forefront of NOI culture.

Cassius Clay dated his first exposure to the Nation of Islam to his participation in the 1959 Golden Gloves Tournament in Chicago, where he saw a copy of *Muhammad Speaks* being sold by an NOI member. He later said, "I didn't pay much attention to it, but lots of things were working on my mind." According to historian Manning Marable, Clay returned to Louisville "clutching a long-playing record of Elijah Muhammad's speeches. Still in high school, he pestered one of his teachers, unsuccessfully, to be allowed to write a paper about the sect."[11] In spite of the negative reputation of the Nation of Islam in the minds of both whites and many blacks, something was very clearly "working" in the young fighter's mind. When Clay visited New York prior to his trip to Rome for the Olympics, he observed a street corner speaker near the Hotel Theresa at 125th Street and Seventh Avenue in the heart of Harlem. The speaker railed against white people, insisting that they were "no good." According to Clay's host, Dick Schaap, the young fighter had never seen or heard anything like the speech. He was "impressed." It's not clear that Clay was directly exposed to the language of the Nation of Islam on this trip, but his first visit to Harlem did give him a new perspective on his relationship to the white world.

Clay attended his first NOI meeting in 1961 in Miami while training for a fight with Texan Donnie Fleeman. In March of that year, he met Abdul Rahaman (Sam Saxon) who was selling copies of *Muhammad Speaks* on the street. Rahaman noted that Clay was a bit familiar with the teachings of the NOI but that he had not yet engaged in any formal study of the religion. He said, "I saw the cockiness in him. I knew if I could put the truth to him, he'd be great, so I invited him to our next meeting at the mosque." On that occasion, Clay said he "felt truly spiritual" on entering the mosque. He said, "A man named Brother John was speaking and the first words I heard were, 'Why are we called Negroes? It's the white man's way of taking away our identities.' I liked what I heard and wanted to learn more."[12] Of his Miami Mosque experience, Clay said he felt he could

> reach out and touch what Brother John was saying. It wasn't like church teaching, where I had to have faith that what the preacher was preaching was right . . . So I liked what I heard, and wanted to learn more. I started reading *Muhammad Speaks* every week, went to meetings, and listened to a phonograph record they gave me called "A White Man's Heaven is a Black Man's Hell." I had respect for Martin Luther King and all the other civil rights leaders, but I was taking a different path.

The young fighter was receptive to the NOI's teachings. In 1961, as lunch counter sit-in participants and freedom riders were severely beaten as they protested for basic rights and black children were denied equal educational opportunities nearly a decade after the *Brown* v. *Board of Education* decision, it was not difficult to accept the idea that white people were the source of most, if not all, evil. Clay's teacher, Jeremiah Shabazz, realized that, in spite of his youth, he was

> a wise young man, so he was able to see what we were teaching had truth. He had trouble worshiping a God other than Jesus, because he'd been raised in a Christian church. But we had a way back then which was, I guess you could say, a system of teaching that had been sophisticated to the point where we could go into history, biology, genetics, and everything to prove our point of black goodness as opposed to white hatred.

Clay's receptivity to his new teachings was based in part on his experiences as a child in Louisville, where he had often seen

> the white man mistreating black people, saw his mother and father being disrespected and mistreated. So the real problem we had with him was not convincing him we were right. It was fear.

Prior to the Liston fight, Clay made a practice of attending Nation of Islam meetings, but he could not do so openly, fearing that if people knew he was there he might not be allowed to contend for the title. He found in the teachings of Elijah Muhammad self-respect and respect for his people. He learned that, even after hundreds of years in this country, many black citizens were unable to exercise their full rights in society, owned little in terms of material possessions, and had no reason to believe that the "American Dream" was possible for them. Instead of preaching a gospel of despair or a theology that stressed "uplift" on white terms, Elijah Muhammad demanded that black people express respect for themselves and each other in their everyday actions. Clay said that the Minister was trying to

> lift us up and get our people out of the gutter. He made us dress properly, so they weren't out on the street looking like prostitutes and pimps. He taught good eating habits, and was against alcohol and drugs.

Clay acknowledged that Elijah Muhammad might have been mistaken when he called all white people devils but he maintained that the NOI leader accomplished a lot in encouraging black self-respect. Once Clay accepted the primacy of Allah and the teaching of Elijah Muhammad that "there was a higher power than the white man," he was ready to accept all of the teachings of the Nation of Islam.[13]

Even before the February, 1964 announcement of his conversion, Clay developed a close personal relationship with Malcolm X, then a popular NOI minister. The two met when Clay and his brother Rudy attended an NOI rally at a mosque in Detroit in 1962.

Malcolm had earned a reputation as a powerful speaker and an outstanding recruiter for the Nation. He was also an independent thinker, a character trait that would lead to trouble, exile, and assassination in the future. Clay saw Malcolm as bright and inspiring, and the two became friends.

On the eve of the heavyweight title fight, Malcolm had come to see Clay's value to the Nation, even though most members ignored or were actively hostile to sports, especially professional boxing. In late 1963, Malcolm and his family spent time in Miami as Clay's guests while he was training to fight Sonny Liston. The fighter and the minister were often seen together in the city, leading to further speculation about Clay's relationship to the Nation of Islam. During this period, under the cloud of his suspension from speaking as a representative of the Nation, Malcolm worked to create a new image of himself as a family man, posing for pictures with his wife and children as well as with Clay. Some of these photos were published in both the *Amsterdam News* in New York and the *Chicago Defender*, presenting a more benign portrait of Malcolm X to a broader urban black public. In Miami, Malcolm assumed the role of Clay's teacher and informal advisor. He wrote in his *Autobiography* that Clay

> did not need to be told how white Christianity had dealt with the American black man. "This fight is the *truth*," I told Cassius. "It's the Cross and the Crescent fighting in a prize ring—for the first time. It's a modern Crusades—a Christian and a Muslim fighting each other with television to beam it off Telstar for the whole world to see what happens." I told Cassius, "Do you think Allah has brought about all this intending for you to leave the ring as anything but a champion?"[14]

In contrast, Liston insisted that the upcoming fight was just a fight. He claimed to be aware of Clay's association with the Nation, saying, "Don't make no difference to me. I don't mess with his personal affairs, he shouldn't mess with mine."[15]

Members of the Nation of Islam were certain that Clay could not unseat the reigning heavyweight champion. The Honorable Elijah Muhammad retained his hostility to sports in general and boxing in particular. According to Manning Marable:

> NOI leaders were convinced that the loudmouthed Clay had no chance to defeat Liston. Publicly embracing him, they believed, would bring only embarrassment after his all but certain loss. But Malcolm, who had developed a solid friendship with Clay, possessed a surer sense of the boxer's skills. He also saw that Cassius was intelligent and possessed a charisma that could attract young blacks to Islam. And it probably occurred to him that, in the event of a showdown with the Chicago leaders, having Clay on his side was a plus.[16]

Both men were motivated by religious conviction, and both were strong strategic thinkers. Clay found a new religious faith, and he also discovered a popular base that did not rely on white institutions or individuals. And Malcolm understood the strategic advantage of recruiting the champ. Clay was receptive to the Nation of Islam message. Writing in 1966, Jack Olsen observed that "Christianity could not satisfy a mystical, unsettled Negro youth weaned on stories about lynching and rape and the lying, deceitful white man." For his part, Clay declared that "Muhammad ain't playing, man! He makes you live clean and righteous. When he catch you, boy, you caught!"[17]

Less than a month before his title fight against Sonny Liston, Clay left his Miami training camp without telling his trainer, Angelo Dundee. This was a most unusual action in the midst of preparing for a high-profile fight. Clay was accompanied by Malcolm X, and his destination was New York. He attended a Nation of Islam rally at the Rockland Palace Ballroom on

155th Street near Eighth Avenue. The concert venue also housed Muhammad Mosque No. 18. Although there were no white people, and certainly no white reporters, at the meeting, Dick Schaap wrote that Clay spoke to the assembled crowd of more than 1,200. He noted that:

> The brash young boxer, who celebrated his 22nd birthday last week, may not be a card-carrying Muslim. But, unquestionably, he sympathizes with Muslim aims and, by his presence at their meetings, lends them prestige. He is the first nationally famous Negro to take an active part in the Muslim movement. Yet he still had not formally announced support for the Muslims.

The *Amsterdam News* also reported on Clay's speech at the Harlem dinner. He told the crowd that he was inspired by what he heard at Muslim meetings because there was "no smoking, no whiskey bottles and a well-disciplined audience. This is a miracle for so-called Negroes, and this is why the white man is so shook up." Speaking of his impending title fight, Clay predicted victory, because, "I'm training on lamb chops and that big ugly bear is training on pork chops."[18] Even as Clay endeavored to make an impression on the New York NOI members, he took the opportunity to blast his future opponent.

The day after his victory over Liston on February 25, 1964, Cassius Clay made public what many had suspected for months. He was now formally affiliated with the Nation of Islam. In spite of the fact that he had been banned from speaking to the press, Malcolm X celebrated Clay's triumph by declaring that

> Clay is the finest Negro athlete I have ever known, the man who will mean more to his people than any athlete before him. He is more than Jackie Robinson was, because Robinson is the white man's hero. The white press wanted him [Clay] to lose. They wanted him to lose because he is a Muslim. You notice nobody cares about the religion of other athletes. But their prejudice against Clay blinded them to his ability.[19]

Cassius Marcellus Clay soon accepted the name Muhammad Ali, and he insisted that people use his new name and reject his "slave name," even though it was not a slave name for him. The champ's identification with the Nation of Islam was now public, and the Nation of Islam now fully accepted him as a member, a brother, and a symbol of their success. Ali was, in the minds of many sportswriters and much of the general public, no longer simply a bragging clown who nevertheless backed up his outrageous claims with his fists. He was now a regarded by many as a fanatic who was intent on fighting a religious race war with white America because of his association with the Nation of Islam, which was for many Americans a dangerous cult whose leaders preached hatred and proposed founding a separate country from which white people would presumably be excluded.

Very soon after Ali's victory over Liston and his declaration of his new religious affiliation, the World Boxing Association considered the situation in which it now found itself. With a new champion who seemed to have a major liability—his connection to an unpopular religious group that many considered a dangerous cult—Association president Ed Lassman proposed that Ali be stripped of his WBA title because his association with the NOI represented conduct detrimental to boxing. Ostensibly, Lassman's demand stemmed from the advance contract for a re-match between the two fighters that was not allowed under WBA rules. But in an editorial in *The Harvard Crimson* a month after Ali's victory over Liston, writer Peter Kann expressed a different point of view:

> Lassman's action is a thinly-disguised political attack on Clay's Black Muslim affiliation. And if the 20 Boxing Commissioners have any common sense, or interest in the future of professional boxing, they would be well advised to leave Cassius his title, and to relieve Mr. Lassman of his.
>
> Part of Lassman's case against Clay is based on the controversial $50,000 contract, signed before the Clay-Liston fight, which gave Sonny's promoters the rights to Clay's first fight if he should become champion. This contract does appear to be a not very subtle effort to circumvent the 1963 WBA regulation prohibiting return clauses in championship fights.
>
> Although few reputable boxing experts have claimed that the Liston-Clay fight was fixed, there may well be grounds for a WBA investigation and perhaps nullification of the contract.
>
> But, Lassman is not calling for an investigation of Cassius Clay's contract; he is demanding the dethronement of Cassius X. The heart of Lassman's case against Clay is the champion's personal behavior and its effect upon "the boxing world" and "the youth of the world," and here Lassman betrays himself as a fool and a bigot.

And the *Crimson* writer made it clear that he saw a clear difference between approving Ali's religious choices and denying him the boxing title he had just earned because of those choices:

> We have every right and probably much reason to regret that Cassius has provided the Muslims with a public forum for their philosophy. We may hope like hell that Floyd Patterson can work his way up the heavyweight ladder, defeat Clay, and then quietly preach the Urban League doctrine from the throne. Or, we might wish for the good old days when fighters fought, kept their social and religious convictions to themselves, and left the civil rights movement for quicker minds to deal with.
>
> Mr. Lassman can subscribe to any of these views, but he has no right to ban Cassius Marcellus Clay, or Cassius "Muhammad Ali" Clay from boxing for expounding the glory of Islam.[20]

Jackie Robinson agreed that Lassman's actions related to Ali's conversion more than his contract. Writing in the *Amsterdam News*, he asked:

> How silly can some people be? We think that Ed Lassman, president of the World Boxing Association, provided a ringing answer to that question recently when he called upon the WBA's Executive Committee to vacate the heavyweight title of Cassius Clay because due to his "general conduct" Clay had become "detrimental to the best interests of boxing." Lassman added that Clay "is provoking world criticism and is setting a poor example to the youth of the world." Since when did boxing become so moral? Any thinking person could see clearly behind Mr. Lassman's artificial and unsuccessful attempt to dethrone Clay.

Robinson continued by pointing out that, when Sonny Liston became the heavyweight champion, Lassman did not call attention to his criminal background. On the issue of whether the new champion would send thousands of young black men to the ranks of the Nation of Islam: "Anyone with basic common sense and even a small knowledge of the nature of the Negro in America," he argued, "ought to realize that the majority of Negroes are not looking for leadership into some segregated and isolated, separate state, as the Muslims recommend." Robinson was no fan of Ali, but he defended the champ's right "to affiliate with the religion of his choice."[21]

Writing in 1968 in *Soul on Ice*, a polemic meant to shake up the sensibilities of white Americans, Eldridge Cleaver made no excuses for Ali and defended him as he was:

> Yes, the Louisville Lip is a loudmouth braggart. Yes, he is a Black Muslim racist, staunch enough in the need of his beliefs to divorce his wife for not adopting his religion; and firing his trainer, who taught him to "float like a butterfly and sting like a bee," for the same reason. But he is also a "free" man, determined not to be a white man's puppet even though he fights to entertain them; determined to be autonomous in his private life and a true king of his realm in public, and he is exactly that.

Cleaver's message was not just a defense of Ali. It was an indictment of the racism that dominated much of American life in the turbulent period of the late 1960s:

> A racist Black Muslim heavyweight champion is a bitter pill for racist white America to swallow. Swallow it—or throw the whole bit up, and hope that in the convulsions of your guts, America, you can vomit out the poisons of hate which have led you to a dead end in this valley in the shadow of death.[22]

The emergence of a new heavyweight champion of the world who was a member of a black separatist group that many saw as dangerous to America created a dilemma for reporters. As Cassius X and then Muhammad Ali, the heavyweight champion was no longer a comical clown who could be tolerated. This new man

> stood erect, often dressed in a dark suit with a bow tie; dignified yet defiant. His stance put him at odds with those who merely tolerated him before. Many cast aspersions upon him or would inflict further insult by refusing to address him by his new moniker.[23]

On March 7, 1964, the *Amsterdam News* reported that Clay (the paper had not yet begun to use his new name) had visited the paper on his return to New York from Miami the previous day. The new champ declared facetiously "Everyone is worried about my religious beliefs. People are no longer curious about my fighting ability," highlighting the interest and even hostility that the announcement of his conversion had inspired. Speaking of Sonny Liston but not mentioning the agreement that already suggested there would be a re-match, Clay said he would fight Liston again: "I used my boxing ability and psychology to defeat him in Miami. If Liston can be talked into getting into the ring with me again the fight will end sooner." And on the subject of his recent conversion, he told the paper that

> Elijah Muhammad is the sweetest man in the world. Malcolm X? I fell in love with him after watching him on television discussing Islam with those educators—leaving them with their mouths wide open . . . I will not be identified as an Uncle Tom. I will be known as Cassius X.

Just as he spoke publicly about his religious convictions at his daily meetings at the Hotel Theresa in Harlem, Clay ended his interview by saying that, "The world recognizes me now that they know my religion is Islam. The religion is the truth, and I am ready to die for the truth." As Clay left the newspaper offices, he shouted his familiar, "I am the greatest!"[24]

The religious conversion of Cassius Clay brought public attention to the Nation of Islam and the reactions ranged from ambivalence to outright hostility. Some reports in the media confirmed that white Americans who knew about the NOI at all regarded it as a dangerous religious group and a cult whose philosophy of separation from whites ran contrary to the integrationist focus of the mainstream civil rights movement. Ali's local Louisville newspaper, the *Courier Journal*, referred to the Nation of Islam as a "Negro-supremacist sect," and the *Chicago Tribune* used the term "cult" to refer to them.[25] Indeed, the NOI's criticism of Dr. King's non-violent civil rights movement, its rejection of integration, and its hostility to white people inspired fear that the NOI could serve as a destabilizing influence among urban Blacks. In 1964, Ali's rants were still more humorous than revolutionary, but his association with Malcolm X, the suspended NOI minister, had sinister implications for many who saw danger in Ali's prominence as a Muslim.

Some writers saw the continuing humor and playfulness in Ali's public posturing, whatever he called himself. Even before Ali's declaration of his new faith, Dick Schaap wrote that, "If Clay shares the anti-white sentiments of the Black Muslims, he has always disguised his feelings well. The only hate he ever exhibits outwardly is for his opponents, and that, despite Clay's boastful lyrics, always shows through as false hate."[26] Writing in the *Saturday Evening Post* in November of 1964, Myron Cope referred to Clay as the loudest black Muslim since Malcolm X who was continuing to act as a clown for the purpose of selling more tickets to his fights. At the same time, Cope acknowledged that Clay might not hate all white people or consider them to be devils, quoting the champion, "They blow up all these little colored people in church, wash people down the street with water hoses. It's not the color that makes you a devil, just the deeds that you do."[27] In this respect, Ali's views were not so far from those of Dr. King's movement, which, like much of white America, condemned the use of fire hoses and police dogs against demonstrators in Birmingham, Alabama in the summer of 1963 and the bombing at the city's Sixteenth Street Baptist Church in September of that year.

But Ali did part company with King's Southern Christian Leadership Conference and other mainstream civil rights groups on the issue of integration, telling Alex Haley that the 1964 Civil Rights Act would not change the hearts of bigoted people. He revealed his personal understanding of the lessons preached by the Nation of Islam when he declared that, while he did not think that white people hated Negroes,

> You just don't never see a rabbit eating with a lion. I think that all this "integration" started backfiring when it put white people on the spot. It ain't going to go much further. I think that the black man needs to get together with his own kind He needs to say, "Let's don't go where we're not wanted." ... The white people don't want integration. I don't believe in forcing it and the Muslims don't either.[28]

The choice to use the name Cassius Clay or Muhammad Ali was an obvious indicator of how the paper or individual writer felt about the brash young champion, his religious conversion, the Nation of Islam, and possibly even about the legitimacy of his heavyweight title. The Louisville *Courier Journal* refused to use Ali's new name, as did the Chicago *Tribune*, Atlanta *Constitution*, and most mainstream newspapers at the time of Ali's announcement of his conversion to Islam. Columnist Robert Lipsyte carried on a long debate with his editors at the *New York Times* in which he would refer to Muhammad Ali and the editors would change the name back to Cassius Clay. Larry Merchant, writing in the New York *Post*, used the name Muhammad Ali, but Dick Young, writing in the New York *Daily News*, was hostile to the champ's new persona and insisted on calling him Cassius Clay. Ali's trainer, Angelo Dundee, commented on the irony of the situation when he wrote that,

> Sportswriters who never had any trouble calling other fighters by their chosen names—like Henry Jackson as Henry Armstrong, or Joseph Louis Barrow as Joe Louis, or Arnold Cream as Jersey Joe Wolcott, or Walker Smith as Sugar Ray Robinson—found they couldn't and wouldn't call him Muhammad Ali, instead continuing to call him Cassius Clay.[29]

But the issue was not easily resolved. As late as 1970, New York's *Amsterdam News* published an editorial decrying sportswriters' inability to adjust to Ali's name change:

> In what seems to us a picayune gesture, many sportswriters (including our own) continue to address Muhammad Ali as Cassius Clay . . . These sportswriters still write Cassius Clay as if they will him to return to the name acceptable by them . . . There have been many boxers, movie stars, and plain John Does who have changed their names and it has been forthrightly accepted. That's why it seems that the bigtime sportswriters who insist in writing Cassius Clay instead of Muhammad Ali which the latter prefers are being small time.[30]

The Nation of Islam, which had previously seen little benefit in developing a relationship with professional athletes, was eager to claim Muhammad Ali as its own once he had attained the heavyweight title. Before the championship fight, Malcolm X was the only major NOI figure who fully supported Clay in his quest to take the title from Sonny Liston. Speaking at a Savior's Day rally in Chicago only a week after giving the champ his new Muslim name, Elijah Muhammad took some of the credit for Ali's victory over Liston:

> I am so glad that Cassius Clay admits he is a Muslim. He was able, by confessing that Allah was the God and by following Muhammad, to whip a much tougher man. Clay had confidence in Allah, and in me as his only Messenger. This assured his victory and left him unscarred.

The Messenger even claimed that his newest convert would become "a major world figure."[31]

By the time Clay accomplished this feat and declared himself a member of the Nation of Islam, Malcolm X had been suspended from the NOI for his inflammatory remark on the assassination of President Kennedy that the president "never foresaw that the chickens would come home to roost so soon." For these remarks, and for the fact that he had become the most recognizable of all the Nation of Islam's ministers, Malcolm was suspended from making speeches in the name of the NOI. Malcolm was beginning to doubt his own fealty to the Nation and to Elijah Muhammad, and this split and Malcolm's epiphany regarding the commonality of human beings irrespective of skin color during his pilgrimage to Mecca led Malcolm to return to the United States and organize new mosques in the Organization of Afro-American Unity. This presented a crisis of faith for Muhammad Ali. He could not remain close to Minister Malcolm and loyal to the Nation of Islam. Ali cast his lot with Elijah Muhammad and the Nation of Islam, turning away from his former friend.

Soon after his momentous victory in the ring, Ali took a much-publicized tour of the United Nations in New York and then declared his intention to visit Africa. In May of 1964, he visited Ghana, Nigeria, and Egypt, to the excitement of the crowds of Africans who lined the streets to get a glimpse of the new champion. He met with the presidents of Ghana and Egypt and had his picture taken riding a camel at the pyramids. As circumstances would have it, Malcolm was preparing to leave Ghana the day of Ali's arrival. Ali did not speak to the minister, snubbing him in the lobby of the Hotel Ambassador in Accra. To Malcolm's greeting, Ali replied, "You shouldn't have quarreled with Elijah Muhammad."[32] Speaking later to reporters, Ali made his disdain for Malcolm clear, asking, "Did you get a look at Malcolm? Dressed in that funny white robe and wearing a beard and walking with that cane that looked like a prophet's stick? Man, he's gone. He's gone so far out, he's out completely. Nobody listens to Malcolm anymore."[33]

In choosing between the powerful Honorable Elijah Muhammad and the charismatic but exiled Malcolm from whom he had previously received instruction and advice, Ali left the former minister with less public support. Jack Newfield even posited the idea that, had Ali stayed loyal to his friend instead of the Nation of Islam, the course of history might have been altered. He wrote that when

> he sided with the cranky, despotic Elijah Muhammad against Malcolm X, it left Malcolm naked to his enemies for the kill. If Ali, as the new heavyweight champion, had remained loyal to his mentor and continued to lend his public support to Malcolm, history might have gone in a different direction. Malcolm might not have lost his power base. Louis Farrakhan might not have taken his place.[34]

Although he later regretted abandoning Malcolm X, Ali at first felt confident that he had made the right choice between the two Muslim leaders. He later reflected that Malcolm's ideas might not have been so divergent from his own:

When Malcolm broke with Elijah, I stayed with Elijah. I believed that Malcolm was wrong and Elijah was God's Messenger. I was in Miami, training, when I heard Malcolm had been shot to death. Some brother came to my apartment and told me what happened. It was a pity and a disgrace he died like that, because what Malcolm saw was right, and after he left us, we went his way anyway. Color didn't make a man a devil. It's the heart, soul, and mind that counts.[35]

In October of 1964, Ali granted a lengthy interview to Alex Haley that was published in *Playboy* magazine. Throughout his long conversation with the co-author of *The Autobiography of Malcolm X*, Ali revealed his feelings about the boxing establishment and what he regarded as the discriminatory action of the National Boxing Association, which had threatened to revoke his title because of his membership in the Nation of Islam. The revocation never took place, but Ali was clear in his opinion about why the NBA threatened his career:

The N.B.A. was going to condemn me, try, me, sentence and execute me, all by themselves. Ain't this country supposed to be where every man can have the religion he wants, even *no* religion, if that's what he wants? It ain't a court in America that would take a man's job, or his title, because of his religious convictions. The constitution forbids Congress from making any laws involving a man's religion. But the N.B.A. would take it on itself to take away my title—for what? What have I done to hurt boxing? I've *helped* boxing. I don't smoke, I don't drink, I don't bother with nobody. Ain't it funny they never said nothing about Liston? He's been arrested for armed robbery, beating up cops, carrying concealed weapons, and I don't know *what* all. And how come they didn't take Gene Fullmer's title? He was a Mormon. His religion believes Negroes are inferior; they ban Negroes from membership. But I guess that's all right. The N.B.A. don't have no power noway. They can't stop nobody from fighting.[36]

Later in the interview, Ali revealed his emerging consciousness of both race and class as determinative issues in American life and politics when he told Haley:

Me being the world Heavyweight Champion feels very small and cheap to me when I put that alongside of how millions of my poor black brothers and sisters are having to struggle just to get their human right here in America. Maybe God got me here for a sacrifice. I don't know. But I do know that God don't want me to go down for standing up.

And in response to the idea that many mainstream civil rights and black community leaders did not support him because he was not a good example for his people, Ali noted that

People are always telling me "what a good example I could set for my people" if I just wasn't a Muslim. I've heard over and over how come I couldn't have been like Joe Louis and Sugar Ray. Well, they're gone now, and the black man's condition is just the same, ain't it? We're still catching hell. The fact is that my being a Muslim moved me from the sports pages to the front pages.[37]

Ali understood the magnitude of his new status. He had earned his title as a fighter, created an image for himself as a braggart who annoyed the public and the press but could nevertheless deliver on his knockout predictions, and he had become the country's best-known member of the Nation of Islam.

Ali worked hard to distinguish his religious conversion from the racial politics of the early 1960s. Most Americans focused on the struggles of the non-violent civil rights movement to gain equal rights in both the Jim Crow South and throughout the country. He distanced himself from mainstream civil rights leaders by declaring that, "integration is wrong. White people don't want it, the Muslims don't want it."[38] For remarks like these, Ali achieved fame, or perhaps infamy, that transcended his earlier clowning and bragging. He had inserted himself into the debate over integration and alienated movement leaders to the point where Roy Wilkins voiced his frustration by saying that Ali "may as well be an honorary member of the white citizens councils." Wilkins represented an older generation of movement stalwarts who had relied on white support and had worked tirelessly to gain legal equality through the courts and Congress. Younger activists voiced a greater appreciation for Ali's bravery in announcing his conversion.

Julian Bond acknowledged the generational differences in civil rights leaders' positions on the Vietnam War, but he went even further in assessing Ali's impact on the anti-war movement by noting that it was Ali's lack of an organizational affiliation and his willingness to stand on his own that made him an especially compelling figure to young opponents of the war. Bond told Thomas Hauser:

> Ali stood on his own, his impact was special. He wasn't pursuing a political agenda; he wasn't bolstered by organizational support.
>
> He was simply a guy, not sophisticated, not well-learned, not an expert in foreign policy, but someone who knew right from wrong and was willing to risk his career for it.[39]

Bond further observed that, through his unwillingness to conform to white images of a non-political and non-controversial black athlete, Ali "was able to tell white folks for us to go to Hell; that I'm going to do it my way." And New York television newscaster Bryant Gumbel praised Ali's effect on others: "He simply refused to be afraid. And being that way, he gave other people courage."[40]

Ali's notoriety came with a price. More than a year after he announced his conversion, he continued to take criticism for his name and his religious beliefs. In July of 1965, after he had defeated Sonny Liston a second time, *Ebony* magazine enumerated the reasons for Cassius Muhammad Ali Clay's public disfavor. Not since the days of heavyweight champion Jack Johnson's white wives and mistresses, the magazine's editors wrote, had the public had so many reasons to view a boxer's behavior as "sinful." The magazine's editors were mocking the abuse that Ali was taking as a result of his religious conversion and his new name. At the same time, they were not quite ready to accept his Muslim name, instead incorporating it into his birth name.

Americans, they said sarcastically, disliked the heavyweight champion because:

> 1) He is young, brash, extremely loquacious, supremely confident, and almost as good as he says he is. 2) He won the heavyweight title some 16 months ago when Champion Sonny Liston refused to come out for the 7th round in Miami. 3) He had to make a somewhat devious agreement with the Sony Liston crowd to guarantee a return bout in order to get his first crack at the title. 4) He inconsiderately developed a hernia and had to be operated on—causing a seven month delay in his return match with Sonny. 5) He is a member of the Black Muslims, a devoted follower of Elijah Muhammad and likes to talk about it. And 6) He was unfortunate enough to knock out Liston with a single right hand punch in somewhat over one minute of the return bout which had been secreted away in an almost unknown town called Lewiston, Maine, where it was seen by only 4,000 spectators at ringside and several million on pay and home TV screens all over the U.S. and Europe.[41]

By 1965, every action taken by Muhammad Ali was interpreted in terms not only of his boxing talent but also of his religious convictions. He was loved in some quarters and reviled in others. He had broken with Malcolm and cast his lot with the Honorable Elijah Muhammad and the Nation. Malcolm was dead, assassinated by members of the NOI, on February 21, 1965. Ali had beaten back a challenge from Liston on May 25 in Lewiston, Maine with a single punch in the first round. As the undisputed heavyweight champion of the world, Ali's life should have been simple. But one of the defining events of the 1960s, the United States' involvement in Vietnam, would complicate Ali's life. His decision to refuse induction into the military would give him a new public persona as a war resister whose actions might affect those of other young black men whose participation in the war was essential. He would soon transcend his prior selves as the brash and plucky challenger and the champion with the unpopular religious choice. Indeed, by 1975, he was no longer a member of the Nation, although he continued to observe many of the practices of traditional Islam. Ali continued to speak his mind as his actions came to symbolize a broader rejection of governmental authority and the primacy of his racial identity.

NOTES

1 Herbert Berg, "Mythmaking in the African American Muslim Context: The Moorish Science Temple, the Nation of Islam, and the American Society of Muslims," *Journal of the American Academy of Religion* Vol. 73, No. 5 (September, 2005), pp. 689–90.

2 "Moorish Science Temple of America," *Encyclopedia Britannica*,http://www.britannica.com/ EBchecked/topic/391620/Moorish-Science-Temple-of-America. Lindsay Jones, ed., "Islam in the United States," *Encyclopedia of Religion*, http://www.islamawareness.net/NorthAmerica/ America/history_of_musinusa.html. "Moorish Science Temple of America," *The American Mosaic: The African American Experience*, ABC-CLIO, 2014.

3 Peter Goldman, *The Death and Life of Malcolm X* (New York: Harper & Row, 1973), cited in in Kevin Baker, "Lost-Found Nation: The Last Meeting Between Elijah Muhammad and W.D. Fard," cited in in Byron Hollingshead, *I Wish I'd Been There* (New York: Random House, 2006), pp. 261–2.

4 Baker, "Lost-Found Nation," pp. 265–7.

5 http://www.noi.org/noi-history/.

6 Herbert Berg, *Elijah Muhammad and Islam* (New York: New York University Press, 2009), p. 38 and "Elijah Muhammad," http://www.discoverthenetworks.org/individualProfile. asp?indid=1581.

7 Mother Tynetta Muhammad, "Nation of Islam in America: A Nation of Beauty and Peace" (March 28, 1996), http://www.noi.org/noi-history/.

8 Internal Memorandum, Federal Bureau of Investigation, "Nation of Islam," www.columbia. edu/cu/ . . . /071659hthp-transcript.pdf.

9 Interview with Herbert Muhammad, *Eyes on the Prize II Interviews*, http://digital.wustl.edu/e/ eii/eiiweb/muh5427.0439.116marc_record_interviewee_process.html.

10 Elijah Muhammad in *Muhammad Speaks* (October 15, 1962) cited in Maureen Smith, "*Muhammad Speaks* and Muhammad Ali: Intersections of the Nation of Islam and Sport in the 1960s," *International Sports Studies* Vol. 21, No. 1 (2001), p. 56.

11 Manning Marable, *Malcolm X: A Life of Reinvention* (New York: Viking, 2011), p. 226.

12 "Muhammad Ali's Pilgrimage to Makkah," *Emel* (January 23, 2014), http://www.emel.com/ article?id=109&a_id=1722&c=32.

13 Thomas Hauser, *Muhammad Ali: His Life and Times* (New York: Simon & Schuster, 1991), pp. 89–97.

14 Malcolm X, *The Autobiography of Malcolm X* (New York: Ballantine Books, 1964), p. 313.

15 Dick Schaap, "The Challenger and the Muslim," *New York Herald Tribune* (January 23, 1964), http://thestacks.deadspin.com/the-challenger-and-the-muslims-1428091998/all

16 Marable, *Malcolm X*, p. 280.

17 Jack Olsen, "Learning Elijah's Advanced Lesson in Hate," *Sports Illustrated* (May 2, 1966), http://cnnsi.com/vault/article/magazine/MAG1078487/index.htm.

18 Dick Schaap, "The Challenger and the Muslim" and "Cassius Clay Almost Says He's a Muslim," *Amsterdam News* (January 25, 1964), p. 1.

19 Malcolm X, quoted in Marable, *Malcolm X*, p. 287.

20 Peter Kann, "The Sporting Scene: Cassius and the WBA," *The Harvard Crimson* (March 23, 1964), http://www.thecrimson.com/article/1964/3/23/the-sporting-scene-psonny-liston-could/.

21 Jackie Robinson, "A WBA Blunder," *Amsterdam News* (April 4, 1964).

22 Eldridge Cleaver, *Soul on Ice* (New York: Dell, 1968), p. 96.

23 John Edward Faulkner, "From Sports Page to Front Page to Legend, Muhammad Ali's Life a Transformational Saga," http://www.kyforward.com/2013/01/from-sports-page-to-front-page-to-legend-muhammad-alis-life-a-transformational-saga/.

24 Les Matthews, "The 'Greatest One' Pays a Visit to the Amsterdam News," *Amsterdam News* (March 7, 1964), p. 1.

25 Daniel Bennett Coy, "Imagining Dissent: Muhammad Ali, Daily Newspapers, and the State, 1966–1971," Master's Thesis, University of Tennessee, 2004, p. 27.

26 Dick Schaap, "The Challenger and the Muslims," *New York Herald Tribune* (January 23, 1964), p. 1, http://thestacks.deadspin.com/the-challenger-and-the-muslims-1428091998.

27 Myron Cope, "Muslim Champ," *Saturday Evening Post* (November 14, 1964), in Jeff Nilsson, "Religion Steps into the Boxing Ring: Ali in '64," http://www.saturdayeveningpost.com/2012/01/21/archives/post-perspective/religion-steps-boxing-ring.html/attachment.

28 Alex Haley, "Interview with Muhammad Ali," *Playboy* (October, 1964), p. 92.

29 Angelo Dundee (with Bert Randolph Sugar), *My View from the Corner: A Life in Boxing* (New York: McGraw-Hill, 2008), p. 108.

30 Editorial, "It's HIS Name," *Amsterdam News* (October 24, 1970).

31 *Muhammad Speaks* (March 13 and April 24, 1964) cited in Maureen Smith, "*Muhammad Speaks* and Muhammad Ali: Intersections of the Nation of Islam and Sports in the 1960s," *International Sports Studies* Vol. 21, No. 1 (2001), p. 57.

32 Devin Gordon, "True Believer," *Newsweek* Vol. 138, Issue 26 (December 24, 2001), p. 38.

33 Hauser, *Muhammad Ali: His Life and Times*, p. 109.

34 Jack Newfield, "The Meaning of Muhammad," *The Nation* (February 4, 2002), http://www.thenation.com/article/meaning-muhammad.

35 Hauser, *Muhammd Ali: His Life and Times*, pp. 111–12.

36 Alex Haley, "Interview with Cassius Clay/Muhammad Ali," *Playboy* (October, 1964), p. 89.

37 Ibid., p. 90.

38 David Zirin, "The Revolt of the Black Athlete: The Hidden History of Muhammad Ali," *International Socialist Review* Issue 33 (January–February, 2004), http://www.isreview.org/issues/33/muhammadali.shtml.

39 Hauser, *Muhammad Ali: His Life and Times*, pp. 186–7.

40 Zirin, "The Revolt of the Black Athlete."

41 "Alas, Poor Cassius!" *Ebony* Vol. 20, Issue 9 (July, 1965), p. 144.

CHAPTER 4

FIGHTING THE GOOD FIGHT

Cassius Marcellus Clay, now Muhammad Ali, found himself embroiled in a new battle after winning the world heavyweight title from Sonny Liston. By April 28, 1967, when he refused to take a step forward across a yellow line as a sign of his induction into the United States Army, Ali had to defend his religious affiliation with the Nation of Islam and his stand against the war in Vietnam. Ali had won the title he coveted, successfully defended it no fewer than nine times, and been stripped of that title for reasons having nothing to do with his prowess in the ring.[1] When Ali refused to accept induction into the military, he was regarded as a brave protester against racial injustice that was revealed in the progress of an increasingly unpopular war, but he was also condemned as a traitor in other quarters. Even as Ali had charted his own course to becoming "The Greatest" as a professional boxer, the path of his career between 1964 and 1971 was filled with many twists and turns. Muhammad Ali soon realized that his most difficult battles would take place outside the ring.

The 1960s was a decade of rapid, dramatic, and unsettling change in the United States and around the world. In many areas of American life such as civil rights, politics, war, music, and the status of women, the decade began not with the calendar but with the unfolding of events. It was not the inauguration of John Fitzgerald Kennedy on January 20, 1961, but his assassination on November 22, 1963 that marked the beginning of a near decade of liberal ascendancy in domestic policy as reflected in Lyndon Johnson's War on Poverty and successful civil rights legislation embodied in the Civil Rights and Voting Rights Acts of 1964 and 1965. American military personnel advised fighters in the Army of the Republic of Vietnam starting with the fall of Dienbienphu in 1954, but it was not until 1964's Gulf of Tonkin Resolution that the fighting in Vietnam was called a "war," in spite of its undeclared nature. War or conflict, Congress gave the president nearly unlimited power to "repel armed aggression" starting in August of 1964, and the use of that power led to the presence of nearly 500,000 military personnel in South Vietnam by 1968. The Beatles and the Rolling Stones were featured on Top 40 radio programming as early as 1963, but much of the music that American teenagers loved in the first years of the new decade sounded more like it belonged to the 1950s. The experimentation and virtuosity in popular music that we associate with the 1960s belongs to the second half of the decade and into the 1970s. Women effectively used the power of protest to demand the legal and social changes of the 1960s but they did so over several years.

The years 1964 and 1965 were critical in race relations and the elevation of the conflict in Southeast Asia to the status as an undeclared war. These were also critical years for Muhammad Ali, who began the period as the newly crowned champ who now had to defend his title. He was also repeatedly called upon to explain his religious beliefs and his choice of a Muslim name. As the champ, Ali confronted issues of race, war, and religion in his personal life. People began to listen to what he had to say on these topics, and his actions were taken seriously, whether people praised or reviled them. Muhammad Ali was now a champion boxer who had risen to celebrity status. He had become a public figure who transcended the sports pages the same way the young men from Liverpool with the mop top haircuts came to dominate popular culture, not just music.

In the summer of 1964, plans coalesced for a Liston–Ali re-match. Set for November 16, the fight was planned for the Boston Garden, thanks to the efforts of Massachusetts Governor Endicott Peabody. Everyone agreed that, as the older fighter, Liston would have to train harder and be in better shape than he had been for the previous fight. Counting on Liston's knockout punch and willingness to train hard, the odds makers made him a 13–5 favorite. Liston's handlers reported to the public that he was taking his training regimen seriously, wearing out sparring partners while training at 170 pounds in preparation for the battle. He spoke of the deeper meaning in retaking the title from the upstart Ali:

> Just the title, just that championship, that's all there is in this world. That title— my title—is there and I'm going to get it and I'm going to keep it a long time. And I'm going to like it and with it I won't be lonely . . . You'll never know what it's like, I hope. One day you are the king. Your friends, or the guys you think are your friends, are all around you. They give you, "Yes, champ; no, champ; you got no worries, champ. No one in this whole world can beat you, champ." Then all of a sudden you're not the champ and you are alone. The guys with the big mouths are out talking about you, not to you, and what they say isn't what they said the day before. It's a big price to pay.[2]

Liston, never regarded as the most intelligent fighter, nevertheless revealed an understanding of his status as a commodity in the sports business, exploited by people who claimed to be acting with his interests at heart.

In contrast, Ali, reveling in his victory over Liston in February, devoted less attention to preparing for the scheduled re-match. He had traveled to Africa and the Middle East, enjoying the adulation of the public, married,[3] and gained enough weight to worry his trainers. At 245 pounds, he was hardly in shape to succeed in a title match. Nevertheless, he boasted that at least a billion people around the world would be praying for his victory. But in late 1964, it made sense to wonder if the new champion would be able to retain his title.

The re-match did not take place as planned. On the morning of Friday, November 13, the weigh-in was a circus. Only an appeal to Ali's better judgment kept him from delivering thirteen black cats to the superstitious Liston. He did arrive at the event with a bear trap shouting that he wanted to catch "the big ugly bear." State police officers escorted Liston into the room, and the weigh-in proceeded, with one of the doctors commenting that, in spite of his age, Liston's reflexes were as responsive as Ali's. Thanks to the older man's obsessive training and the young champion's preoccupation with other things, the two appeared to be an even match. But by the evening, after a substantial meal, Ali was writhing in agony and demanding that his brother Rahman call an ambulance. He was suffering from an incarcerated inguinal hernia that required emergency surgery at Boston City Hospital. The hernia was the result of a congenital defect and would not have been noted in the pre-fight physical examination. Doctors who faced the press agreed that this condition could have surfaced at any time. But the conspiracy theorists had a field day. Did the Muslims slip something into Ali's food? Did he cause the hernia himself because he was afraid of fighting Liston? Was he unhappy with the promised gate for the fight? Did his vomiting cause the hernia instead of the other way around? These ideas all fell into the realm of idle speculation, of course. The fight would have to be postponed. Ali said of this development, "By the time I'm back in the ring, it'll be next year."[4]

The Liston–Ali re-match was problematic from its inception. Ali seemed to understand that neither he nor Sonny Liston was especially popular, noting, "We both villains. So, naturally, when we get in the ring, the people, they would prefer if it could happen for it to end in a double knockout because they don't want either one of us to win."[5] Reflecting the dismal state of the sport after the first Liston–Ali fight, the World Boxing Association had quickly suspended Ali's title and taken Liston's name off its world rankings, ostensibly because the two had signed a contract for a re-match without its approval. As the fighters prepared to do battle again, the Association influenced most of its member state boxing commissions, with the exception of

New York, California, and Pennsylvania, to pass on the proposed re-match. When the Massachusetts Boxing Commission agreed to sanction the fight, the WBA suspended the Massachusetts organization. Nevertheless, until Ali's illness intervened, the fight was scheduled to take place at the famous Boston Garden. The fight was now scheduled for May 25, 1965, but concern by Boston public officials that the promoters might have connections to organized crime led to an investigation by Suffolk County District Attorney Garrett Byrne, who attempted to enjoin Inter-Continental Management, the fight's promoters, from promoting the fight in Massachusetts on the grounds that the group did not have a state license to do so. The suspicion of an organized crime presence was not unreasonable, given boxing's, and Liston's, unsavory reputation. In the end, the promoters withdrew from the Boston deal. What remained of the plan for a Liston–Ali re-match was a heavyweight champion, a former champion who was now the challenger, and a date, but no venue for the fight. Inter-Continental worked with Maine Governor John H. Reed to settle on the small city of Lewiston, an old industrial town with 41,000 residents. St. Dominic's Hall, a junior hockey rink that held 4,900 spectators, was the chosen location. Only 2,434 appeared for the fight in this remote location, but Inter-Continental made its money from closed-circuit television revenues.[6]

To prepare for his postponed title defense in Lewiston, Ali stepped up his training program, lost weight, and got himself into good shape. He was much better prepared than he would have been had the fight occurred on its originally scheduled date in late 1964. As for Liston, he claimed not to be worried about Ali, telling *Sports Illustrated* in February of 1965 that "Clay is not a good fighter . . . If I had to do it again, I would go out for that last round. It was my trainer who told me not to go out. He said I might damage the shoulder so bad I might never fight again."[7] In addition to rationalizing why he had lost more than a year earlier, Liston convinced himself that he had trained hard for the fight, but this was far from true. Reflecting after the fight, *TIME* magazine reported on Liston's hubris, noting that the older fighter "had persuaded quite a few people—including the underworld characters hanging around his training camp—that he would button the lip of the twinkle-toed loudmouth who took his title away in Miami last year. Odds makers made him the 6–5 favorite."[8] Rumors abounded that sparring partners were well-paid to take the abuse as mere punching bags, and more than one quit in disgust.

Security for the fight emerged as a high priority, given the background of both fighters and the shady reputation of boxing itself. Ali's backers were concerned about rumors that followers of Malcolm X would make an attempt on Ali's life in retribution for the assassination of their leader on February 25. Sonny Liston reported that he had received threats from members of the

Nation of Islam, and he was worried that, should an attempt take place on Ali's life, the shooter would miss and hit him instead.[9] Fruit of Islam bodyguards were present to protect Ali, and the FBI had a twelve-man presence in Lewiston to insure that the fight was held in a secure environment.

On May 25, 1965, at 1:44 of the first round, after stunning Liston with an unexpected right cross, Ali knocked his opponent to the canvas with a strong right hand punch. Liston got up on one knee but then rolled back to the floor. The time keeper failed to start the clock that would have determined a knockout and ended the fight, and the referee, former heavyweight champion Jersey Joe Walcott, was unable to move Ali to a neutral corner. Instead, the champ was standing over Liston, yelling, "Get up and fight, sucker!" If Liston was listening for a count that would give him an idea of when to get up, he did not hear it. The fight was officially ended at 2:12. Writing in *Sports Illustrated*, Jim Murray wrote that, "Sonny Liston hit the floor like a guy slipping on a cake of soap getting out of the bathtub. This is the second time this fight has ended with several thousand people looking at each other and asking: 'What happened?'" Liston had not expected the blow, and he never recovered, making him easy prey for the second punch that some writers called the "phantom punch." The fight was over almost as soon as it began. Murray concluded his comments with an assessment of Liston's place in the boxing pantheon: "Two years ago we were saying this guy was the best heavyweight in history. Now, he's not even the best heavyweight in Lewiston. And if you think that this isn't a comedown, you're never been to Lewiston."[10]

Not surprisingly, rumors, speculation, and conspiracy theories emerged to substantiate the idea that the fight had been fixed. Ali himself was unsure at first that he had connected with the punch, although he later claimed credit for an "anchor punch," originally used by fighter Jack Johnson and reportedly learned from actor Stepin Fetchit, that took Liston down. In his post-fight interview, Liston said the punch made him groggy and unable to get up because he had lost his balance and could not hear the count. A week later, when asked why he fell, Liston said, "I was stunned," and his reply as to why he didn't get back up again right away was, "Just lost my balance, I guess."[11]

Liston's vague explanation only fueled speculation that the outcome of the fight was determined before the first bell. Even before the fight was officially over, future Ali challenger George Chuvalo climbed into the ring, shouting that the fight had been fixed, and announcer Don Dunphy declared that "If that was a punch I'll eat it. Here was a guy who was in prison and the guards used to beat him over the head with clubs and couldn't knock him down." The obvious conclusion was that Liston had thrown the fight, most likely to make money for mobsters who had bet against him. *New York Times* columnists Dave Anderson and Arthur Daley were less sure, declaring that Liston was really no match for the younger Ali and that he "didn't have it anymore." Tex Maule in *Sports Illustrated* thought he provided conclusive evidence that Ali had won the fight with his powerful right hand:

> For the few qualified observers who had a clear view of the knockout punch, there was no doubt about its power. Immediately after it landed, Floyd Patterson, seated at ringside in the most advantageous position to see the blow, said, in answer to a direct question: 'It was a perfect right hand.' Jose Torres, the light heavyweight champion, agreed. 'A very strong right hand,' he said. Indeed, for all those who had a good view of the punch—and, unfortunately, there could not have been more than 1,200—there was never any doubt as to the stunning power of the blow. It was perfectly delivered against an opponent who was moving toward it, so that the effect was of a head-on collision.[12]

But the issue was far from settled. Some argued that Liston had been weakened by Ali's fierce right hand and was then knocked to the canvas by a punch that was so quick that few actually saw it. Others intimated that the former champ fell to the canvas and threw the fight because he feared the NOI, the Mafia, followers of Malcolm X who might be gunning for Ali, or the wild man Ali himself. The story of Jack Johnson's "anchor punch" only added to an air of incredulity about the fight. Writer Dave Kindred noted the obvious contradiction between the image of actor Stepin Fetchit and the persona of Muhammad Ali: "Stepin Fetchit? Whose life work in Hollywood had been the exploitation and perpetuation of a stereotype of black men as subservient, ignorant, and cowardly?" Howard Cosell, who interviewed Ali soon after the fight, responded to the Johnson–Fetchit–Ali trajectory of the punch, commenting that, "If boxing can survive this, it can survive anything."[13] For some mainstream sportswriters, the argument has been settled by videotape, but the controversy will not disappear. In May of 2001, Wallace Smith wrote in the *New York Post*: "Muhammad Ali flicked a right hand punch in the direction of Sony Liston and ended a heavy-weight title fight barely one minute after it began. That was 36 years ago today, and there are people who will swear to you the punch hasn't landed yet."[14]

Ali will be remembered for this unconventional victory and many others. Unlike most fighters in the first half of the twentieth century, Ali carries a reputation derived not only from his prowess in the ring but also his political and cultural influence, cast when he refused induction into the armed forces during the Vietnam War. By the mid-1960s, Black athletes were beginning to speak publicly on issues of race and equality, and their voices were influential because of their success as athletes. Black college and professional athletes reminded the public that they had frequently been required to stay in separate hotels from their white teammates and that, sometimes, they were pulled from competition with teams in the South in order not to offend local sensibilities. Writing about the conditions that led to what came to be called "the revolt of the Black athlete," Othello Harris described even less obvious but no less demeaning forms of treatment meted out to black athletes, which included derogatory stereotyping and even attempts to regulate interracial dating. The new generation of athletes was less likely to accept or ignore such treatment. While black athletes of earlier decades were inclined to ignore or privately complain about their treatment,

> black athletes in the sixties began to confront racial injustice. Accommodationists were on their way out. A new black athlete was evolving, one who, like Ali, was assertive, defiant, proud of his or her blackness, and willing to sacrifice profits and rewards to maintain dignity. The sports world would be permanently altered.[15]

For the most part, black athletes supported integration and Dr. Martin Luther King, Jr.'s non-violent movement. Ali was nearly alone in his affiliation with the Nation of Islam. Basketball player Lew Alcindor converted to Islam as a college student in the late 1960s, but he did not change his name to Kareem Abdul-Jabbar until May 1, 1971, and his political positions, while no less powerfully anti-racist than those of Muhammad Ali, were articulated with greater subtlety and less bravado. Because many people accepted the influence of professional athletes on young people who regarded them as heroes, athletes were increasingly under scrutiny not only for their accomplishments in sports but also for their publicly expressed views on broader social issues. With the emergence of more dominant black athletes, race was among the most important of those issues.

It was not surprising that Muhammad Ali's religious and political views would become fair game for his opponents. Indeed, Floyd Patterson, who had established his status as a contender to fight Ali and earn the heavyweight title for the third time, couched his criticism in religious and political terms. Ali was not bad for boxing because of his fighting style, and he was not an embarrassment to the sport because of his bad poetry. He was, according to Patterson, a negative influence on the sport because he was a member of the Nation of Islam. Patterson said he felt

> very strongly about this, boxing most certainly could use a new image right now. I say it, and I say it flatly, that the image of a Black Muslim as the world heavyweight champion disgraces the sport and the nation. Cassius Clay must be beaten and the Black Muslims' scourge removed from boxing. I have much respect for Clay as a fighter, but I lost a lot of respect for him as a person when he joined the Black Muslims, particularly when he gave them credit for helping him win the championship. Cassius has made no secret of his devotion to Black Muslimism. He boasts of it, parades and flaunts it whenever he can. He constantly raises racial issues. By calling me a "Black White Hope" and by several other ill-advised and intemperate remarks, he has continually damaged the image

of American Negroes and the civil rights groups working on their behalf. No decent person can look up to a champion whose credo is "hate whites." I have nothing but contempt for the Black Muslims and that for which they stand.[16]

Patterson's criticism focused on Ali's willingness to embrace a religious ideology of black separatism rather than the more mainstream focus on integration that had gained acceptance with a broad public because of the sacrifices of the civil rights movement and the identification of the movement with progressive Christian reform. Ali would have none of this, and he was reviled for his position.

But a champion needs a challenger, and Patterson was the obvious challenger for Ali. Set in Las Vegas on November 22, 1965, the bout ended in a technical knockout in the twelfth round. Shortly after the fight, Gilbert Rogin wrote that, "Although he never put a valorous Floyd Patterson down for the count, Cassius Clay displayed an awesome range of skills as he battered his opponent at will and proved to a sometimes skeptical public that he is, as he says, 'The Greatest.'" Rogin acknowledged that Ali probably could have ended the fight much earlier by scoring a knockout. Whatever the outcome, Rogin felt that Patterson's reputation remained intact. He wrote that Ali "was seeking to humiliate Floyd Patterson but Cassius Clay, known to his fellow Black Muslims as Muhammad Ali, only succeeded in ennobling him." But a few weeks later, Rogin acknowledged that, however noble the now-retired champ might be, he had not prepared well to fight Ali. Patterson said he had possessed "no plan" for approaching the heavyweight champion. Rogin observed that perhaps there was no way for Patterson to have developed a plan, but "standing in the middle of the ring as though you are waiting for a number 5 bus was definitely not it."[17] Try as some sportswriters did to find energy and excitement in this battle for heavyweight supremacy, the overwhelming conclusion was that this had been a long and ultimately boring fight. Ali won the battle, but Patterson remained honorable in the minds of many writers and fans. Rogin argued that critics and fans felt so unsatisfied because there was little dramatic action in the ring and even less appreciation of Ali's skill and finesse among fans outside the ropes. "What critics want," he wrote, "is theater, a TV show, a series of events arranged so that they have dramatic unity and interest—in other words, a fixed fight, but one where everybody had the winner the day before. This fight was the way life is, often intolerable and overwhelming, unsuspected, a letdown."[18] Boxing may still have been corrupt, but, with the defeat of fighters like Patterson, it had lost some of its appeal to traditionalists. The new champ was a man of his time who was in the process of pushing issues of religion, race, and war into the ring, on television, and into the public mind.

After Ali's defeat of Patterson, his next logical contender was Ernie Terrell, and the bout was scheduled for March 29, 1966 in Chicago. But events in Selective Service offices and in court altered the champ's plans and placed him at the center of a controversy that he could not resolve with his fast footwork and lightning punches. The non-war in Southeast Asia had been justified by the 1964 Gulf of Tonkin Resolution and had enjoyed wide public support. But starting in 1965 with teach-ins on college campuses, protests in the streets, and even the beginning of a GI anti-war movement, resistance to the conflict and to the draft was increasing. Americans objected to the war as an unnecessary action that masked an imperialist venture, they expressed personal reservations about intervening in a civil war in a faraway country against people of color, and they resisted the draft on grounds of religion or conscience. Ali became one of the most famous draft resisters on religious grounds. The controversy that ensued positioned Ali not just as a championship athlete but also as an African-American man protesting an unjust war as he defended his religious principles and his right to take an unpopular position on a matter of great public significance. His actions put him at odds with many fans, sportswriters, and the United States government. From his 1-A classification in 1966 to his vindication by the United States Supreme Court, Ali's successes in the ring and his frustrations outside of boxing were inexorably intertwined.

Like all young men in the United States in the 1960s, Cassius Clay was required to register with the Selective Service. On April 18, 1960, he had reported to Local Board 47 in Louisville, Kentucky. There was no further action regarding his draft status until he was classified 1-A on March 16, 1962. That classification made Clay eligible to be drafted and, on January 24, 1964, he took the first step toward joining the military by reporting to the Armed Forces Induction Center in his new home in the Miami area for examination. He failed the mental aptitude test at that time and again in March of that year with an Army IQ score of 78, placing him well below the minimum standard for induction. On March 26, 1964, he was re-classified 1-Y, or "not qualified for current standards for service in the armed forces." The Secretary of the Army, responding to public outrage over what appeared to be special treatment for the champ, wrote that:

The requirements of today's Army do not allow for acceptance of those personnel not offering a reasonable value to the defense effort. The induction standards must be such that the new members of the Army are capable of learning new skills and applying them. In summary, it was my decision that Cassius Clay should be rejected for induction due to his inability to meet prescribed minimum standards.[19]

Ali revealed his embarrassment at being considered not intelligent enough for military service to Alex Haley in *Playboy*:

> The fact is I never was too bright in school. I just barely graduated. I had a D-minus average. I ain't ashamed of it, though I mean, how much do school principals make a month? But when I looked at a lot of the questions they had on them Army tests, I just didn't know the answers. I didn't even know how to *start* after finding the answers. That's all. So I didn't pass. It was the Army's decision that they didn't want me to go into the service. They're the boss. I don't want to say no whole lot about it . . . I have said I am the greatest. Ain't nobody ever heard me say I was the smartest.[20]

Ali told Louisville *Courier Journal* reporter Larry Boeck that "The test was tough. But I did my best – I don't want anyone to think I'm crazy."[21] That a famous and controversial person was given a "pass" on military service while ordinary men who scored only a bit better on the aptitude test were sent to fight in Vietnam must have seemed unfair, but in 1964 the war had not yet galvanized much opposition and was not yet on the nightly network news broadcasts for more than a few minutes. Ali experienced two years of relative peace regarding his draft status. On February 17, 1966, after having spent the previous two years classified as unqualified for the draft, Ali was declared eligible, which made it likely that he would be sent to Vietnam, if only to entertain the troops like many other celebrities. Ali was re-classified at a time when draft calls were increasing in response to demands for more troops. He had already become a controversial figure, first by defeating Sonny Liston and then for announcing his membership in the Nation of Islam. His unwillingness to accept conscription only increased the controversy that surrounded the name Muhammad Ali.

This was the context in which the Ali–Terrell fight was planned for March of 1966. In January of that year, Ali had announced that his fights would now be organized and promoted by Main Bout, a new company in which, he said, "Negroes are not used as fronts, but as stockholder, officers, and production and promotion agents." Ali well understood that economic power was at the heart of true progress toward racial equality. Two of the major stockholders in Main Bout were Herbert Muhammad, son of Elijah Muhammad, who served as the organization's president, and John Ali, the Nation of Islam's national secretary, who was the treasurer. These two NOI leaders controlled 50 percent of Main Bout's stock and half of the votes on the organization's board, thus allocating majority control of the organization that would control the financial fortunes of boxing's biggest draw to members of the NOI. Mike Malitz, who ran closed-circuit television networks, served as vice president, and attorney Bob Arum was Main Bout's secretary. They were the only white members of the governing structure, and each man owned 20 percent of the total stock and controlled one vote on the board. Jim Brown, who was still active as a professional football player, handled publicity for Main Bout. He owned 10 percent of the company's stock and controlled one vote. Brown emphasized the broader economic goals of the organization even beyond promoting Ali's fights when he declared that, "Our goal is to use the money we make—and hope to make in future ventures—to support the founding of businesses by Negroes." After his retirement from football, Brown continued his support of black businesses with the founding of the National Negro Industrial and Economic Union.[22]

Main Bout began its efforts to promote Ali's next fight against Ernie Terrell in Chicago. But once Ali was re-classified and made clear his unwillingness to fight "those Viet Cong," plans for the bout quickly fell apart. Sportswriters were quick to express their disdain for Main Bout because of its obvious connection to the Nation of Islam. Jimmy Cannon asserted that the fight was more than just a boxing match, it was "a fete to celebrate a religion that throws hate at people." Doug Gilbert wrote that "if the Muslims own Clay, and also own television rights to all of his fights, they have what amounts to a hammerlock on all that's lucrative in boxing," and Gene Ward declared that the fight would be a "death blow" to the fight game. Apocalyptic visions abounded in the Chicago newspapers, and the *Tribune* and the *Daily News* prevailed upon Illinois Governor Otto Kerner to ban the fight. The Illinois State Boxing Commission demanded an apology from Ali for his "unpatriotic remarks," which he refused to offer. The Commission cancelled the fight, after the state's Attorney General, William Clark, declared it to be illegal.[23] Bob Arum tried unsuccessfully to re-locate the bout in the United States. He was able finally to secure Maple Leaf Gardens in Toronto, Canada. That transaction was also characterized by controversy, as Conn Smythe, the outspoken director of the arena, resigned rather than allow a fight that featured a "draft dodger." Terrell withdrew because the renegotiated contract provided him with a smaller purse than he wanted. His last-minute replacement was the Canadian fighter George Chuvalo.[24]

In the first Heavyweight Championship fight held in Canada, 13,540 fans saw the challenger Chuvalo stay with Ali for the scheduled fifteen rounds. The gate of $120,000, plus closed-circuit television and foreign broadcast rights yielded a total purse of $180,000, of which Ali earned $90,000 and Chuvalo $40,000. This was a relatively small purse for Ali, but this was not surprising, considering the controversy that had surrounded the fight from the moment it was announced. Chuvalo, the son of immigrants from Bosnia-Herzegovina, was a self-taught boxer who was described as "the prototypical 'coulda been,' with a promising career that regularly saw him near the top of the heavyweight boxing rankings, but seemingly unable to put it together in the high profile fights." Odds makers favored Ali 7–1, and many sportswriters thought the bout was a joke. In spite of the controversy surrounding the fight and the apparent mis-match, fans were treated to "an exciting, violent, memorable bout." After the fight, Ali declared that Chuvalo was "the toughest guy I ever fought. I kept saying he was tough, tougher than Sony Liston, tougher than Floyd Patterson, tougher than Ernie Terrell, but people thought I was just trying to build up the gate. Now you know I was right."[25] Ali left Toronto with his championship intact. He had taken more of a beating than anticipated but had prevailed nonetheless.

Shortly after Ali's victory in Toronto, the Federal Bureau of Investigation began gathering information on the heavyweight champion, interviewing his family and friends, checking law enforcement records, and placing him under surveillance. This investigation transcended the issue of the draft to reveal seven traffic violations in five years in four different states. In addition, FBI agents discovered that Ali had purchased a firearm, a .22 caliber Colt derringer, at a pawnshop in Miami in September of 1964. Even though Ali's friend, Sam Saxon, was reported to have thrown the gun into the Atlantic Ocean, the traffic violations and purchase of a gun all pointed to character issues that could be damaging to Ali's image. In addition, the FBI turned its investigative attention to Main Bout. The organization dissolved in June of 1967, after seventeen months.[26]

Two months after the Chuvalo fight, Ali returned to London to fight Henry Cooper for the second time at Arsenal Football Stadium. This was the first Heavyweight Championship fight staged in England in fifty-eight years. Before the fight, Ali engaged in his typical banter on British television:

> I'll tell Henry Cooper, he's watching this show, to come to the fight and be ready to fight because I'm coming to get you. I'm coming to London to get you. And after I'm through beating him, I think he'll have to join The Beatles and be a singer. I'm coming to get you, Henry. I don't like the way you knocked me down the last time. No man knocks me down and gets away with it, so you be ready for it, you hear? Be ready because I'm coming to get you. Now you go home and tell him that. I'm not joking.[27]

Cooper had knocked Ali to the canvas in their non-title, pre-Liston fight in June of 1963. Through the first five rounds of this battle, the scoring was a draw, with Cooper winning the first two rounds and Ali taking the fourth and fifth rounds after the third was declared even. After prevailing in the fifth round, Ali punched Cooper hard enough in the sixth round to open a cut above his left eye that was eventually closed with sixteen stitches. The referee, George Smith, called the fight as blood gushed from Cooper's brow and covered both fighters. Cooper maintained after the fight that he and Ali had accidentally butted heads, opening up an artery. It did not matter; the blood gushed and the referee called the fight, declaring a victory for Ali.[28]

Three months later, on August 6, 1966, Ali returned to London to fight the thirty-two-year-old "Blackpudlian," Brian London, at the Earls Court Arena. Ali won the fight with a knockout in the third round before a crowd of 13,000. Ali accepted the challenge and the guarantee of $252,000 and a percentage of television revenue for the fight because he needed money for alimony and was sure he could win the fight against a "punching bag" who had been defeated by Henry Cooper and Floyd Patterson. Ali was taller, heavier, and faster, so his victory was no surprise. After the fight, London said that he would like a return match, but only if Ali would "put a 50-pound weight on each ankle."[29]

By mid-1966, the public perception of the Vietnam War was changing. Draft calls increased, as did protests against the war and efforts to avoid conscription. The Army lowered its minimum standard on the mental aptitude test from the sixteenth to the thirteenth percentile, making Ali draft eligible. On March 17, 1966, Ali went back to his Louisville draft board, and, through his attorneys, he argued that he was a conscientious objector. He said on many occasions that he "had no quarrel with them Viet Cong." He also argued that he should be exempt from military service because he supported his mother and paid alimony to his ex-wife, saying "I may never be able to overcome this time of loss of boxing sharpness and come back from the service and earn the kind of money required to pay off these financial obligations." In addition, Ali claimed that he was entitled to conscientious objector status because his Muslim religion required that he refrain from taking part in a war with "infidels or any nonreligious group."[30]

Draft Board 47 did not accept Ali's arguments and denied his request for draft exemption, referring his case to the Department of Justice for prosecution. It was common practice for such cases to be referred to an independent investigator before proceeding to court. In this instance, on August 23, 1966, Ali made his case to the investigator, retired state circuit Court Judge Lawrence Grauman, in a twenty-one-page letter as well as his personal testimony. The validity of Ali's conscientious objector claim rested on three criteria: his objection to serving in the military had to be sincere; his objection had to be based on sincere religious belief and training; and he had to voice objection to all wars, not just the conflict in Vietnam. In a surprising ruling, given the increase in draft calls and the animosity directed at Ali for his rejection of the draft and his acceptance of Islam, Judge Grauman accepted Ali's claim of conscientious objection, noting that Ali was a man of good character and integrity whose objection to participation in war was sincere. Nevertheless, the Department of Justice took the case to the 5th Circuit Court on the grounds that Ali's objections to war were specific rather than general and that his objection to fighting in Vietnam was political rather than religious in nature.

Ali understood the broader implications of his re-classification. He was a black man. He was famous. He had spoken out against the war and the draft. And he was a Muslim. In a television interview in April of 1966, Ali railed against the Selective Service and the process by which we was suddenly qualified for military service:

> It was not me who said that I was classified 1-Y the last time . . . It was the government who said that I'm not able . . . Now in order to be 1-A I do not remember being called nowhere to be reclassified as 1-A. These fellows got together and made the statement that I'm 1-A without knowing if I'm as good as I was the last time or better. Now they had 30 men to pick from in Louisville, and I'm also sure that there are at least 30 young men that they could have picked from. Instead they picked out the heavyweight champion of the whole world. There's just one in my class. You have a lot of men in baseball they could have called. You have a lot of men in football they coulda called. You have a lotta men that they coulda called that are of school age and have taken the test that are 1-A. Now, I was not 1-A the last time I was tested. All of a sudden they seem to be anxious to push me in the Army.[31]

In response to Judge Grauman's ruling and Ali's continuing posturing, Congressman L. Mendel Rivers, the new Chairman of the House Armed Services Committee, did some posturing of his own. In a speech to the Veterans of Foreign Wars in New York on August 25, 1966, Rivers called Ali a "theologian of Black Muslim power." He told the veterans that, if the champ's appeal were successful, Congress would surely act:

> We're going to do something if that board takes your boy and leaves Clay home to double talk. What has happened to the leadership of our nation when a man, any man regardless of color, can with impunity advise his listeners to tell the President when he is called to serve in the armed forces. "Hell, no, I'm not going."[32]

Sports columnists frequently criticized Ali's stance against the war. *New York Post* and *Journal American* writer Jimmy Cannon, one of the most famous columnists of the 1940s and 1950s, but something of a relic by the mid-1960s, asserted that Ali was a bad influence on boxing and that he had turned the sport into "an instrument of mass hate . . . Clay is using it as a weapon of wickedness."[33] Cannon was particularly angered by Ali's position on the war and the draft:

> He fits in with the famous singers no one can hear and the punks riding motorcycles with iron crosses pinned to their leather jackets and Batman and the boys with their long dirty hair and the girls with the unwashed look and the college kids dancing naked at secret proms held in apartments and the revolt of students who get a check from Dad every first of the month and the painters who copy

the labels off soup cans and surf bums who refuse to work and the whole pampered style-making cult of the bored young.[34]

Americans who agreed with Cannon flew American flags and placed "My Country: Love It or Leave" bumper stickers on their cars. Opinions about the war represented an increasingly polarized nation, divided along racial, class, and generational lines.

Throughout 1966 and early 1967, Ali was preoccupied by his conflict with the draft, which had become very public. Writing in *Sports Illustrated*, Jack Olsen characterized Ali as a "hardheaded bigot," even as he acknowledged that Ali's objection to the draft was a matter of conscience. Olsen observed that, within a few days of Ali's assertion that he would refuse induction into the armed forces,

> newspaper editorial writers and columnists and statesmen and Bowery bums were telling the world heavyweight champion what they thought about him in some of the strongest language ever used to describe a sports figure. He was "a self-centered spoiled brat of a child," "a sad apology for a man," "the all-time jerk of the boxing world," "the most disgusting character in memory to appear on the sports scene." "Bum of the month. Bum of the year. Bum of all time."

The insults were not confined to "man in the street" remarks. According to Olsen, the Governor of Illinois called Ali "disgusting," and the Governor of Maine said the fighter "should be held in contempt by every patriotic American." There were racial epithets, anonymous threats, and every manner of anonymous insult directed at Ali for stating his unpopular views. Olsen did convey a bit of irony when he described the "choleric" campaign against the possibility that Ali's next fight might be held in Chicago. He joked that, "The newspaper's attitude seemed to be that thousands of impressionable young Chicagoans would go over to the Viet Cong if Cassius were allowed to engage in fisticuffs in that sensitive city." Thanks to the *Chicago Tribune's* campaign against Ali and negative commentary from radio and television commentators, "little old ladies, from Champaign-Urbana, bookmakers and parish priests, armchair strategists at the Pentagon and politicians all over the place joined in a crescendo of get Cassius clamor." Olsen also noted the primacy of race as an issue in the discussion of Ali's character. He quoted an anonymous "amateur psychologist," who said, "The thing is, Americans have become so guilty about Negroes that they bend over further than they want in their attitude toward them. Then along comes somebody like Cassius, and they feel free to unload their resentment and pour it on."[35] If Ali was expected to play the part of the "good Negro," people with that expectation were bound to be disappointed. Amid all the publicity, Ali continued to train and to fight in the ring as his battles in court continued.

Under the guidance of his attorney, Hayden Covington, Ali claimed in August of 1966 that he should be exempt from the military draft not only on the basis of his own conscientious objection, a claim that had been rejected by Selective Service officials, but also because he was a "minister of the Lost and Found Nation of Islam." This claim proved difficult for the press to accept, especially as Ali pursued a new opponent in the ring every few months. He was reviled for his affiliation with the Nation of Islam in addition to his status in the public mind as a draft dodger. Between August of 1966 and April of 1967, Covington filed a number of appeals that delayed administrative action, and the heavyweight champion continued to fight less than distinguished opponents.

One of these opponents was Karl Mildenberger, the European heavy-weight champion in the first heavyweight title match held in Germany. Frankfurt's Waldstadion was the scene of the scheduled fifteen-round battle in which Ali, who was still called Cassius Clay by the mainstream press, knocked the challenger down in the fifth, eighth, and tenth rounds. Ulti-mately, the British referee Teddy Waltham ended the fight in the twelfth round. *Sports Illustrated* described the bloody end to the fight in an article titled, "A Muslim Ministers to a Southpaw." Martin Kane wrote that at one minute, fifty seconds of the twelfth round:

> Mildenberger was caught with another straight right, and though he did not fall, he was so clearly stunned and helpless that Referee Waltham rightly stopped the fight. By that time Mildenberger was a bleeding mess. There is scar tissue on both his brows, and there is a thin scar under his left eye. Clay broke the latter wide open just before the bell rang to end the fifth round. Later he opened the brow above it. It was clear then that Mildenberger, who is not known as a puncher, could not hope to win even with his desperate attempts at a knockout, but it was also clear that he was making a far better fight than anyone had looked for.[36]

Ali's seventh challenger was Cleveland "Big Cat" Williams. For the first time since his two Liston bouts, he was fighting an American on Ameri-can soil in Houston's Astrodome. Williams was the hometown favorite and a fighter whose record of 65 wins in 71 fights, 51 of those by knockout, made him a formidable opponent. Ali's pre-fight discourse differed from the bombast he had delivered before previous bouts—he talked of back pain, of weariness with the fight game, and of his desire to devote himself full-time to his Muslim ministry. At the same time, Williams's manager Hugh Benbow bellowed, "The Cat and me will take care of Clay in three." 35,460 fans saw Ali control the fight from beginning to end. At the end boxing historian Bert Randolph Sugar described the scene: "blood poured down from his nose while Ali savaged him with a left, a right and another left. Referee Kessler jumped in. He had had enough, even if the Big Cat hadn't." The fight lasted a mere three rounds, after which Ali asked the press, "Are there any questions you want to ask about my fighting ability?" *TIME* magazine concluded that there was no question of Clay's ability, noting that Williams left the fight with his "face bruised, one eye puffed nearly shut, five stitches in his cut lip." The Big Cat announced his retirement from boxing. "He is leaving it [the ring] the same way he found it— penniless." In contrast, Ali's victory "marked the end of a year in which he had beaten five opponents and earned $2,000,000. It also left Cassius with only one logical contender: Ernie Terrell, the World Boxing Association's heavyweight champion."[37]

Issues of race, religion, and politics came to the fore in Ali's next title defense, a fifteen-round battle with Terrell. A native of Belzoni, Mississippi, Terrell amassed an impressive record of forty-six wins in his fifty-five fight career. In the weeks leading up to the February 6, 1967 contest, Ali expressed increasing anger at Terrell's insistence on calling him Cassius Clay. His pre-fight rhetoric was tinged with more anger than humor when he declared, "I'm gonna whup him. I'm gonna give him a humiliation. I'll keep hittin' him, and I'll keep talkin." A week before the fight, Terrell referred to the champ as Clay, and he responded angrily. "Why do you call me Clay? You know my right name is Muhammad Ali. It takes an Uncle Tom Negro to call me by my slave name."[38] The stage was set for an angry fight, and *TIME* magazine provided a description of the brutal fight and the anger over a name that accompanied the punches:

> He did not knock Terrell out—or even down. Instead Cassius carefully closed Ernie's left eye, opened a bloody gash over his right eye that later required seven stitches, and generally made mincemeat of his man. Then, with Terrell dazed and helpless, Clay screamed, "Uncle Tom!" Nigger! "What's my name?" he demanded again and again. "That's it, baby!" shouted Clay's Muslim handlers. "Make him say your name!" Terrell refused, and took his licking.[39]

It was clear that the battle was not just an athletic contest for victory and a championship title. Ali, a self-declared Muslim for nearly three years, was still fighting for respect as a member of an unpopular religion. In addition, he was fighting for respect as a man who had requested exemption from the draft. The Vietnam War was highly controversial by 1967, with protests against the war reaching communities beyond just college campuses, but labels like "draft dodger" stung, and Ali's case that he deserved a deferment because of his work as a minister for the Nation of Islam was mired in administrative and procedural appeals and going nowhere.

Ali was the undisputed heavyweight champion. But sports writers began to observe a difference in the fighter and the man. Tex Maule, who had written about Ali since his early professional fights, noted changes in the public persona of the champion:

> Muhammad Ali, who has grown from a cheerful, ingenuous boy into a cruel man, proved beyond any question that he is the heavyweight champion of the world when he destroyed Ernie Terrell in Houston's Astrodome Monday night. He fought with elan and power and with a consummate sense of timing and distance, and when the fight was over he had punished Terrell unmercifully. It was a wonderful demonstration of boxing skill and a barbarous display of cruelty.[40]

Ali had another chance to defend his title on March 22, 1967 in Madison Square Garden, this time against Zora Folley, the Korean War hero who had begun his boxing career in the Army. At age thirty-four, Folley was likely nearing the end of his career. *TIME* magazine called him a "pug who had already been beaten by Sonny Liston, Henry Cooper, and Ernie Terrell—all of whom Clay had kayoed."[41] Folley was among the first fighters to accept Ali's Muslim name, and the two fighters respected each other. Writing in *Sports Illustrated*, Mark Kram wrote that, unlike previous encounters outside the ring, there was so little animus between the two men before the fight that the gate was in danger. With the announcement that, after his numerous appeals had failed, Ali would be required to report for induction into the Army in April of 1967, interest in the fight was revived, and Ali played a new part for the press—he was now the man who was willing to sacrifice himself for his religious beliefs. Mark Kram conveyed as much in *Sports Illustrated* before the fight:

> "This may be the last chance," he said, "to see Muhammad Ali in living color, so if you have always been wanting to see me you'd better come to the Garden." Later he said: "Perhaps in one to three years I will fight again." The "one to three" seemed to indicate he would choose a jail sentence to military service. He would not disclose his decision, but his hints were cleverly camouflaged. "My life, my death, all my sacrifices," said Ali, who has a curious bent toward martyrdom, "are for Allah. I am the tool of Allah and because of my sacrifice it will come out that hundreds of Muslims are in jail rather than fight in the Army. Or even just to go into the service."

Clearly, politics and religion were at the heart of conversations about the Folley fight, which ended with a knockout in the seventh round. Ali cancelled his next fight against Oscar Bonavena scheduled for May 27 in Tokyo. There was more interest in the outcome of his induction proceedings and future court appearances than in the fights themselves. Sportswriter Kram recognized that, even in the shady boxing world, Ali was anathema. People criticized his performances in the ring, but their real difficulty was not with

Muhammad Ali the fighter but with the black man whose religion they did not understand and whose politics with regard to the Vietnam War they abhorred:

> Whatever the outcome, Ali is and has been a gifted champion. Yet polemics and debate precede and follow each of his fights, and the judgments, usually discrediting, are frequently colored by personal distaste. Even among boxing people, who accept any behavior short of having their wallets lifted, Ali is anathema, and they, like much of the press, couch their prejudices with tiresome criticisms: Ali can't punch, Ali can't take a punch, and, anyway, everyone he fights is just a pug who would be knocked down by a spring wind.[42]

Just after Ali defeated Folley in the ring, he requested a transfer of his draft board from Louisville to Houston, Texas. At the same time, he argued in Louisville that there was an absence of African-American representation on local draft boards, in effect challenging the constitutionality of the Universal Military Training and Service Act. If he could prove his case, he could then argue that local draft board did not have the authority to draft young black men. On March 29, 1967, the United States District Court for the Western District of Kentucky ruled that the champion's complaint could not be adjudicated because he had not yet actually appeared for induction, so the process could not be reviewed. He filed the same suit in the District Court for the Southern District of Texas with a similar result.[43] Ali's next move was an appearance scheduled for April 28, 1967 at the Induction Center in Houston. His biggest fight was yet to come.

NOTES

1 Ali also won two non-title fights and lost to Joe Frazier during this period.
2 "This Just In: Ali's Hernia Killed Liston" (November 13, 1964) posted by Paul Gallender (November 20, 2012), http://www.boxing.com/this_just_in_alis_hernia_killed_liston.html.
3 Ali was married four times. He knew his first wife, Sonji Roi, for only a month before they married on August 14, 1964. They were divorced on January 10, 1966, in part because Sonji object to the NOI's restrictions on women's dress. Nineteen months after his divorce, Ali married Belinda Boyd on August 17, 1967. She converted to Islam and changed her name to Khalilah Ali. The couple had four children, Maryum (1968), Jamillah and Rasheda (1970), and Muhammad Ali, Jr. (1972). This marriage ended in the summer of 1977, in part because of Ali's affair with Veronica Porsche. Veronica is the mother of Hana (1974) and Laila (1977). This marriage ended in 1986. Ali married Yolanda (Lonnie) Williams on November 19, 1986. They have an adopted son, Amin. Lonnie has been Ali's care-giver as his Parkinson's Syndrome symptoms have progressed.
4 Huston Horn, "The 400,000 Bellyache," *Sports Illustrated* (November 23, 1964), http://www.si.com/vault/article/magazine/MAG1076631/index.htm.
5 Tex Maule, "The Baddest of All Looks Over the Universe," *Sports Illustrated* (February 15, 1965), http://sportsillustrated.cnn.com/vault/article/magazine/MAG1076902/index.htm.
6 "Muhammad Ali vs Sonny Liston (2nd meeting)," *BoxRec Encyclopedia*, http://boxrec.com/media/index.php/Muhammad_Ali_vs._Sonny_Liston_%282nd_meeting%29.

7   Maule, "The Baddest of All Looks Over the Universe."

8   "Prizefighting: Theater of the Absurd," *TIME* (June 4, 1965), http://content.time.com/time/magazine/article/0,9171,898360,00.html.

9   This theme emerged again when Floyd Patterson published a long article in *Sports Illustrated* explaining why his goal to defeat Ali (whom he continued to call Cassius Clay) had risen to the level of a "moral crusade." Patterson, too, feared a stray bullet in the ring, saying, "Suppose someone did try to kill Clay while we were fighting. I'm not kidding. Two fighters move around quickly, and if a bullet is fired I *might* move right into the range and get killed instead of Clay." Floyd Patterson and Jack Mahon, "Cassius Clay Must be Beaten," *Sports Illustrated* (October 11, 1965), http://cnnsi.com/vault/article/magazine/MAG1077772/index.htm.

10 Jim Murray, "Ascent of a King," *Sports Illustrated* (June 7, 1965), http://sportsillustrated.cnn.com/vault/article/magazine/MAG1155947/index.htm.

11 "Prizefighting: Theater of the Absurd."

12 Tex Maule, "A Quick, Hard Right and a Needless Storm of Protest," *Sports Illustrated* (June 7, 1965), http://sportsillustrated.cnn.com/vault/article/magazine/MAG1077300/index.htm.

13 "Muhammad Ali vs Sonny Liston (2nd meeting)," *BoxRec Encyclopedia*, http://boxrec.com/media/index.php/Muhammad_Ali_vs._Sonny_Liston_%282nd_meeting%29, and Dave Kindred, Sound and Fury (New York: The Free Press, 2006), p. 96.

14 "Muhammad Ali was Great, but not the Greatest," *New York Amsterdam News* (December 19, 2002), p. 15.

15 Sociologist Harry Edwards published his groundbreaking study, *The Revolt of the Black Athlete*, in 1969. See Othello Harris, "The Revolt of the Black Athlete," in Elliott J. Gorn, *Muhammad Ali: The People's Champ* (Urbana and Chicago: University of Illinois Press, 1997), p. 60.

16 Patterson and Mahon, "Cassius Clay Must be Beaten."

17 Gilbert Rogin, "Champion as Long as He Wants," *Sports Illustrated* (November 29, 1965), http://sportsillustrated.cnn.com/vault/article/magazine/MAG1077948/index.htm and Gilbert Rogin, "Not a Great Fight, But it Was a Real One," *Sports Illustrated* (December 6, 1965), http://sportsillustrated.cnn.com/vault/article/magazine/MAG1077979/1/index.htm.

18 Rogin, "Not a Great Fight, But it Was a Real One."

19 Army Secretary Stephen Ailes's comments appeared in a letter to Representative Carl Vinson, Chair of the House Armed Services Committee. They appeared in the *Louisville Courier Journal* (April 19, 1964) in Thomas Hauser, *Muhammad Ali: His Life and Times* (New York: Simon & Schuster, 1991), p. 143.

20 Alex Haley, "Interview with Cassius Clay/Muhammad Ali," *Playboy* (October, 1964), p. 89.

21 Kindred, *Sound and Fury*, p. 100.

22 Michael Ezra, "Muhammad Ali's Main Bout: African American Economic Power and the World Heavyweight Title," avery.cofc.edu/wp-content/uploads/2012/08/Charleston-Ali.pdf.

23 Ibid.

24 "Muhammad Ali vs George Chuvalo," *BoxRec Encyclopedia*, http://boxrec.com/media/index.php/Muhammad_Ali_vs._George_Chuvalo. Kevin Plummer, "Historicist: The Heavyweight Showdown, George Chuvalo Squares off against Muhammad Ali at Maple Leaf Gardens in 1966," *Torontoist* (March 23, 2013), http://torontoist.com/2013/03/historicist-the-heavyweight-showdown/.

25 "Historicist: The Heavyweight Showdown."

26 Hauser, *Muhammad Ali: His Life and Times*, pp. 150–2.

27 "Muhammad Ali vs Henry Cooper (2nd meeting)," *BoxRec Encyclopedia*, http://boxrec.com/media/index.php/Muhammad_Ali_vs._Henry_Cooper_%282nd_meeting%29.

28 Ibid.

29 "Muhammad Ali vs Brian London," *BoxRec Encyclopedia*, http://boxrec.com/media/index.php/Muhammad_Ali_vs._Brian_London. "Prizefighting: Feats of Clay," *TIME* (August 12, 1966), http://content.time.com/time/magazine/article/0,9171,842624,00.html.

30 Hauser, *Muhammad Ali: His Life and Times*, pp. 142–4 and Michael Meltsner, "Me and Muhammad," *Marquette Sports Law Review* Vol. 12, Issue 2 (Spring, 2002), pp. 584–5.

31 Jack Olsen, "A Case of Conscience," *Sports Illustrated* (April 11, 1966), http://sportsillustrated. cnn.com/vault/article/magazine/MAG1078395/3/index.htm.

32 *New York Times* (August 26, 1966) in Hauser, *Muhammad Ali: His Life and Times*, pp. 154–5.

33 Dave Zirin, "Fifty Years Since the Fall of Sonny Liston and the Birth of Muhammad Ali," *The Nation* (February 24, 2014), http://www.thenation.com/blog/178521/50-years-fall-sonny-liston-and-birth-muhammad-ali#.

34 Dave Zirin, "Rumble, Young Man, Rumble: Muhammad Ali and the 1960s," http://daily-struggles. tumblr.com/post/16010802743/rumble-young-man-rumble-muhammad-ali-and-the-1960s.

35 Olsen, "A Case of Conscience."

36 Martin Kane, "A Muslim Ministers to a Southpaw," *Sports Illustrated* (September 19, 1966), http://sportsillustrated.cnn.com/vault/article/magazine/MAG1079034/index.htm.

37 "Prizefighting: Skinning the Cat," *TIME* (November 25, 1966), http://content.time.com/time/ magazine/article/0,9171,843106,00.html; Bert Randolph Sugar, "Greatest Knockouts: Ali vs Williams," ESPN.com (September 28, 2006), http://sports.espn.go.com/sports/boxing/news/ story?id=2606152; Martin Kane, "The Massacre," *Sports Illustrated* (November 21, 1966), http://sportsillustrated.cnn.com/vault/article/magazine/MAG1079283/index.htm.

38 "Prizefighting: Hate & Love," *TIME* (February 17, 1967), http://content.time.com/time/ magazine/article/0,9171,839462,00.html and "Prizefighting: The Mouth," *TIME* (January 6, 1967), http://content.time.com/time/magazine/article/0,9171,843187,00.html.

39 "Prizefighting: Hate & Love."

40 Tex Maule, "Cruel Ali With All the Skills," *Sports Illustrated* (February 13, 1967), http://si.com/ vault/article/magazine/MAG1079523/1/index.htm.

41 "Prizefighting: The Impossible Dream," *TIME* (March 31, 1967), http://content.time.com/ time/subscriber/article/0,33009,941087,00.html.

42 Mark Kram, "After Muhammad, A Graveyard," *Sports Illustrated* (April 3, 1967), http:// sportsillustrated.cnn.com/vault/article/magazine/MAG1079695/2/index.htm.

43 Andres F. Quintana, "Muhammad Ali: The Greatest in Court," *Marquette Sports Law Review* Vol. 18, Issue 1 (Fall, 2007), p. 185.

CHAPTER 5

"... AND STILL CHAMPION"

The turbulence in Muhammad Ali's career took place as the United States was becoming increasingly embroiled in an undeclared war in Southeast Asia. By 1967, Americans were no longer asking, "Viet Where?" and the draft, with its racial and class implications, was on the front pages of local and national newspapers. Local draft boards struggled to meet the quotas authorized by Congressional action that steadily increased the number of military personnel actively engaged in combat and support operations in Southeast Asia. The increases in troop strength were dramatic, from 184,000 in 1965 to 536,000 in 1968.[1]

Increasingly, the specter of the draft was haunting hundreds of thousands of young American men. On June 30, 1967, President Johnson signed a bill ending draft deferments for new graduate students after the 1967–68 academic year. This law also limited deferments for current graduate students to one year for those pursuing a master's degree and no more than four years for those working toward a Ph.D.[2] On December 1, 1969, the Selective Service held the first draft lottery that affected men born between January 1, 1944 and December 31, 1950 who were not otherwise deferred. Undergraduate student (2-S) deferments ended after President Nixon signed a bill on September 29, 1971 that made the men of the Class of '75 the first undergraduates since World War II to be subject to military induction.[3]

As draft calls increased, so too did resistance to both the rationale for the fighting and the mechanism for conscripting soldiers. Even with the institution of the Selective Service Lottery, which was intended to insert a greater element of fairness into the process, the draft still more frequently captured poor and non-white citizens who had less access to legal and social alternatives. Increasingly, young Americans perceived the draft as unfair.[4]

Between April 28, 1967, when Ali refused induction, and his victory in the Supreme Court on June 28, 1971, he received more public attention as a draft resister or conscientious objector and member of the Nation of Islam than as a professional boxer. Ali was stripped of his title and had lost his license to fight and, thus, his livelihood because of his decision to resist induction. His actions were still in the news, but the venues for his battle were now the Selective Service Administration and the federal courts. He simultaneously, perhaps inadvertently, became a symbol of resistance for Americans who had come to oppose the presence of the United States in Vietnam.

Ali, like other draft resisters, faced public disapprobation, if not outright hatred. Many sportswriters and members of the public thought that his refusal to step forward and accept induction into the Army and the public manner in which he articulated his opposition to the Vietnam War crossed the line of decency. To make matters worse, Ali had changed his name and professed his faith in a religion that most Americans associated with black separatism, hatred, and anti-Americanism. Writing in 2001 in *U.S. News and World Report*, Brian Duffy described the public reaction to Ali in 1967 as "almost otherworldly, a potent brew of naked racism, angry jingoism, and a weird xenophobic spasm at the public injunction of such a foreign, and to many frightening religion."[5] Ali's stand on the war polarized the sporting world just as the war itself polarized the nation.

Ali's refusal to step forward was part of a long train of events that revealed increasing opposition to American participation in the war in Vietnam. Anti-war sentiment increased as troop numbers in Southeast Asia grew, peaking in about 1971, as the Nixon administration implemented a policy of "Vietnamization" of the war by withdrawing troops and declaring an impending "peace with honor." The first attempts to raise an anti-war consciousness came from Quakers and others who saw the hypocrisy and futility of American support of Ngo Dinh Diem, a corrupt and oppressive leader in South Vietnam. As images of Vietnamese Buddhist monks setting themselves on fire in protests of Diem's repression of their religious rights appeared on television in this country, Americans began to ask what was going on in the small nation on the other side of the world, but there were few efforts to answer that question or suggest that the United States might not want to involve itself in the civil war there.

At the same time that Cassius Clay returned from the Rome Olympics with a gold medal, the Students for a Democratic Society (SDS) was founded to little fanfare. Even the dissemination of the group's 1962 Port Huron Statement that declared the 1960s to be the decade in which young people would lead the way to a more peaceful and equitable society drew little attention at the time of its writing. In 1962, the troop numbers and

American body counts were not yet high enough to draw the attention of an American public imbued with the crusading spirit of Cold War liberalism and the imperative to contain or obliterate communism throughout the world.

When Clay conquered Sonny Liston to become the heavyweight champion of the world in 1964 and then embraced a new name and a new religion, activism in far-flung places called attention to both the civil rights and anti-war movements. The University of California at Berkeley's Free Speech Movement and the Mississippi Freedom Summer made news every night as Mario Savio declared his demands for free speech, including activism on campus against the war. At the same time, black and white activists were jailed and Andrew Goodman, Michael Schwerner, and James Chaney were murdered in Philadelphia, Mississippi in June. With the escalation of the fighting and increases in draft calls, the anti-war movement was taking hold on college campuses, focusing its attention on the rapidly escalating American involvement in a land war in Asia.

The bombing of North Vietnam that began with Operation Rolling Thunder in February of 1965 led to teach-ins on college campuses and anti-war marches and rallies that increased in size as the conflict grew in intensity. On April 17, 1965, SDS organized a march on Washington that attracted approximately 20,000 people at the capitol building. This was an orderly march that took place just after the United States had sent its first combat troops to South Vietnam. In April of 1967, 300,000 people marched against the war in New York City. On October 21 of that year, more than 100,000 marchers came to the Pentagon and the Lincoln Memorial. Activist Abbie Hoffman insisted that the energy of the protesters would "levitate the Pentagon." Yippie hype notwithstanding (the building remained earthbound), the turnout was impressive, and the march received significant press coverage. By 1967, 13,000 Americans had died in Vietnam, and the war was front page news. Two years later, at the height of the fighting, it was possible to attract 250,000 (some estimates were as high as 500,000) to a march in Washington on November 15, 1969. The May Day protest of 1971, after the killings at Kent State the year before and the recent incursion into Laos, attracted 200,000 protesters, including members of the Vietnam Veterans Against the War. Moratorium Day protests that involved nearly 2,000,000 people throughout the country, local marches, and a growing interest in those who refused to be inducted or who protested the war from within the military contributed to a climate of mistrust of American government policy and the conduct of the war that the United States seemed to be unable to win. Muhammad Ali's draft resistance occurred in a context of a massive anti-war movement in the United States and throughout the world.[6]

Although Ali did not immediately associate himself with the anti-war movement, anti-war activists wanted to associate their cause with his. Indeed, his opposition to the war energized the movement. Father Daniel Berrigan, a prominent anti-war activist, declared that Ali's refusal "was a major boost to an antiwar movement that was very white. He was not an academic, or a bohemian or a clergyman. He couldn't be dismissed as cowardly."[7] As the war intensified and as protest against the war grew in scope, Ali placed himself closer to the anti-war movement as a speaker who was in demand on many college campuses.

Ali also took a step closer to the mainstream civil rights movement, whose demands for integration and legal equality he had previously dismissed. A month before his induction appearance in Houston, Ali visited Louisville, his hometown. At the same time, the board of Dr. King's organization, the Southern Christian Leadership Conference (SCLC), was meeting in the city. In a statement following the meeting, the SCLC criticized the war as "morally and politically unjust" and the draft as discriminatory. The board further stated that the Selective Service placed African-Americans "in the front lines in disproportionate numbers and from there to racially segregated cemetery plots in the deep south." Ali and King met during the SCLC board meeting on March 29–30, 1967, and the champ spoke publicly in support of the struggle in Louisville for fair housing practices. It was also during this visit that he made a connection between the anti-war and civil rights struggles, asking rhetorically why he should travel "ten thousand miles from home and drop bombs and bullets on brown people in Vietnam while so-called Negro people in Louisville are treated like dogs and denied simple human rights?" Citing the oppressive conditions under which his friends and neighbors lived in his hometown, Ali went on to declare, in response to a reporter's question, that:

> This is the day when such evils must come to an end. I have been warned that to take such a stand would put my prestige in jeopardy and could cause me to lose millions of dollars which should accrue to me as the champion. But I have said it once and I will say it again. The real enemy of my people is right here. I will not disgrace my religion, my people, or myself by becoming a tool to enslave those who are fighting for their own justice, freedom, and equality.

Like many civil rights and anti-war activists, Ali affirmed his willingness to go to jail for his convictions.[8]

Ali did not present himself as a martyr. Rather, he asserted that in resisting the draft he was behaving in a manner that was consistent with the principles of the Nation of Islam. But others did see the former champion as a martyr of sorts. The cover of *Esquire* in April of 1968 portrayed the former champion as St. Sebastian, a Christian martyr. The cover was the inspiration of the magazine's art director, George Lois, who described how he let Ali know about the famous saint:

> I had looked at hundreds of pictures of the great paintings of Saint Sebastian and they are all really bright. But I told Ali, "I want you to pose where your body is very quiet but your head is in pain because I don't want to show your body like that. I want to show your body strong, but your head is in pain."

On learning that the famous saint was a Christian, Ali said "George, I can't pose as a Christian." Lois replied:

> It's a symbolic thing. Anyone in the world can look at this thing and understand the imagery. And the imagery doesn't say you're a Christian, the imagery says that you are a martyr. And what I'm saying is that you are a martyr to your race, you are a martyr because of the war. It's a combination of race, religion, and war in one image, you're symbolizing it in one image.[9]

But Ali was unmoved. He could not see himself portrayed as a Christian martyr. Finally, Lois asked Ali to get Elijah Muhammad on the phone:

> It takes about two minutes, but Ali gets him on the phone, so I pick up and have about a 15 minute talk about what religion I am, how old I am, etc. (etc.) . . . I'm talking to him about symbolism, how Ali is a martyr, blah, blah, blah. Finally, Elijah asks to speak to Ali. Then, Ali gets off the phone with him and says, "Let's do it."

The *Esquire* cover pictured Ali as the Roman soldier who was killed for converting to Christianity. Ali was pictured in his characteristic white trunks and shoes with arrows in his body. The cover was a huge success and was reproduced and sold as a protest against the war and Ali's prosecution for draft evasion.[10] It was an elegant and powerful use of art to make a political statement.

The strength of Ali's convictions would soon be tested. On April 28, 1967, Ali appeared at 8:00 a.m. at the Armed Forces Examining and Entrance Station in the United States Customs House in downtown Houston. He was accompanied by his attorneys and was met by supporters on the streets, some of whom carried signs in support of Ali's actions while others simply called for an end to the draft and the Vietnam War. Forty-seven men who had passed their physical examinations and been classified as eligible for service reported that morning. Forty-six of them stepped forward and accepted induction into the armed forces. Unlike his fellow draftees, Ali had argued that he was entitled to an exemption from military service on the basis of his religious convictions, his status as a conscientious objector, and his role as a Muslim minister whose "preaching and teaching" was a full-time, if unpaid, job supported by the "avocation" of professional boxing. He had also filed a challenge to the entire Selective Service system on the basis of race discrimination that was pending before the United States District Court in Houston.

When asked to step forward and accept induction, Ali refused three times, after which he was advised that his action could lead to an indictment on felony charges. Lieutenant Colonel J. Edwin McKee, the supervisor of the induction center, informed Ali that if he were convicted of federal charges of refusing induction, he would be subject to a penalty of up to five years in prison and a fine of $10,000. After his refusal, Selective Service officials informed Ali that he was likely to be prosecuted for violation of the Selective Service and Training Act.

Ali's prepared statement, delivered to reporters outside the induction center, described the federal government's effort to draft him into the military as a "continuation of the same artificially induced prejudice and discrimination." This was clearly a response to the numerous denials of his requests for exemption from the draft by the Selective Service system and the federal courts. By emphasizing prejudice and discrimination, Ali reminded Americans that the work of the civil rights movement was far from finished and that he was one of many voices that challenged both the wisdom of integration and the propriety of a war against people of color.

In 1967, these were words that many Americans were unprepared to hear, and it was not surprising that words like "traitor" were frequently used to describe the now former heavyweight champion. In his statement, Ali stressed that his decision was "a private and individual one and I realize that this is a most crucial decision. In taking it I am dependent solely upon Allah as the final judge of these actions brought about by my own conscience." Of course, many Americans refused to believe that Ali acted on his own and considered him to have been influenced by the Nation of Islam, for many a dangerous cult. Asserting that he had acted on his own, Ali asserted his right to dissent, saying, "I insist upon my right to pursue my livelihood with the same rights granted to other men and women who have disagreed with the policies of whatever administration was in power at the time."[11]

Ali petitioned the Texas Southern District Court for injunctive relief from the actions of the Selective Service system, as well as National Director Lieut. General Lewis Hershey and Commissioners Judge Henry Gwiazda, Dr. Kenneth W. Clement, and Charles Collatos. The Court began its ruling, written by Judge Allen Hannay, in *Muhammad Ali et al. v. John B. Connally, Governor of Texas, et al.* by stating that it was axiomatic that the Selective Service Act was constitutional as an exercise of both the emergency and the war powers of Congress. The rulings of the Selective Service Board must be considered final. Judge Hannay, using the same logic as had the District Court judges in Louisville, stated: "The legal remedy for any wrongful action by the Board is not pre-induction injunctive order." Ali had not been harmed by the system because he had neither submitted to the draft nor had he been subjected to punishment for refusing to be inducted. According to the ruling, Ali could not seek relief until after his conviction, should that occur. The judge observed that, "The selectee if he refuses the final step toward military induction must face the criminal sanctions and prosecution authorized by law therefor and his remedy lies in whatever defense he claims as against the actions of the Selective Service Board."[12]

As Ali's legal battles continued, one of his few supporters in the press was ABC announcer Howard Cosell, who used his forum as a broadcaster with a national audience to represent the champion's position:

> The action he [Muhammad Ali] has taken is based on his deepest personal convictions and he is aware of the possible implications and consequences ... He says he hopes to immediately resume his boxing career, that he won his title fairly within the four corners of the ring and that this is the only way he can be deprived of it. He is also aware that certain authorities in the world of boxing will seek to strip him of his title.[13]

It took only a few hours for the World Boxing Association to do just that. On the same day, when news of Ali's refusal to step forward became public, Edwin Dooley, chairman of the New York State Athletic Commission, announced that Ali no longer held a valid license to box in the state and that New York athletic authorities concurred with the WBA that Ali was no longer the heavyweight champion. Dooley told the press that he thought it was "a pity that Clay has loused up his image and the image of boxing ... I once thought he would emerge as a combination of Joe Louis, Jack Dempsey, Rocky Marciano, and Willie Mays. However, he's thrown it away." He further asserted that continuing to allow Ali to fight in New York was "detrimental to the best interests of boxing."[14] Other state boxing authorities quickly followed New York's example and suspended or revoked Ali's license to fight in their states. Bob Evans, President of the World Boxing Association, said, "I feel Ali has violated the laws of the United States regarding Selective Service. His action today leaves me no alternative." Very soon after the WBA action, the British Boxing Board of Control and the European Boxing Union took away Ali's designation as heavyweight champion.[15]

In New York, State Athletic Commissioner Dooley suggested that a tournament be organized to crown a new champ. Ali stated his feelings about this proposal in no uncertain terms:

> I had the world heavyweight title not because it was given to me, not because of my religion, but because I won it in the ring. Those who want to take and start a series of auction-type bouts not only do me a disservice, but actually disgrace

themselves . . . Sports fans and fair-minded people throughout America would never accept such a title-holder.[16]

With this statement, Ali turned the tables on his detractors who had called him a disgrace to the sport of boxing.

Howard Cosell referred to the boxing authorities' actions as "an outrage; an absolute disgrace . . . Due process of law hadn't even begun, yet they took away his livelihood because he failed the test of political and social conformity."[17] Cosell was right: Ali's crime, for which he was being tried and sentenced in the court of public opinion, was the crime of non-conformity, resisting the authority of the United States, and practicing an unpopular religion.

In early May, Ali was indicted by a federal grand jury in Houston for draft evasion. His attorneys attempted to prevent a trial, but their request was denied in court. The trial took place in the United States District Court for the Southern District of Texas on June 20, 1967. After only five hours of testimony, it took an all-white federal jury only twenty-one minutes to convict the heavyweight champion. Ali requested an immediate sentencing for his own peace of mind and in order to pursue his appeals in a timely way. Judge Joe McDonald Ingraham refused a request for leniency from United States Attorney Morton Susman, who noted that Ali had no significant criminal record. The judge elected to make an example of the champ, sentencing him to the maximum penalty of five years in prison and a fine of $10,000.[18]

Ali's conviction was one factor, along with increases in troop strength, growing numbers of American deaths and casualties, and the rapidly increasing cost of the conflict, that helped to galvanize resistance to the Vietnam War. A few weeks before Ali's trial in Houston, Rev. Martin Luther King, Jr. had declared in New York City's Riverside Church that:

> it should be incandescently clear that no one who has any concern for the integrity and life of America today can ignore the present war. If America's soul becomes totally poisoned, part of the autopsy must read Vietnam. It can never be saved so long as it destroys the deepest hopes of men the world over. So it is that those of us who are yet determined that America will be led down the path of protest and dissent are working for the health of our land.[19]

Dr. King's break with the Johnson Administration was a major step in the evolution of his thinking on Vietnam. His words in support of the peace movement inspired others to re-think their support of the war, and Ali's actions no doubt had a similar effect. Activist Julian Bond credited Ali's conviction with helping to raise consciousness and skepticism about the war. He wrote that Ali's conviction "reverberated through the whole society . . .

You could hear people talking about it on street corners. It was on everyone's lips. People who had never thought about the war before began to think it through because of Ali. The ripples were enormous."[20] Protests against the war continued to grow, but it would be unfair to over-estimate the impact of anti-war expressions on compliance with the draft law. Even in the presence of a GI anti-war movement, military recruits and conscripts generally obeyed the law. A week after Ali's famous refusal, *TIME* magazine downplayed his influence on present and future draftees:

> Though such gaudy objectors to the draft as Cassius Clay and draft-card burners suggest that Americans in unprecedented numbers are resisting military service, statistics convincingly show that the opposite is the case. Americans evading the draft or deserting once they are inducted still number considerably less than in previous wars. Last year only 353 of 1,100,000 eligible men were convicted as draft dodgers compared with one-year totals of 8,422 in World War I, 4,609 in World War II and 432 in the Korean conflict. Similarly, the AWOL desertion rate for 1966 was .08 for every 1,000 draftees against 3.7 in World War II and .89 in Korea.[21]

There was no question that Ali would appeal his draft evasion conviction to the Supreme Court, if necessary. He was confident that he would prevail in court, although the District Court rulings in Louisville and Houston had not provided evidence to support that confidence. Ali repeatedly told reporters that they were wrong to assume that he would either submit to the demands of the Selective Service and go into the Army or continue to resist and go to jail. He presented a third alternative that few actually expected, suggesting that he would be vindicated:

> I have searched my conscience ... I take my stand in rejecting the call to be inducted in the armed services. I do so with the full realization of its implications and possible consequences ... In the end I am confident that justice will come my way for the truth must eventually prevail.[22]

As a famous person who opposed a now-controversial war, Ali found himself with support around the world, in Muslim and non-Muslim countries in the Middle East and Africa. He began to see himself as an international figure whose fame transcended the boxing ring. He told reporters:

> Boxing is nothing, just satisfying to some bloodthirsty people. I'm no longer Cassius Clay, a Negro from Kentucky. I belong to the world, the black world. I'll always have a home in Pakistan, in Algeria, in Ethiopia. This is more than money.[23]

This statement was true. Ali was no longer the braggart of his younger days. He understood that he was gaining fame and respect throughout the world as well as expressions of hatred and revulsion for his actions in his own country. He realized that his voice would be heard and his ideas taken seriously.

In August of 1967, Ali attempted to arrange a fight with Oscar Bonavena in Tokyo, but he soon realized that his ability to earn a living had been compromised even beyond the borders of the United States. When Ali appealed to Judge Ingraham in Houston for permission to travel to Japan, the judge refused to allow him to leave the United States and ordered him to surrender his passport. The World Boxing Council and the Orient Boxing Council revoked Ali's title. The champ was stuck.

Ali understood that he had raised fundamental issues of race, and he credited his association with the Nation of Islam for raising his personal consciousness. Ali said in 1970:

> When I didn't go to Vietnam, I was by myself almost. Now everybody is against it. Right? I wasn't wrong then. I used to always say: "I'm pretty." "I'm beautiful." And now the black folk have signs saying "black is beautiful." They're just now getting around to seeing it. But I saw it many years ago because I follow the real leader.[24]

With a suspended license, no title, the threat of a federal indictment, and the disapprobation of almost every sports writer who chose to comment publicly on his situation, Ali found himself without a livelihood and no discernible means of supporting himself and his family. Bill Gleason of the *Chicago Sun Times* noted the connection between Ali's actions and his race: "The white race finally had a cause they could vindicate as just. Here was an avowed racist who said he would not fight in the war for reasons of his own. The crowd roared for the blood of Ali."[25]

Despite the support he received in some quarters for his stand against the Vietnam War, the loss of his livelihood was a serious setback, and Ali was forced to turn to the college lecture circuit. His stature grew among many young people, black and white, who had begun their own collective challenge to government policy in Vietnam. Campus marches and protests were common by 1967. In April of 1967, the Black Power committee at Howard University, a historically black university in Washington, DC, invited Ali to speak. The campus had recently been the scene of Black Power demonstrations, so the mood was tense when Ali spoke at the Frederick Douglass Memorial on campus before an audience of nearly 1,000 members of the Howard community. Ali's address, popularly called his "Black is Best" speech, emphasized the theme of respect for black identity and the need for a homeland. He told the students, "All you need to do is know yourself to set yourself free. We don't know who we are. We call ourselves Negroes, but have you ever heard of a place called Negroland?" Ali encouraged the enthusiastic crowd to reject the "white is beautiful" paradigm:

> See, we have been brainwashed. Everything good and of authority was made white. We look at Jesus, we see a white man with blond hair and blue eyes. We look at all the angels, we see white with blond hair and blue eyes. Now, I'm sure if there's a heaven in the sky and the colored folks die and go to Heaven, where are the colored angels? They must be in the kitchen preparing the milk and honey. We look at Miss America, we see white. We look at Miss World, we see white. We look at Miss Universe, we see white. Even Tarzan, the king of the jungle in black Africa, he's white!

To prove his point, Ali concluded his Howard address with the assertion that "Black dirt is the best dirt. Brown sugar causes fewer cavities, and the blacker the berry, the sweeter the juice."[26] Ali was now earning his living promoting Black Power instead of battling in the ring.

Black Power and identity were Ali's favorite topics on campus, and he rarely talked about his legal battles or the Vietnam War. At the University of Washington on May 30, 1968, Ali spoke about race, Islam, and love. Sometimes, he even offered advice that was inconsistent with the socially experimental tenor of the times. As a member of the Nation of Islam, Ali was hardly an advocate for drug use or sexual experimentation. His conservative admonitions about sex and drugs, reflecting his Muslim teachings, were generally met with polite, tolerant applause. But college crowds loved Ali nevertheless, and his talks frequently ended with a familiar call-and-response refrain:

> Can my title be taken away without my being whupped?
> NO!
> One more time!
> NO!
> Who's the heavyweight champion of the world?
> You are!

In the few instances when Ali spoke about his own case, he linked his resistance to the draft to growing calls for black liberation throughout the world. His campus speeches sounded a familiar refrain: "I'm expected to go overseas to help free people in South Vietnam at the same time my people here are being brutalized and mistreated."

He appeared at an anti-war rally in Los Angeles in June of 1967. Taking his place before the crowd on an overturned garbage can, he said, "Anything designed for peace and to stop the killing of people I'm for 1,000 percent. I'm not a leader. I'm not here to tell you what to do. But I encourage you to express yourselves."[27] Ali also gained personal affirmation and support from his college audiences. According to ESPN's Michael Silver:

> The defrocked champion may have been barely literate but he certainly was not verbally challenged. His lively lectures were well received. He spoke about his views on race, religious philosophy, and the war. Since the boxing establishment had already started the process of crowning a new heavyweight champion Ali always ended his speeches by asking the audience to tell him who the real heavyweight champion was. He was obviously pleased to hear the familiar chant of "Ali, Ali." The counter culture had a new hero.[28]

Ali's stand against the draft was a source of inspiration for organizers who had been working to end the war and the draft for years. Dagmar Wilson of Women Strike for Peace described Ali as "one of the heroes of our time." In March of 1968, Joe Frazier fought Buster Mathis for the Heavyweight Championship sanctioned by the World Boxing Association. Protesters gathered outside Madison Square Garden in support of Ali, claiming that he was the real champion. John Wilson of the National Black Anti-War, Anti-Draft Union summarized the sentiment represented by the protest: "We feel that white America cannot . . . decide for black people who the world champion is."[29]

Ali's views on the war and racism energized other athletes who dared to speak out against racism in athletics in their own way at a time of growing racial consciousness and opposition to the Vietnam War. On June 4, 1967, football player Jim Brown brought together a group of current and former black sports stars to meet with Ali. This group included basketball stars Bill Russell and Lew Alcindor (later Kareen Abdul-Jabbar) and professional football players Willie Davis and Bobby Mitchell. According to *Cleveland Plain Dealer* writer Bransen Wright, this group of elite athletes "wanted to know just how strong Ali stood behind his convictions as a conscientious objector. The questions flew fast and furious. Ali's answers would determine whether Brown and the other athletes would throw their support behind the heavyweight champion." They concluded that Ali had taken a sincere and principled stand, and they held a press conference with Ali to declare their support for his position against the war. The original intent of the meeting had been to question whether Ali would submit to the draft on the theory that he would be given easy duty and could keep his title, which would not compromise his ability to earn a living. But the group, most of whom had graduated college and some of whom had served in the military, was soon convinced of his sincerity. A few months after the meeting, Bill Russell commented: "I envy Ali . . . He has something I have never been able to attain and something very few people possess. He had absolute and sincere faith. I'm not worried about

Muhammad Ali. He is better equipped than anyone to withstand the trials in store for him."[30]

Amateur athletes also began to contribute to the national conversation regarding racism and equality. The Olympic Project for Human Rights was organized in the fall of 1967 to organize a boycott of the upcoming games in Mexico City. Professor Harry Edwards, himself a former discus thrower at San Jose State University in California, was a prime mover in the Olympic boycott movement. The Olympic protest served to articulate specific grievances relating to unequal and substandard housing, education, and employment, all issues that advocates of Black Power were bringing to public attention. The Project hoped to demonstrate that black athletes were being used to promote values of athleticism, friendly competition, and sportsmanship in a society that did not treat them as full citizens and human beings who deserved respect.

The Project demanded first that Ali's title be reinstated, a demand that also reflected the athletes' opposition to the war. Further, the Project demanded the removal of Avery Brundage from his position as the head of the United States Olympic Committee because of his racist views. Brundage had been called a "racist, an anti-communist, and an authoritarian bully" who had been an admirer of Adolf Hitler since the 1936 Olympic Games. Finally, the group demanded that Rhodesia and South Africa be banned from the Olympic Games because of their apartheid regimes. The International Olympic Committee acceded to the final demand, and the two segregationist countries were not permitted to send athletes to the Games. Even though the proposed boycott did not succeed, Black Power and racism were never far from the center of popular discussion about the Mexico City Olympics.[31] Ali himself became involved in the conversation about the proposed Olympic boycott. In an appearance at Fairleigh Dickinson University in New Jersey in April of 1968, a student asked him about his view of the possibility that American athletes would refuse to represent their country in the Olympic Games as he had done in 1960. Ali told the audience of 750, "Some think it's a way of protesting, their way of sacrificing ... I'm an example of that myself, so naturally I'd be for it ... My stand started it."[32] Indeed, Ali's position on the war had influenced other athletes to think critically about their "place" in the world. Although the boycott did not succeed, there were athletes who took independent action.

On October 16, 1968, the second day of the Mexico City Olympics, John Carlos and Tommie Smith voiced their protest against racism with Black Power salutes as they received their medals.[33] Images of Carlos and Smith on the medal stand with their fists raised appeared all over the world as a symbol of resistance to racism. But not all Americans perceived the athletes in heroic terms. Writing in the *Chicago American*, Brent Musburger called

Carlos and Smith "a pair of black-skinned storm troopers." He also appealed to some of America's worst racist instincts when he wrote, "One gets a little tired of having the United States run down by athletes who are enjoying themselves at the expense of their country." Brundage's response, although it was couched in the high-minded rhetoric of Olympic tradition, revealed no empathy with the position of the protesters: "The untypical exhibitionism of these athletes also violates the basic standards of good manners and sportsmanship, which are so highly valued in the United States, and therefore the two men involved are suspended forthwith from the team and ordered to remove themselves from the Olympic Village."[34] Brundage seemed not to understand that protests against racism and calls for empowerment had long ago transcended polite requests for equality to become part of an increasingly insistent demand for justice that encompassed legal equality, economic and social equity, and resistance to the Vietnam War. From the innocence of Cassius Clay's 1960 gold medal to the furor caused by the sprinters' public protest in 1968, black American athletes had come a long way in their willingness to voice their objections to the pervasive racism in American society and American sports.

To stay in the public eye, Ali accepted a role in the short-running Broadway musical, "Buck White," which ran for seven performances between December 2 and 6, 1969. With music, lyrics, and direction by Oscar Brown, Jr., the play also featured performances by Donald Sutherland, who played a character named "White Man." Ali played "Buck." The *Playbill* synopsis was almost as short as the play's run: "A militant black lecturer addresses a meeting organized by a black political group in this musical adaptation of Joseph Dolan Tuotti's play *Big Time Buck White*." Ali's musical talents did not match his prowess in the ring, but he did perform the song "We Came in Chains" on the Ed Sullivan Show. The poster from the show reveals Ali in a fake beard and Afro haircut. In spite of its song and dance numbers (Ali did not dance), the play was a scripted Black Power lecture. Ali recited lines such as:

> Now if we continue to be held down and tied to ghettos of hopelessness, then our anger is someday going to burst in an explosion and that explosion is going to unify all colored people in the world. Colored people are seeing the white man's quest for power as a definite threat to them . . . the black people and the brown people and the yellow people and all the disaffected, disillusioned people . . . they are making a commitment.[35]

Even in a less-than-successful Broadway production, it was clear that, by 1969, Muhammad Ali had gone far beyond his non-political and purely religious anti-war stance to become a forceful advocate for profound social and political change.

When he declared his conversion to the Nation of Islam, Ali became a spokesperson for the NOI. According to Jeremiah Shabazz, the leader of Mosque No. 12 in Philadelphia and a close advisor to Ali:

> When Elijah Muhammad spoke, his words were confined to whatever city he had spoken in. But Ali was a sports hero, and people wanted to know what he had to say, so his visibility and prominence were of great benefit to the Nation. His voice carried throughout the world, and that was a true blessing for us. There's no doubt, our following increased enormously, maybe a hundred percent, after he joined the Nation.[36]

As long as Ali was in the news for his accomplishments in the ring, and as long as he sang the praises of the Nation of Islam, he was valuable. After his conviction for draft evasion, Ali's position in the Nation of Islam began to change. Ali's status in the Nation was further compromised by a comment he made in a 1969 interview. When Howard Cosell asked the deposed champ if he would return to boxing, he replied, "Why not? If they come up with enough money."[37]

For this comment, Ali was suspended from the Nation of Islam, which issued the following statement:

> We tell the world we're not with Muhammad Ali. Muhammad Ali is out of the circle of the brotherhood of the followers of Islam . . . for one year. Mr. Muhammad Ali shall not be recognized with us under the holy name Muhammad Ali. We will call him Cassius Clay.

Jeremiah Shabazz further explained the thinking of Hon. Elijah Muhammad:

> It was like Ali was saying he'd give up his religion for the white man's money. The Messenger sent for Ali, and I went with him to Chicago. I was there when the Messenger told Ali he was taking his name back and suspending him from the faith, that he didn't want to be included with anyone so weak as to go crawling on hands and knees to the white man for a little money.[38]

The action of the NOI was reported in the *Amsterdam News*, which quoted the words of Hon. Elijah Muhammad at length. The paper reported the NOI leader's explanation of Ali's suspension:

> THIS MEANS that Muhammad Ali (Cassius Clay) is not respected in the society, and circle of Islam for the next year, from the date of this statement and issue of MUHAMMAD SPEAKS Newspaper.

In a warning to those who might question his actions, Elijah Muhammad further stated:

> You are not the judge in this matter. This is for Allah (God) and myself to judge and not the world.[39]

Ali accepted Elijah Muhammad's ruling. Even after having been rejected by his religious leader, he remained loyal to the organization, telling *The Black Scholar* in June of 1970:

> Yes, I'm under a year's suspension because I said I was going back to boxing just for the money. As if to say that my god and what I believe can't take care of me. I cannot talk to any Muslim in the country, or go to any meetings. They will not speak to me on the street. They have nothing to say to me until I'm back in good standing. This is what makes the Honorable Elijah Muhammad so great. There's no favoritism.[40]

In spite of his suspension, Ali retained his conviction that the teachings of Elijah Muhammad and the Nation of Islam were responsible for his perspective on race in American society. While Ali has maintained his Muslim faith to the present day, he has not been as closely tied to the organization as he was in the mid- to late 1960s. Ali left the NOI in 1975.

Unbeknownst to him, Ali was also a minor figure in a developing constitutional issue relating to the Fourth Amendment and the emerging practice of conducting warrantless searches as part of foreign intelligence surveillance during the 1960s. Although the Supreme Court had established that law enforcement authorities could not conduct a search of a private residence without a specific warrant authorized by a judge in the case of *Mapp* v. *Ohio* (1960), federal agencies such as the Federal Bureau of Investigation had a long-established practice of conducting surveillance and wiretaps without warrants because they were able to establish that the searches related to national security. The Supreme Court had not yet ruled on the reasonableness of such searches, and the process for obtaining permission for warrantless searches, most of which were wire taps, had not yet been developed under the Foreign Intelligence Surveillance Act (FISA), which was enacted in 1978.

As Ali was appealing his draft evasion conviction to the Supreme Court, federal government sources revealed that he had been a party to five telephone conversations that had been monitored and recorded. Although Ali was not the target of the government's investigation in this instance (Dr. Martin Luther King, Jr. was the target of the FBI's surveillance), the propriety and legality of the wiretaps to which he had been subjected had not been fully established, and exceptions to the requirement that searches be authorized by a warrant had not been clarified. This was the basis on which Ali claimed that his conviction might have been tainted.

Recently released documents reveal that Ali was also on a National Security Agency watch list that included Dr. King, *New York Times* columnist Tom Wicker, humorist Art Buchwald, and Senators Frank Church and Howard Baker. The MINARET program began as a vehicle for tracking the activities of drug dealers and people who might threaten the president but soon expanded to include surveillance on a number of prominent people who had questioned or expressed opposition to the Vietnam War on the grounds that they might be "domestic terrorists." MINARET was virtually unsupervised and its operatives had so few rules that even the National Security Administration itself called the operation "disreputable if not outright illegal." Attorney General Elliot Richardson shut down MINARET in late 1973, and its abuses contributed to the establishment of the FISA courts by Congress in 1978. At the time of Ali's draft resistance case, few people knew of the scope of MINARET's surveillance activities. On the basis of the five wiretapped phone calls that had been revealed, the Supreme Court vacated Ali's conviction on March 24, 1969, sending his case back to Judge Ingraham in the Texas District Court where Ali's trial had occurred to determine if that conviction had been the result of illegally obtained information.[41]

Judge Ingraham personally reviewed the surveillance logs of the five conversations and ordered that Ali and his attorneys receive the records of four of the conversations. He ruled that the defendant did not have the right of access to the fifth conversation because it was the result of lawful surveillance activity. But the disclosure of the wiretaps did not help Ali's case, as the judge ruled that the content of the conversations was immaterial to Ali's conviction. The FBI had wiretapped the heavyweight champion, but the content of the conversations did not relate to Ali's refusal to be drafted. This was an important development because the Fifth Circuit Court upheld the right of the president as commander-in-chief to engage in foreign intelligence operations that included warrantless wiretaps in the interest of national security. As a result of his determination that the surveillance had not affected Ali's case, Judge Ingraham re-imposed his original sentence, and Ali was headed back to the Supreme Court to appeal his conviction.[42] Throughout his legal struggles, Ali was defended by Hayden Covington, a noted white defense attorney who had achieved thirty-seven victories in cases before the Supreme Court. Among Hayden's more famous clients was the Watch Tower Bible and Tract Society, the publication of the Jehovah's Witnesses.[43]

As Ali was fighting his legal battles, he still had to consider how he was going to earn a living and support his family. On September 22, 1969, Ali applied to the New York State Athletic Commission to renew his license to fight in the state. One of his supporters was Joe Frazier, who gave the former champ small sums of money privately and offered support in his battle to regain his license to box in New York. Nevertheless, the Commission voted unanimously to deny Ali's application because of his "refusal to enter the service and [his felony] conviction in violation of Federal law regarded by [the] Commission to be detrimental to the best interests of boxing, or to the public interest, convenience or necessity."[44] Ali filed suit in federal court for the southern district of New York, arguing that his denial on the basis of his conviction denied his First (freedom of religion), Fourteenth (equal protection under the law and denial of his property right to earn a living), and Eighth (protection against cruel and unusual punishment) Amendment rights. Judge Marvin E. Frankel ruled that the Commission had a right enshrined in the statute that had created it to suspend or revoke a boxing license on the basis of an applicant's prior felony conviction. While denying Ali's claim that he should have been issued a license renewal, Judge Frankel left open the possibility that Ali could bring his case back to court if he could provide more specific evidence to support his claim.[45]

Ali's attorneys, with help from the NAACP Legal Defense Fund, got to work. They found 244 cases in which boxing licenses had been issued or renewed for applicants who had been convicted of either felonies or misdemeanors. The felons alone included convicted robbers, murderers, arsonists, and embezzlers. His case was heard in the courtroom of Judge Walter R. Mansfield, who ruled that the denial of a boxing license on the basis of factors that were not relevant to the profession of boxing constituted a violation of Ali's rights under the Equal Protection Clause of the Fourteenth Amendment. The Judge's opinion included the following statement:

> If the Commission in the present case had denied licenses to all applicants convicted of crimes of military offenses, plaintiff would have no valid basis for demanding that a license be issued to him. But the action of the Commission in denying him a license because of his refusal to serve in the Armed Forces while granting licenses to hundreds of other applicants convicted of other crimes and military offenses involving moral turpitude appears on its face to be an intentional, arbitrary, and unreasonable discrimination against the plaintiff.

Judge Mansfield went on to say that, "It is not suggested that any rational basis exists for singling out the offense of draft evasion for labeling as 'conduct detrimental to the interests of boxing' while holding that all other criminal activities such as murder, rape, arson, burglary, and possession of narcotics are not so classified." Even though he was still a convicted felon, the champ finally gained a victory in court on September 14, 1970. The New York State Athletic Commission did not appeal Judge Mansfield's ruling, and Ali was entitled to re-claim his license to box in New York State.[46]

The political and social tides were changing. By 1970, support for the war was diminishing further, resistance to the draft did not seem so unreasonable, and Ali's views on the conflict in Vietnam were closer to the mainstream than to a radical fringe. Thanks to the efforts of state senator Leroy Johnson, Georgia's first African-American political office holder in nearly a century, and the fact that the state of Georgia did not have a boxing commission to permit or allow the fight, Ali received a license to fight from the City of Atlanta Athletic Commission on August 12, 1970. Ali agreed to fight Jerry

Quarry from Bakersfield, California in the City Auditorium in Atlanta on October 26. Reflecting on the social and political as well as the athletic importance of the fight, *The Ring* writer Lee Groves noted that, "One of the most important comebacks in boxing history began when Muhammad Ali emerged from a 43-month exile to score a three-round TKO over Jerry Quarry. Ali's return wasn't just a sporting spectacle but it was also a social happening that struck at the heart of a deeply divided nation." Civil rights leader Julian Bond wrote:

> It was like nothing I'd ever seen. The black elite of America was there. It was a coronation; the king regaining his throne. The whole audience was composed of stars ... You had all these people from the fast lane who were there, and the style of dress was fantastic. Men in ankle-length coats; women wearing smiles and pearls and not much else. It was more than a fight, it was an important moment for Atlanta, because that night Atlanta came into its own as the black capital of America.[47]

In spite of Atlanta's status as the embodiment of the "New South," Georgia Governor Lester Maddox held some staunchly conservative, Old South, segregationist views. Maddox told the *Atlanta Journal-Constitution*, "We shouldn't let him fight for money if he didn't fight for his country." The Governor failed to mount a boycott of the fight, so he declared October 26 to be a "day of mourning." In spite of his efforts to divert interest from the fight, reporters and the public were enthusiastic about seeing what Ali could do after his long exile from the ring. Ali himself understood the importance of the fight:

> People are coming from Pakistan and China ... From Philadelphia and from Detroit, from Watts. Satellites are flying around the sky just to take this fight to Africa and Asia and Russia. Millions and millions of people, watching and waiting—just to see me jump around a ring ... I'd better win.[48]

Ali did win in typical Ali style. His jabs were effective, and he was able to snap back his head with almost every one of Quarry's efforts to land a punch. Ali hit Quarry above his right eye, which had been scarred in a previous fight. The cut gushed blood, and Quarry was not able to recover. Lee Groves remembered that, at the end of the third round,

> The left side of Quarry's face was a mess, and his head-down, hunched-over posture reflected his discouragement. Referee Perez monitored the situation as Quarry's seconds worked over the cut. But only 20 seconds into the rest period the fighter leaped off the stool as if launched by rocket fuel. The reason for Quarry's reaction was that Perez had stopped the fight, affixing Quarry's fifth loss and confirming Ali's 30th victory.[49]

Only five weeks later after the reinstatement of his New York license, Ali fought Argentinian fighter Oscar "Ringo" Bonavena for the vacant North American Boxing Association heavyweight title. He received a guarantee of $200,000 against 42.5 percent of the total receipts, and Bonavena's guarantee was about half of that. More than 19,000 spectators watched the fight in Madison Square Garden, and there were closed-circuit television presentations in 150 cities. Prior to the fight, Bonavena baited Ali by calling him a "chicken" for his refusal to go into the Army, and Ali responded by saying, "Please! Tell everyone to get to your theaters. I have never had a man I wanted to whup so bad!" Ali also made one of his famous predictions, saying, "He'll be mine in nine." That prediction proved false, as the fight went into the fifteenth round. Ali was ahead in the judging, and in the fifteenth round, he was able to knock Bonavena down three times. This forced a stoppage of the fight, the first time this had happened to Bonavena in his sixty-eight-fight career.[50] The win was a technical knockout, and it was not as easy as Ali had predicted, but it was a win. The champ was back.

In 1971, Joe Frazier, whose record was 26–0 with twenty-three knockouts, was the recognized heavyweight champion of the world, having defeated both Buster Mathis and Jimmy Ellis during Ali's forced exile from the ring. He did so in the World Boxing Association's tournament that brought to the ring a number of contenders who battled for a title without having to face the deposed champion. Ali had not fought for a title, except for his recent victory over Oscar Bonavena for the vacant NABF title, since his defeat of Zora Folley in 1967. His professional record was 31–0, with twenty-three knockouts, which made a potential matchup between the two undefeated heavyweight champions uniquely compelling. Once again, Ali was involved in a cultural clash as well as a boxing match. Writing in *Sports Illustrated*, Richard Hoffer noted the contrast between the two fighters:

> Ali represented the counterculture, becoming the mouthpiece of a new generation. Frazier, for simplicity's sake, was cast as the establishment figure, his roots as a sharecropper's son from South Carolina turned slaughterhouse worker in Philadelphia obliged to stand in for the status quo. It was, additionally, Ali's flash vs Frazier's brawn, a contest between style and substance. And it was even more: To Frazier's everlasting puzzlement, Ali introduced race into their budding rivalry, calling Frazier an Uncle Tom.[51]

In fact, Frazier had been one of the few fighters to support Ali during his exile from professional boxing. Although he had taken advantage of Ali's absence to advance his own career and win a version of the Heavyweight Championship, he also privately gave Ali small amounts of money when he needed help.

The two fighters met in Madison Square Garden on March 8, 1971 in a much-heralded "Fight of the Century." Reflecting back on the excitement generated by the fight, ESPN columnist Michael Silver noted that:

> Fifty countries had purchased rights to the telecast. The fight was broadcast from ringside in 12 different languages. When the final tallies were added up it was estimated that 300 million people around the globe had watched the fight. It was the largest audience ever for a television broadcast up to that time. More people had tuned into the fight than had watched the moon landing two years before.[52]

The bout lived up to its pre-fight hype. The "Fight of the Century" was not a specifically political event, but it was difficult not to portray Ali as the representative of the Back Power and anti-war movements and Frazier as the fighter of the boxing establishment and conservative America. According to the official website of the International Boxing Hall of Fame, "Ali was still held in contempt by much of the country. He was viewed as a brash, draft- dodging Muslim who embodied the defiance and the spirit of both the anti-war movement and the radical chic. Frazier—who read the bible and liked to sing—was held up as the conscientious, blue-collar champion."[53] Odds makers gave Frazier a slight edge with 6–5 odds in his favor, and Ali made his own prediction: "Frazier will fall in six," and he returned to his old form with a poem for the occasion:

> Joe's gonna come out smokin'
> But I ain't gonna be jokin'
> I'll be pickin'and pokin'
> Pouring water on his smokin'
> This might shock and amaze ya
> But I'm gonna destroy Joe Frazier.

The poem was far from Ali's best, but the fight was a major draw. Madison Square Garden held 20,455 spectators that night for a fight that was called "electric" with a total gross of gate and television revenue of between eighteen and twenty million dollars.

For ten rounds, the fight was exciting and a "draw" in the eyes of many observers. Silver called it a "grudge match" in which each man was "fighting as if he had a point to prove." At the end of the eleventh round:

> Frazier caught Ali with a tremendous left hook to the jaw that caused his knees to sag. He tried to fool Frazier into thinking he was just playing possum but he was genuinely hurt. He barely made it to the end of the round. The pace slowed a bit in the next two rounds as both men seemed to be conserving what energy they had left for the homestretch. In the 14th round, Ali, drawing on some

mysterious inner resource, staged a miraculous comeback and pounded Frazier with some of his best punches of the fight.

But in the fifteenth round, Frazier caught Ali's jaw once again and he was knocked to the mat. A left hook had "dropped Ali for only the third time in his career."[54] Joe Frazier was now the title holder by virtue of a technical knockout. Both men spent time in the hospital after the fight as a result of their grueling battle in the ring.[55] Ali lost his first professional fight that night.

In defeat, the now former heavyweight champion was gracious toward Frazier, perhaps in recognition of Frazier's character and kindness toward Ali when he had been exiled from boxing. When a reporter referred to him as "champ," Ali replied:

> "I ain't the champ," he said quietly. "Joe's the champ, I call him champ now, not before but I do now. I ain't protestin'. He's a good, tough fighter. Not a great boxer but great at his own thing. He puts pressure on you all night, cuts off the ring, and he's the best hitter I ever met. I always thought of him as a nice fella. What I said before, that was to do with the fight. Just the fight. I got to know him pretty good from traveling up from Philadelphia before he fought Jimmy Ellis. I was low on money that day and he loaned me a hundred dollars. He's a nice man with a family, just another brother workin' to make a living."[56]

Ali may have suffered defeat in the ring, but he would soon be vindicated in court.

According to the Supreme Court, a conscientious objector must be opposed to war in any form, must base his opposition to war on religious or moral beliefs, and be sincere in his objection to war. The Court ruled on Ali's appeal of his conviction for draft evasion on June 28, 1971 in *Clay* v. *United States*. In its advice to Ali's draft board, the Justice Department had asserted that Ali did not meet any of the criteria that would qualify him for conscientious objector status. However, when the case went to the Supreme Court, the government allowed that Ali was sincerely opposed to war on religious grounds and based its case solely on the requirement that a conscientious objector must be opposed to all war. Ali had previously said that war "is against the teachings of the Holy Qur'an. I'm not trying to dodge the draft. We are not supposed to take part in no wars unless declared by Allah or The Messenger. We don't take part in Christian wars or wars of any unbelievers." That statement alone, which appeared to make Ali a potential participant in *some wars*, would have disqualified Ali as a conscientious objector.

When the first vote was taken, Justice Marshall did not participate because he had served as the solicitor general at the inception of the case, and the vote was 5–3 to uphold Ali's conviction, which would likely have resulted in a prison sentence. Justice Harlan, who had been assigned to write the opinion, became convinced of Ali's sincerity and that the Justice Department had presented its case differently to the draft board and the court. Harlan changed his vote, and the court was now evenly divided. The focus now shifted to the thinking of Justice Potter Stewart, who noted that Ali's local draft board had not indicated the specific reason for denying his claim for conscientious objector status. According to Thomas Hauser, members of the draft board could, at least theoretically, have held that

> Ali's position was not sincerely held or not based upon religious training and belief—positions that the government itself now conceded were wrong. Stewart's argument appealed to the conservatives on the Court, because it meant that Ali's conviction could be reversed without ruling that members of the Nation of Islam were entitled to conscientious objector status. Only chief Justice Warren Berger refused to go along with the proposal; and in the end, he too succumbed to Stewart's logic.[57]

The Court's 8–0 ruling was important not only for Ali but for future claimants because the justices stipulated in the opinion that draft boards are required to state specific reasons for their denial of conscientious objector status. The justices wrote that:

> (W)e feel that this error of law by the Department, to which the Appeal Board might naturally look for guidance on such questions, must vitiate the entire proceedings at least where it is not clear that the Board relied on some legitimate ground. Here, where it is impossible to determine on exactly which grounds the Appeal Board decided, the integrity of the Selective Service System demands, at least, that the Government not recommend illegal grounds.[58]

Ali also received positive affirmation for the sincerity of his position by Justice William O. Douglass, who wrote in his concurring opinion that Ali was, by virtue of his religious convictions, "conscientiously opposed to participation in war of the character described by his religion. That belief is a matter of conscience protected by the First Amendment."[59]

Although Ali was no longer the heavyweight champion, he was a winner in the eyes of Americans who opposed the war; members of the Nation of Islam whose cause Ali espoused; and African-Americans, many of whom had come to see him as their standard-bearer. He had followed in the steps of Dr. King in opposing the Vietnam War, and he had prevailed against a government that attempted to conscript him and a press and public that frequently reviled him. This was an important case for the champ and for others who might follow him with similar claims. While Ali fought as an individual in the ring, he battled with and on behalf of others outside it. He ultimately prevailed in both arenas.

NOTES

1 Department of Defense Manpower Data Center, http://www.americanwarlibrary.com/vietnam/vwatl.htm.

2 Robert J. Samuelson, "LBJ Signs Draft Law Cutting Graduate 2-S," *The Harvard Crimson* (July 3, 1967), http://www.thecrimson.com/article/1967/7/3/lbj-signs-draft-law-cutting-graduate/.

3 Peter Shapiro, "Freshman Deferments End as Nixon Signs New Draft Legislation," *The Harvard Crimson* (September 29, 1971), http://www.thecrimson.com/article/1971/9/29/freshman-deferments-end-as-nixon-signs/.

4 White, middle-class men who faced conscription had access to advice about how to obtain medical deferments, information about traveling to Canada or Sweden, and access to alternative service such as the military reserves.

5 Brian Duffy, "Muhammad Ali," *U.S. News and World Report* Vol. 131, Issue 7 (August 20–27, 2001).

6 See Mark Barringer and Tom Wells, "The Antiwar Movement in the United States," http://www.english.illinois.edu/maps/vietnam/antiwar.html and Jeff Leen, "The Vietnam Protests: When Worlds Collided," *Washington Post* (September 27, 1999), p. A1, http://www.washingtonpost.com/wp-srv/local/2000/vietnam092799.htm.

7 David Zirin, "Revolt of the Black Athlete: The Hidden History of Muhammad Ali," *International Socialist Review* Issue 33 (January–February, 2004), p. 5.

8 Nick Marquesee, *Redemption Song: Muhammad Ali and the Spirit of the Sixties* (London and New York: Verso, 2005), pp. 212–15.

9 "The Passion of Muhammad Ali," http://stevenlebron.com/post/27340789545/the-passion-of-muhammad-ali.

10 Ibid. and "Showing Muhammad Ali as a Martyr for Refusing to Fight in a Bad War," http://www.georgelois.com/pages/Esquire/Esq.Ali.html.

11 Robert Lipsyte, "Clay Refuses Army Oath: Stripped of Boxing Crown," *New York Times* (April 28, 1967), http://www.nytimes.com/books/98/10/25/specials/ali-army.html.

12 Andres F. Quintana, "Muhammad Ali: The Greatest in Court," *Marquette Sports Law Review* Vol. 18, Issue 1 (Fall, 2007), pp. 185, and 266 Supp. 345: *Muhammad Ali v. Connally*, United States District Court S. D. Texas, Houston Division.

13 Christopher Ross, "Cosell Backed Ali from the Start," *ABC Sports Online*, http://espn.go.com/abcsports/wwos/objector.html.

14 Thomas Rogers, "New York Lifts Crown in Swift Move," *New York Times* (April 29, 1967) in Daniel Bennett Coy, "Imagining Dissent: Muhammad Ali, Daily Newspapers, and the State, 1967–1971," Master's Thesis, University of Tennessee, 2004, pp. 70–1.

15 Thomas Rogers, "New York Lifts Crown in Swift Move," *New York Times* (April 29, 1967) and Bennett Coy, "Imagining Dissent."

16 "From the Archive, 29 April 1967: Muhammad Ali Refuses to Fight in Vietnam War," *Guardian* (April 29, 2013), http://www.theguardian.com/theguardian/2013/apr/29/muhammad-ali-refuses-to-fight-in-vietnam-war-1967.

17 *Ali v. Division of State Athletic Commission*, 308 F. Supp. 11 12 (S.D.N.Y. 1969) in Michael Meltsner, "Me and Muhammad," *Marquette Sports Law Review* Vol. 12, Issue 2 (Spring, 2002) and Ross, "Cosell Backed Ali from the Start."

18 Quintana, "Muhammad Ali: The Greatest in Court," p. 186.

19 Martin Luther King, Jr., "Beyond Vietnam: A Time to Break Silence," Speech to Clergy and Laity Concerned delivered at Riverside Church (April 4, 1967), http://www.hartford-hwp.com/archives/45a/058.html.

20 Dave Zirin, "This Day in History in 1967: When Muhammad Ali Took the Weight," http://www.thenation.com/blog/161565/day-history-when-muhammad-ali-took-weight.

21 "The Draft: Gaseous Cassius," *TIME* (May 5, 1967), http://content.time.com/time/subscriber/article/0,33009,899478,00.html.

22 Robert Lipsyte, "Clay Refuses Army Oath: Stripped of Boxing Crown," *New York Times* (April 29, 1967), http://www.nytimes.com/books/98/10/25/specials/ali- army.html.

23 Zirin, "This Day in History."

24 "*The Black Scholar* Interviews Muhammad Ali," *The Black Scholar* (June, 1970).

25 "Muhammad Ali," *Military Times*, http://www.homeofheroes.com/DG/08d_ali.html.

26 Patrick Kiger, "Muhammad Ali's Speech at Howard University 1967," http://blogs.weta.org/boundarystones/2014/04/14/muhammad-alis-speech-howard-university-1967.

27 Mike Marqusee, *Redemption Song: Muhammad Ali and the Spirit of the Sixties* (New York: Verso, 1999), pp. 239–40 and "Muhammad Ali Speaks at UW on May 30, 1968," http://www.historylink.org/index.cfm?DisplayPage=output.cfm&file_id=1459.

28 Michael Silver, "Where Were You on March 8, 1971?" *ESPN Classic* (November 19, 2003), http://espn.go.com/classic/s/silver_ali_frazier.html.

29 David L. Hudson, Jr., "Muhammad Ali and the First Amendment," *First Amendment Center*, http://www.firstamendmentcenter.org/muhammad-ali-and-the-first-amendment.

30 Branson Wright, "Remembering Cleveland's Muhammad Ali Summit, 45 Years Later," *Cleveland Plain Dealer* (June 3, 2012), http://www.cleveland.com/sports/index.ssf/2012/06/gathering_of_stars.html. Bill Russell and Tex Maule, "I'm Not Worried About Muhammad Ali," *Sports Illustrated* (June 19, 1967), http://sportsillustrated.cnn.com/vault/search?term=Muhammad+Ali+June+19%2C+1967.

31 David Zirin, "The Revolt of the Black Athlete: The Hidden History of Muhammad Ali," *International Socialist Review* Issue 33 (January–February, 2004), http://www.isreview.org/issues/33/muhammadali.shtml.

32 "Muhammad Ali at Fairleigh Dickinson," *The Amsterdam News* (April 20, 1968).

33 William C. Rhoden, "In Ali's Voice from the Past, a Stand for the Ages," *New York Times* (June 20, 2013), http://www.nytimes.com/2013/06/21/sports/in-alis-voice-from-the-past-a-stand-for-the-ages.html?_r=0.

34 See Neil Faulkner, "Review: The John Carlos Story," *International Socialist Organization* (August 8, 2012), http://internationalsocialist.org.uk/index.php/2012/08/review-the-john-carlos-story/; Dave Zirin, "After Forty-Four Years, It's Time Brent Musburger Apologized to John Carlos and Tommie Smith," *The Nation.com* (June 4, 2012), http://www.thenation.com/blog/168209/after-forty-four-years-its-time-brent-musburger-apologized-john-carlos-and-tommie-smith#; and David A. Love, "45th Anniversary of John Carlos-Tommie Smith 'Black Power Salute' at '68 Olympics," *TheGrio.com* (October 16, 2013), http://thegrio.com/2013/10/16/45-year-anniversary-of-black-power-salute-at-68-olympics/#s:tommie-smith-and-john-carlos-16x9.

35 "Buck White," *Playbill*, http://www.playbillvault.com/Show/Detail/3713/Buck-White and http://dangerousminds.net/comments/check_out_muhammad_alis_broadway_chops_as_he_performs_a_number.

36 Jeremiah Shabazz quoted in Mattias Gardell, *In the Name of Elijah Muhammad: Louis Farrakhan and the Nation of Islam* (Durham, NC: Duke University Press, 1996), p. 68.

37 Mikal Gilmore, "How Muhammad Ali Conquered Fear and Changed the World," *Men's Journal* (November, 2011), http://www.mensjournal.com/magazine/how-muhammad-ali-conquered-fear-and-changed-the-world-20130205?page=6.

38 Dave Zirin, "Knocked the Hell out by 'The Trials of Muhammad Ali,'" *The Nation.com* (August 17, 2013), http://www.thenation.com/blog/175804/knocked-hell-out-trials-muhammad-ali# and Mychal Denzel Smith, "The Meaning of Muhammad," *The Nation* (January 17, 2002).

39 "Muslims Suspend Ali; He's Cassius Clay Again," *Amsterdam News* (April 12, 1969).

40 "*The Black Scholar* Interviews Muhammad Ali," *The Black Scholar* (June, 1970).

41 See "Disreputable if Not Outright Illegal: National Security Agency versus Martin Luther King, Muhammad Ali, Art Buchwald, Frank Church et al.," *National Security Archive* (November 14, 2008), http://www2.gwu.edu/~nsarchiv/NSAEBB/NSAEBB441/ and "Declassified NSA Files

Show Agency Spied on Muhammad Ali and MLK," *Guardian* (September 26, 2013), http://www.theguardian.com/world/2013/sep/26/nsa-surveillance-anti-vietnam-muhammad-ali-mlk.

42 Quintana, "Muhammad Ali: The Greatest in Court," pp. 186–7.

43 "Hayden C. Covington," *Wikipedia*, http://en.wikipedia.org/wiki/Hayden_C._Covington.

44 *Ali v. Div. of State Athletic Commission of N. Y.*, 308 F. Supp. 11, 14 (S. D. N. Y. 1969), in Quintana, "Muhammad Ali: The Greatest in Court," p. 188.

45 Quintana, "Muhammad Ali: The Greatest in Court," p. 189.

46 Ibid., p. 190 and *Muhammad Ali* v. *Division of State Athletic Commission of New York*, No 69 Civ. 4867, 316 F. Supp. 1246 (1970).

47 Lee Groves, "Ali Quarry Remembered," *The Ring* (October 26, 2013), http://ringtv.craveonline.com/tag/ali-quarry.

48 Quintana, "Muhammad Ali: The Greatest in Court," pp. 190–1 and Mikal Gilmore, "How Muhammad Ali Conquered Fear and Changed the World," *Men's Journal* (November, 2011).

49 Groves, "Ali Quarry Remembered."

50 "Muhammad Ali vs Oscar Natalio Bonavena," *BoxRec Encyclopedia*, http://boxrec.com/media/index.php/Muhammad_Ali_vs._Oscar_Natalio_Bonavena.

51 Richard Hoffer, "Joe Frazier 1944–2011," *Sports Illustrated* (November 11, 2011), http://sportsillustrated.cnn.com/vault/topic/article/Joe_Frazier/1900–01–01/2100–12–31/dd/index.htm.

52 Silver, "Where Were You on March 8, 1971."

53 http://www.ibhof.com/pages/archives/alifrazier.html.

54 Silver, "Where Were You on March 8, 1971."

55 Quintana, "Muhammad Ali: The Greatest in Court," p. 193.

56 Hugh McIlvanney, "When the Mountain Came to Muhammad," *Guardian* (March 9, 1971), http://www.theguardian.com/sport/2011/nov/08/joe-frazier-muhammad-ali-1971.

57 See *Cassius Marcellus Clay also known as Muhammad Ali, Petitioner*, v. *United States*, 403 U.S. 698 (1971) and Thomas Hauser, *Muhammad Ali: His Life and Times* (New York: Simon & Schuster, 1991), p. 239.

58 *Cassius Marcellus Clay also known as Muhammad Ali, Petitioner*, v. *United States*, 403 U.S. 698 (1971).

59 Justice Douglass, Concurring Opinion in *Cassius Marcellus Clay also known as Muhammad Ali, Petitioner*, v. *United States*, 403 U.S. 698 (1971).

CHAPTER **6**

ONCE AGAIN A HERO

Muhammad Ali's loss to Joe Frazier on March 8, 1971 was one major turning point in the champ's long career. In the previous eleven years, he had fought a total of thirty-two times, in non-title fights for recognition, respect, and money, and in bouts in which he won and retained the Heavyweight Championship. Although he ventured as far as Frankfurt, Germany, Toronto, Ontario, and Lewiston, Maine, his professional fights more frequently took place in his hometown of Louisville, his adopted home, Miami, or in the boxing capital of the country, New York's Madison Square Garden. In just over a decade, he had won and lost a title, changed his religious identification, been convicted of a felony for refusing induction into the Army, and finally earned vindication in the Supreme Court. He changed his name once and his image numerous times to fit the circumstances of his life and career. After his loss in the "fight of the century," it was not unreasonable to wonder what the former champ had left.

Ferdie Pacheco, a doctor who had been part of Ali's entourage since the beginning of his professional career, offered his own perspective to the meaning of the champ's defeat. Compared to the adversity that Ali had faced since he first declared himself to be "the greatest," the "fight of the century" was just another obstacle to be faced, a battle to be won or lost. Pacheco asserted that the lessons learned from all of Ali's previous struggles had helped to carry him through the fight and his defeat. He told George Plimpton that the public, Ali's friends and adversaries alike

> was brainwashed. They thought a loudmouth like Ali would react to being beaten by wincing and moaning and carrying on like a child. They forget that the past three years he's had to go through a number of very severe confrontations—socially, religiously, politically, monetarily—in each of which he's been raked over

the coals. Socially, he's learned what it is to be despised by his countrymen. He was tossed out of a religious organization he feels strongly about. His politics got him into such trouble that jail continues to be a possibility. His money-making potential was taken away by the boxing commissions. Well, all this hurting must have helped carry him through the fight.[1]

Ali understood that he had just been through a difficult ordeal, and he credited the experience with giving him a more mature perspective on his life and career. Reflecting on the loss to Frazier, Ali noted that:

The whole time I wasn't allowed to fight, no matter what the authorities said, it felt like I was the heavyweight champion of the world. Then I lost to Joe Frazier. And what hurt most wasn't the money that losing cost me. It wasn't the punches I took. It was knowing that my title was gone. When I beat Sonny Liston, I was too young to appreciate what I'd won. But when I lost to Frazier, I would have done anything except go against the will of Allah to get my title back again.[2]

The champ would have to work long and hard to achieve his goal of regaining the heavyweight title. He would need all of his residual strength, as he left the ring more severely injured than in any of his previous bouts. In the immediate aftermath of the fight, Ali spent a few hours having his severely swollen jaw X-rayed at the Flower and Fifth Avenue Hospital. He refused to stay in the hospital overnight, not wanting the public to think that Joe Frazier's blows had incapacitated him. Soon after the fight, the now former champ reflected on his loss, noting that he "wasted" a few rounds that he could have won, suggesting that his strategy of dancing in the ring to avoid his opponent had not been effective in tiring out Frazier. While expressing respect for his opponent, Ali maintained that, even in victory, Frazier had taken the worst blows that night:

We both have respect for the other, more than when we started . . . But Frazier do one thing that he should not do if he expect to keep fighting. He accepts too many punches to get in. It messes up your face, takes too much out of you. He look much worse than me after the fight. I hit him three times what he hits me. Of course, that left hook of his leave a swole . . . but nothing else. When that swole go down, I won't have a mark, not a bruise.

Insisting that the fight "could have gone another way," Ali reflected on the greater meaning of the fight and the loss of the championship:

Fighting is more of a business now than the glory of who won. After all, when all the praise is over, when all the fanfare is done, all that counts is what you have to show for. All the bleeding; the world still turns. I was so tired. But I didn't shed a tear. I got to keep living. I'm not ashamed.[3]

Once Again a Hero • 135

Between March of 1971 and December of 1981, when Ali finally retired from boxing at the age of thirty-nine, he replicated the grueling pace of the first half of his career, fighting twenty-nine times. He won and retained the heavyweight title sanctioned by the North American Boxing Federation, lost that title and then regained it. He later regained and successfully defended his world heavyweight boxing title, lost that title and regained it again, and ended his career with a loss to Trevor Berbick in a non-title fight. He fought all over the world, from the Philippines to Zaire (now the Democratic Republic of the Congo) as well as a variety of locations in the United States and the Caribbean. He left the Nation of Islam, yet he strengthened his faith and earned respect for his stand against the Vietnam War as the conflict came to an end and Americans sought to reconcile the imperatives of Cold War containment with the fact that the United States had suffered a defeat. Ali's stand against the war and the military was, if not popular, at least closer to mainstream American opinion at the dawn of the 1980s. The champ was on his way to becoming an American hero. In this chapter, we will explore Ali's character and image as he sought to re-make himself after his 1971 defeat at Frazier's hands to his victory over Frazier in the second of their three battles.

A mere four-and-a-half months after the Frazier defeat, Ali was back in the ring, this time against his childhood friend, Jimmy Ellis. Ali scored a technical knockout in the twelfth round to win the fight and claim the NABF heavyweight title, but the story is much more interesting in human terms, bringing together friendship, money, pride, and respect among people who counted themselves as friends of Muhammad Ali. Born in February of 1940, nearly two years before Cassius Clay, Jimmy Ellis grew up in Louisville, Kentucky in the same "nice nasty" world of genteel racism. Both boys found a focus as amateur boxers, and they even appeared together on Joe Martin's local television program, "Tomorrow's Champions." During Ali's exile from professional boxing, Ellis won the WBA's eight-man tournament with victories over Leotis Martin, Oscar Bonavena, Jerry Quarry, and Floyd Patterson. After a period of fifteen months during which Ellis did not fight because of a severely broken nose, he was brutally defeated by Joe Frazier in five rounds.

The lives and careers of Ali and Ellis were connected in a variety of ways. Ellis served as Ali's sparring partner for years, fighting hundreds of rounds and giving him a unique perspective on Ali's strengths and possible weaknesses. In addition, Ellis was featured on the undercard of Ali's fights against Henry Cooper, Sonny Liston, George Chuvalo, Karl Midlenberger, Cleveland Williams, and Zora Folley. Angelo Dundee trained both fighters, and this gave Ellis additional familiarity with Ali's style and perhaps the confidence to think he could win the fight. Both fighters had something to prove: Ellis needed to show that he could compete with the best fighters in the world, and Ali needed to demonstrate that he had not lost his ability as a fighter and that he was on his way to regaining his title. On the night of the fight, in a moment that could have been either humorous or tragic, Ali's assistant trainer and "cheerleader," Drew Bundini Brown, neglected to bring the former champ's trunks, although he was able to locate substitute attire in the right color but the wrong size before the opening bell. Ali was very particular about the color of his boxing attire (he always wore white), and he was no doubt unhappy about wearing a pair of boxing trunks that were two sizes too big.

The fight was held in the Houston Astrodome, where 31,947 fans watched Ali, who was a 7–2 favorite, take control after three even rounds. In the fourth round, he hit Ellis with a blow from his right hand that weakened Ellis for the remainder of the fight. Spectators in 200 locations in North America and in thirty-four other countries watched Ali dance all over the ring, even sometimes dropping his hands and avoiding Ellis's attempts to hit him by throwing back his head. Ali's guaranteed purse was $450,000 against 45 percent of the total of all receipts, while Ellis was promised 20 percent. As a trainer, Angelo Dundee was entitled to a fee for his services, but he could not be considered the trainer for both fighters. This complication was actually rendered simple by the fact that Dundee was also Ellis's manager. Managers earned more than trainers, and Ali's gave his permission for Dundee to work with Ellis for the fight, thereby earning a larger share of the proceeds from the bout. Ali was handled in the ring by trainer Harry Wiley. Ali, who later described himself as "a little pulpy," weighed in at 221 pounds, while Ellis tipped the scale at 189 pounds, and there was a significant difference in strength as well as size.

Ali showed that he could best his former sparring partner, and he also demonstrated that he had the stamina to fight more than a few rounds. There was also an element of pride in this competition, as the NABF heavyweight title, which had recently been relinquished by George Foreman, was on the line. But, for Ali, his ability to dominate in the ring was more important than the title. According to Tex Maule in *Sports Illustrated*:

> The right hand may have had much to do with the outcome, but Ali's ability to stay on his toes and move around the ring for almost the whole 12 rounds was really decisive. Against Joe Frazier, Ali often had looked lethargic, shuffling aimlessly and depending on the speed of his hands to contain the continuing charge of his opponent. Against Ellis he was, in ballet terms, on point, moving from side to side on his toes and changing direction quickly and easily. At the end of the fight he was moving more gracefully than at the beginning. "He wanted to

prove he could go 12 rounds on his toes and he did," said Dundee, "Ain't many men who could do that, not at his age."[4]

Ali clearly controlled the fight after the fourth round, but he made no effort to finish off his opponent. Tex Maule reported that, when Ali was asked why he let the fight continue until the twelfth round, he replied:

> I could see in his eyes he was really hurt bad . . . Ain't no reason for me to kill nobody in the ring, and if I hit him a couple of more shots, I might kill him. I was just waitin' for someone to stop it. I ain't there to kill people.
>
> Because he is your friend?
>
> No, because he is a man, like me.[5]

Friendship, money, status, and pride all motivated Ali. At the same time, the once and future champ continued to project a new, more measured image to a public that wondered what he would do next.

Within four months, Ali was back in the ring again, this time as a 7–1 favorite to best Buster Mathis. Ali returned to the Astrodome in Houston weighing 227 pounds. His opponent, who had not fought in more than two-and-a-half years, weighed 256 pounds, prompting some sportswriters to call this fight the "Battle of the Bellies." Mathis, who, from time to time was called "The Behemoth" or "A Fat Bastard," got a new nickname for this fight when promoters in Houston printed posters that exhorted fans to "Be There When the Mountain Comes to Muhammad."

Although he was an accomplished professional who achieved a record of 30–4 in his career, Buster Mathis was a hard-luck fighter. He waged a decades-long fight with his weight, declaring that, "For some people, it's booze or drugs. For me, it's always been food." As a young amateur fighter, Mathis qualified for the United States Olympic team by defeating Joe Frazier but lost his spot on the team to Frazier after breaking his hand.

As a professional fighter, Mathis compiled an impressive 23–0 record against less-than-impressive opposition. When the World Boxing Association filled Ali's vacant title through a tournament won by Jimmy Ellis, the New York State Boxing Commission staged its own version of a Heavyweight Championship fight that brought Mathis and Frazier together again on March 4, 1968. The referee stopped the fight in the eleventh round, declaring Frazier the winner of the New York State Athletic Commission title by a technical knockout. After six consecutive wins, Mathis lost to Jerry Quarry in April of 1969. He did not fight again until he faced Ali in Houston on November 17, 1971.

Before the fight, Ali declared, "This will be Buster's last stand. I will do to Buster what the Indians did to Custer. I'm gonna wipe him out."

Once again, his prediction came close to the fight's true outcome. After ten rounds that Tex Maule called "dull," Ali won by unanimous decision in the twelfth round after he had knocked his opponent down three times. In that round, Ali exhausted Mathis, and the fans were clearly looking for a knock-out punch. Ali's trainer, Angelo Dundee, exhorted his fighter to "take him out," but the champ refrained from using his powerful right hand to end the fight by a knockout. After the fight, Ali asked reporters, "How am I goin' to sleep if I just killed a man in front of his wife and son just to satisfy you writers?" He declared that he did not care about looking good "to the fans or to Angelo. I got to look good to God. I mean Allah." When asked if he had changed his approach from the unrelenting cruelty he had loosed on previous opponents like Floyd Patterson and Ernie Terrell, he replied that he had matured and that he had a different attitude toward his opponents. "Them was the days of the draft thing and the religion thing and black against white, all that. Now them days have gone forever. I don't need to do like I did then. I'm more educated and more civilized."[6] Ali hoped to project a more mature and reflective image as he battled in the ring to regain his title.

Reflecting on his performance in Houston, Mathis said he felt vindicated as a fighter who had done his best after the long interval since his dramatic loss to Jerry Quarry. He summed up his feelings, saying, "Nobody can call me a dog anymore." After his bout with Ali, Mathis fought only twice more, beating Humphrey McBride on September 5, 1972 and losing to Ron Lyle on the 29th of that month. Ali continued his turbulent career, with twenty-six more fights. Mathis died in 1995 at the age of fifty-two, having suffered two strokes and a heart attack.

The Mathis fight was far from Ali's best, and he was so heavily favored that the promoters feared that both ticket sales and closed-circuit television revenue would fall far short of expectations. Bobby Goodman, who handled the publicity for the fight, described the situation:

> We had a problem. The guys liked each other, it didn't shape up as the most competitive fight in the world, and ticket sales were lagging behind because we couldn't get Buster riled up. They were both such sweet guys. And every time they were together for an interview or press conference, Buster would start laughing; he couldn't control himself. So I went to Muhammad and said, "We've got to come up with something. This is a closed circuit fight; we have to generate some news."[7]

Not surprisingly, Ali came up with a plan that was as creative as it was outlandish. He proposed that Goodman arrange to have him "kidnapped." He would hide out in the woods with a cook and a sparring partner and re-appear in time for the fight. Thinking like a fight promoter, Goodman told Ali that if he were kidnapped, no one would want to buy tickets to a fight that might not take place. And, thinking like a reasonable person, he reminded the former champ that his plan involved fraud, among other possible felonies. Even though the "kidnapping" never took place, it was typical of Ali's talent for self-promotion in the interest of publicizing a fight. Once again, he demonstrated that he had learned his lesson from Gorgeous George about how to work a crowd.

On the day after Christmas in 1971, just five weeks after his victory over Buster Mathis, Ali traveled to Zurich, Switzerland, where he fought Jurgen Blin, a minor fighter from what was then West Germany, in the Hallenstadion Arena. Fighting for a purse of $250,000, compared to a guarantee of $45,000 for Blin, Ali seemed to have entered the ring for the money, as there was no title on the line and Blin was not considered a major competitor on Ali's path back to a Heavyweight Championship. Ali had a twenty-two pound advantage over his opponent, who was not averse to throwing a lot of punches, some of which connected with Ali's face and body and forced him to the ropes. Nevertheless, in the fifth round, Blin suffered cuts under both eyes that bled profusely. He lasted until the seventh round, when Ali knocked him down with a powerful right. The German fighter could not continue, and the referee ruled that Ali had won by a knockout. Roy Martin summed up the importance of the fight in paving Ali's path to a future championship:

> Muhammad Ali really put on a good show in Switzerland. Note that I said show and not fight. He spent the whole night playing around making Blin look like a fool, falling through the ropes and taking more punishment from the ring posts he ran into than Blin's jabs. However, I am not complaining. When Ali wanted to fight for thirty seconds or so every round it was great and when he fooled around it kept the crowd entertained. This was the end for Jurgen Blin.[8]

Ali fought six times in 1972, winning battles against McArthur Foster in Tokyo on April 1 in fifteen rounds and a re-match with George Chuvalo in Vancouver in twelve rounds on May 1. He scored technical knockouts against Jerry Quarry in Las Vegas in seven rounds on June 27, Alvin Lewis in Dublin, Ireland in eleven rounds on July 19, and the thirty-seven-year-old Floyd Patterson in New York in seven rounds on September 20. Then, he knocked out Bob Foster in Stateline, Nevada in the eighth round on November 21. These fights helped to restore Ali's reputation at the same time that Joe Frazier appeared to be losing his edge. Frazier had taken some time off after his defeat of Ali to perform with his band, "The Knockouts." Now he, like Ali, was back in the fight game. The difference, of course, was that, while Ali claimed to be "the People's Champion," Frazier still held the title.

In the first fight ever held in the Far East featuring major heavyweight boxers, Ali took on McArthur (Mac "The Knife") Foster in Tokyo's Budokan Arena, a venue that had been constructed for karate matches in the 1964 Olympics. Ali made his usual pre-fight prediction that he would defeat his opponent in the fifth round. He even carried a card labeled "Five-R" into the ring. But Foster did not cooperate, taking the fight to the full fifteen rounds before Ali scored a unanimous decision. Ali, who was three years older and fifteen pounds heavier than his opponent, outlasted the ex-Marine, and the decision was never in question.[9]

Just a month later, Ali fought George Chuvalo, "The Toronto Hard Rock." Since his fifteen-round loss to Ali in 1966, Chuvalo had been badly beaten by both George Foreman and Joe Frazier, who had broken his right orbital bone with a brutal punch in 1967 that required surgery to place his eye back into its socket. Chuvalo was thirty-four and definitely past his prime. Nevertheless, the Canadian claimed, "I'm a better fighter than I was in 1966 and he's not as good a fighter as he was then," and he demonstrated, as he had throughout his career, that he could take serious punishment in the ring. Ali won by a unanimous decision as he pummeled his opponent, but he was not able to knock Chuvalo down. Ali retained his NABF heavyweight title. Amazingly, in his ninety-three professional fights, George Chuvalo never hit the canvas.[10]

Muhammad Ali first fought Jerry Quarry in October of 1970, when he scored a technical knockout in the third round. The June 27, 1972 fight also ended in a technical knockout. This card featured both Quarry brothers: Jerry lost to Ali in the heavyweight bout while his younger brother lost a light heavyweight fight to Bob Foster. Both fights were successful title defenses and the evening was dubbed, "The Soul Brothers versus the Quarry Brothers." Ali dominated his fight with a barrage of punches. According to boxing writer Tom Gray, Ali was "in fabulous form and landed at will throughout a one-sided encounter. The famous jab set up a kaleidoscope of power shots as crosses, hooks, and uppercuts nailed Quarry with alarming regularity." Ali even taunted the challenger by pretending to be in pain when he took an occasional punch. Ali maintained his NABF title in preparation for a rematch against Joe Frazier.[11]

When Ali arrived in Dublin, Ireland in the summer of 1972 to fight Detroit native Alvin ("Blue") Lewis, he was an immediate celebrity. His outsized personality and eagerness to please a crowd made him popular, but the revelation that he had an Irish great-grandfather, Abe Grady, insured that he would be treated like a native son. Lewis, an ex-convict, was one of Ali's occasional sparring partners, and he knew his opponent's style well. Nevertheless, Ali pummeled Lewis at will, and the referee stopped the fight in the eleventh round. The real story of the fight was outside the ring, as 7,000 spectators crashed the gate at Croke Park to protest the excessively high prices for tickets. Despite the riot, Ali returned to the United States with growing confidence in his ability to re-take the Heavyweight Championship crown.

When Muhammad Ali faced Floyd Patterson for the first time in November of 1965, it was an acrimonious affair. The two fighters traded insults, with Patterson attacking Ali's new religious affiliation and asserting, "The image of a Black Muslim as the world heavyweight champion disgraces the sport and the nation." For his part, Ali taunted Patterson as an "Uncle Tom" and denigrated his friendship with whites and decision to live in a white neighborhood.[12] With battle lines drawn, the two faced each other in the ring, and Ali won the bout in twelve rounds.

They fought again in Madison Square Garden on September 20, 1972. It was a fairly even match for four rounds, although Ali did not seem to be working very hard. In the sixth round, he landed a punch that cut Patterson's eye. Ali's assault was so powerful that the doctor in charge stopped the fight after the seventh round. After the fight, Ali demonstrated his respect for Patterson when he commented, "Patterson is a great, great fighter. I thought he'd be nothing, but he surprised me. I didn't knock him out. I didn't get him on a TKO. All I did was close his eye."[13]

Ali's contentious relationship with Patterson surfaced again, and this time the issue was a proposed fight in a segregated country thousands of miles from Madison Square Garden. Ali's fame and reputation continued to rest on his political courage in resisting the military draft in addition to his boxing prowess. In the summer of 1972, the apartheid government of South African Prime Minister B.J. Vorster invited the former champion to visit the racially segregated nation to deliver a series of ten lectures between December 20 and January 2, 1973 for a proposed fee of $300,000. Ali demonstrated a lack of sensitivity to the evils of apartheid when he indicated that he would accept the invitation if he could obtain the proper visa. Ali never explained his willingness to accept Vorster's invitation, nor did he offer an explanation for why he ultimately did not deliver the lectures. At about the same time, the South African government invited Floyd Patterson to fight in the country. Patterson tuned down the invitation, saying that, even if he did agree to fight, he would give the proceeds of the bout to groups in the country engaged in the anti-apartheid struggle

In October of 1972, *Boxing News* reported that Ali had accepted an invitation to fight Al Jones, an unknown American fighter, before 80,000 fans in South Africa on November 18 of that year. After initially accepting the invitation, Ali made the absurd statement that "it's different if I go, instead of Floyd, because I'm a real Black man."[14] In the end, neither Patterson nor Ali fought in South Africa. It is possible that Ali was influenced by conversations with Dennis Brutus of SANROC (the South African Non-Racial Olympic Committee), an organization that had worked for years to push for an end to apartheid in sports and society, and Ambassador Abdulrahim Rahim of Somalia, who chaired the United Nations Special Committee on Apartheid.

The two leaders no doubt reminded him that the nations of the world were increasingly turning against a country whose racial policies rested on segregation and discrimination.[15] Ali's willingness to travel to South Africa in the early 1970s, when the international tide was turning against apartheid, was certainly intellectually and ethically inconsistent. He may have felt that the need for money trumped his political reputation, or perhaps he felt that his presence in South Africa would help the anti-apartheid cause. Of course, the government would not have permitted any utterances that challenged the apartheid regime, even from a heavyweight champion.

The South African fight that never took place also reveals a complex story about money, race, and politics. Ali's potential opponent, Al Jones, "South Florida's brightest heavyweight hope" whose major claim to fame was his right hand that was broken no fewer than four times in his short career, was far from famous and no challenge for the former champ. In South Africa, Reliable N.E. Promotions handled the arrangements, while the American promoter was Top Rank, a new venture started by Bob Arum, formerly of Main Bout Promotions. The arrangement failed because Reliable N.E. Promotions proved unable to produce letters of credit. In addition to convincing arguments against apartheid, the fight in South Africa foundered on a less-than-stable financial foundation.

While *Boxing News* reported that the fight would be held in front of an audience that would be seated according to race, the promotional contract revealed that the audience was to be seated on an integrated basis or, if segregated, seating would be available on an equal basis for both white and non-white fight patrons. This arrangement evoked the "separate but equal" doctrine that was actually a rationalization for racism, but even such a small move toward racial equality was a major step forward for a country locked into a system of rigid segregation. Even more interesting is the position of the Nation of Islam, which had reinstated Ali after his one-year suspension. Herbert Muhammad articulated his father's views when he said that:

> The position of the Nation of Islam was that Ali was a fighter, and that as champion of the world, he should be able to fight anywhere on earth. We didn't get into that thing about South Africa. My father didn't look no different at South Africa than he did at the United States; he believed both of them were run by devils. And to say they don't fight in South Africa because they're doing wrong; well, some of the same crimes are done in the United States against black people. So my father didn't have the attitude that you could fight in the United States but not in South Africa.[16]

In effect, the Nation saw enemies in all white societies but also saw opportunities to exploit relationships with those enemies if they could advance the career of the NOI's most famous member.

Even though Ali did not fight in South Africa, he did face Bob Foster in November of 1972 in Stateline, Nevada. Foster had earned his reputation as a light heavyweight, and there was a forty-pound differential between the two fighters, with Ali weighing in at more than 220 pounds. The fight was remarkable only insofar as Foster landed a punch that opened a cut over Ali's left eye, drawing blood from a cut for the first time in his professional career. In spite of the injury, Ali knocked Foster down six times in the first seven rounds. When he did so again in the eighth round, the referee counted Foster out, giving Ali a win by knockout.[17]

In the midst of the controversy over the South Africa fight and the eventual bout in Nevada, Bob Arum proposed an entirely new venture for Ali. Actor and director Warren Beatty planned to re-make *Here Comes Mr. Jordan*, a 1941 film about a boxer who dies before his time and has the chance to come back to earth. Beatty hoped to cast Ali as the lead in the new film, which was to be called *Heaven Can Wait*. Negotiations proceeded between Arum and Warner Brothers Studio, salary amounts and guarantees were agreed upon, and the parties even stated that Ali would receive "star" billing. With a screenplay by Francis Ford Coppola, the project seemed like it would be a popular success. The problem with the project was the basic premise that the deceased fighter would come back to life in another person's body, which contradicted the basic principles of the Nation of Islam. Elijah Muhammad would never approve Ali's participation in the film because Muslims did not accept the idea of life after death. Arum wrote to his business partner that, "this ends the project, since there is no way anyone can get into a theological discussion with Elijah."[18] Ali would continue to pursue celebrity in and outside the ring, but he would not do so in *Heaven Can Wait*. Warren Beatty played the role and changed the character from a boxer to a football player.

For the next eleven months, between February of 1973, when Ali beat Joe Bugner in Las Vegas, and his January of 1974 victorious re-match with Joe Frazier at Madison Square Garden, Ali continued his quest for victory in the ring and for the publicity that he craved. Joe Bugner, the Hungarian-born fighter who fell to Ali in twelve rounds on Valentine's Day in 1973, characterized him as "the greatest of all time, in my opinion." Indeed, Ali was special, in and out of the ring. Ali could sell anything to anyone, so he marketed his own fights. In that respect, he was a promoter's dream. Bugner related an incident that demonstrated Ali's extraordinary talent for "selling anything" and attracting attention:

> Intelligence wise, in the ring and out, he was incredible. Before both our fights he asked me to give him a wink if a member of the press was nearby and I suppose I should have known better. I winked at him and suddenly he jumped out of his chair and screamed, "He just called me a nigger!" I was stunned, just a kid at the time, and didn't know what to say. Moments later Ali came over to me and said,

"Hey Joe Bugner. Was I good?" I told him he'd made me look like a racist and he replied, "That was the whole idea. Joe Bugner we're selling tickets!" He was close to the bone but there was always method behind his madness.[19]

Ali demonstrated time and again that he could maintain his celebrity with his quick wit as well as his fists.

For the next seven months, Ali's life was dominated by his defeat and then his victory over Ken Norton. In March of 1973, Ali held the NABF heavyweight title and was the number 1 contender for the world heavyweight title. He was a 5–1 favorite to defeat Norton, who was ranked number 6. Norton was an accomplished fighter who had learned his craft in the Marine Corps. By the time he faced Ali, he had compiled an impressive 30–1 record without winning a title or earning a purse larger than $8,000. Referred to as "Ken somebody," Norton was not given much of a chance against Ali in San Diego. Norton's boxing style was unorthodox but effective. According the Gene Kilroy, Norton's former manager, "Instead of jabbing from above like most fighters, he would put his hand down and jab up at Ali," and trainer Angelo Dundee offered his own assessment of why Norton was difficult to fight: "With that lurching, herky-jerky, splay footed movement of his, you couldn't just time him."[20] Still, few people actually expected him to beat Muhammad Ali.

Before the fight, Ali's record was 41–1 with thirty-one knockouts. He expressed some respect for Norton's talents. Although he said he would "annihilate" his opponent, he declined to make one of his famous predictions, saying, "I'm not going to call the round on him. He's too good for that." It was common knowledge that Norton consulted a therapist who used hypnosis to help the fighter gain confidence and focus. Hypnotist Michael Dean (whose real name was Dr. Sanford I. Berman) told the Associated Press that he helped Norton by telling him, "The big difference between success and failure isn't big at all. It's one millionth of an inch." Norton also read self-help books such as Napoleon Hill's *Think and Grow Rich*, which helped him to prepare mentally for his fights. He said, "I train for my fights mentally as well as physically. One thing I do is only watch films of the fights in which I've done well or in which my opponent has done poorly." That preparation and focus, encouragement under hypnosis, and relaxation techniques that he could use in the ring, such as stepping away from his opponent and rolling his shoulders back, helped Norton to improve his performance.[21] To the surprise of the boxing pundits, those techniques, along with a powerful right hand, insured Norton's victory in the twelfth round.

The fight was one of Ali's most violent battles, and this time he was the recipient of a blow that caused major physical damage. He entered the ring with confidence, wearing a robe that had been a gift from Elvis Presley that was festooned in rhinestones and the words "People's Choice" embroidered on the back. Even though Ali was favored to win the fight, it was possible to find an interesting parallel between Elvis, the former rock and roll bad boy who now entertained aging Las Vegas audiences by singing his former hits and performing garish production numbers in a tight white suit, and Ali who, although he was clearly on a comeback path, may not have been the fighter and was certainly no longer the outsized personality he had been before the loss of his heavyweight crown.

On the evening of March 31, 11,884 spectators crowded San Diego's Sports Arena to see the Ali–Norton matchup. Ali was guaranteed to receive $210,000, while Norton's purse was $50,000.[22] Norton had prepared for the fight by sparring with Joe Frazier, who had defeated Ali in 1971. Trainer Eddie Futch encouraged Norton to push Ali back with a series of quick jabs before launching a full-blown attack. The punch that broke Ali's jaw landed in the second round, although Norton later told an ESPN interviewer that his fist must have hit its mark much later in the fight because it would have caused too much pain for Ali to have continued for another ten rounds.[23] In spite of his trainer Angelo Dundee's plea to let him stop the fight, Ali persisted for an additional ten rounds. At the end of twelve rounds, Norton was awarded the victory in a split decision.

Was Ali's career over? With his defeat, he lost the NABF title, and it was certainly possible to suspect that his amazing career would come to a close without his regaining the World Heavyweight Championship. Howard Cosell, one of Ali's biggest supporters, suggested that the champ might have reached the end of his career in San Diego: "It was the end of the road as far as I could see. So many of Ali's fights had incredible symbolism, and here it was again. Ken Norton, former marine against the draft dodger in San Diego, a conservative naval town. It seemed Ali would never get his title back."[24]

But Ali had other ideas. Both men trained hard for a scheduled re-match on September 10 in Inglewood, California. Ali recuperated and trained at his camp in Deer Lake, Pennsylvania, while Norton sparred and meditated in the obscure town of Gilman Hot Springs, California, that boasted a population of 395. Ali predicted that he would knock out his opponent but once again declined to predict the round in which the battle would end. The fight went the full twelve rounds, with Ali declared the victor by a split decision. Norton felt that he was ahead on points, but the judges gave the edge to Ali, who unleashed a flurry of punches in the final round. With this victory, he regained the NABF title. Once again, Ali was back.

Less than six weeks later, Ali fought Rudi Lubbers, the Dutch national champion, at the Senayan Stadium in Jakarta, Indonesia. Before a crowd of 25,000, Ali landed several punches but did not knock his opponent down.

He scored a unanimous decision in a fight with no title implications. It was clear that this fight was a warm-up effort in advance of Ali's scheduled match with Joe Frazier, which was to take place on January 28, 1974. Although Frazier was no longer the world heavyweight champion, having lost his title to George Foreman, he remained a formidable physical and psychological foe for Ali, who needed a tune-up, a good purse, and a relatively easy victory.

Ali and Joe Frazier fought three times in the ring. They also engaged in a publicity-gaining, fine-inducing scuffle in the *ABC Wide World of Sports* studios on January 23, just a few days before the fight. Former *Life* magazine sports editor, Dave Wolf, described the scene as the two fighters watched a tape of their previous fight:

> The fight was real. Joe was angry. Ali had called him ignorant once too often, but there was more to it than that. Rahaman (Sam Saxon) had been heckling Joe from the first round of the tape on. He was only about ten feet from the stage and every time the tape showed Ali landing a punch, Rahaman would shout, "Amen! Praise Allah! There it is again!" And Joe started burning. If we'd known how loose the security was going to be and that Rahaman would be allowed to act the way he did, there's no question that Joe wouldn't have gone. Rahaman was more of an instigator than Ali that afternoon.[25]

As a result of this altercation, each man paid a fine of $5,000 levied by the New York State Boxing Commission. For the publicity value of this unplanned altercation, it was no doubt worth the cost to both camps.

The two men next met in New York's Madison Square Garden. Ali was regarded as the number 1 contender against Foreman and Frazier was ranked number 2. Each man had a score to settle—Ali against Frazier and Frazier against Foreman—so the fight was attractive to the boxing public, even though Ali was convinced that he was in better shape than his opponent. Dr. Ferdi Pacheco described the feeling in Ali's camp before and during the fight:

> Heavyweight boxing was in a lull period at that time. There were no compelling fights for Ali at that point and Frazier had suffered an astounding defeat at the hands of George Foreman, who bounced him off the canvas like a basketball. What Ali needed was an easy fight and suddenly Joe Frazier looked like an easy fight. The money was big but a lot of fans felt they were being overcharged for a questionable non-title bout.

Although Frazier had appeared "listless" in his fight with Joe Bugner, he was prepared for his second Ali battle, and he looked forward to a second triumph over "The Greatest." But Ali and his handlers did not see Frazier as a significant threat. Pacheco described the mood: "Suddenly you couldn't sell Joe Frazier as a viable opponent and inside the Ali camp we fell into the same stupor. Try not to hurt Joe was the phrase on everyone's lips, poor old broken down Joe. Essentially Ali was getting ready to beat the shit out of a damaged Joe Frazier."[26] Ali's camp was right. Ali did win, by a unanimous decision. Once again, he felt he was ready to compete for the Heavyweight Championship title, this time against George Foreman.

Notes

1 George Plimpton, "No Requiem for a Heavyweight," *Sports Illustrated* (April 5, 1971), http://cnnsi.printthis.clickability.com/pt/cpt?expire=&title=The+filght.

2 Thomas Hauser, *Muhammad Ali: His Life and Times* (New York: Simon & Schuster, 1991), p. 234.

3 Plimpton, "No Requiem for a Heavyweight."

4 Tex Maule, "End of a Beautiful Friendship," *Sports Illustrated* (August 2, 1971), http://www.si.com/vault/1971/08/02/611673/end-of-a-beautiful-friendship.

5 Ibid.; "Muhammad Ali vs Jimmy Ellis: The Inevitable Fight – 40 Years On," *SecondsOut.com*, http://www.secondsout.com/usa-boxing-news/usa-boxing-news/muhammad-ali-vs-jimmy-ellis-the-inevitable-fight---40-years-on; "Muhammad Ali vs Jimmy Ellis," *BoxRec Encyclopedia*, http://boxrec.com/media/index.php/Muhammad_Ali_vs._Jimmy_Ellis.

6 Tex Maule, "Got to Look Good to Allah," *Sports Illustrated* (November 29, 1971), http://www.si.com/vault/1971/11/29/613926/got-to-look-good-to-allah.

7 Roy Martin, "Ali vs Blin," http://home.comcast.net/~heavyweights/Roy_MartinlivsJurgenBlin.htm.

8 Ibid.

9 See Leslie Nakashima, "Muhammad Ali Unanimous Winner in Japanese Fight," *UPI* (March 31, 1972); "Muhammad Ali vs Mac Foster," *BoxRec Encyclopedia*, http://boxrec.com/media/index.php/Muhammad_Ali_vs._Mac_Foster; Tom Gray, "Muhammad Ali: The People's Choice 1972," *SecondsOut.com*, http://www.secondsout.com/features/main-features/muhammad-ali-the-peoples-choice-1972.

10 "Muhammad Ali vs George Chuvalo (2nd meeting)," *BoxRec Encyclopedia*, http://boxrec.com/media/index.php/Muhammad_Ali_vs._George_Chuvalo_%282nd_meeting%29.

11 "Ali, Foster Get Wins over Jerry and Mike Quarry," *Natchez News Leader* (July 2, 1972); "Muhammad Ali vs Jerry Quarry (2nd meeting)," *BoxRec Encyclopedia*; Gray, "Muhammad Ali: The People's Choice 1972."

12 Patterson made his remarks in *Sports Illustrated* (October 14, 1965). See Hauser, *Muhammad Ali: His Life and Times*, p. 139.

13 "Muhammad Ali vs Floyd Patterson (2nd meeting)," *BoxRec Encyclopedia*, http://boxrec.com/media/index.php/Muhammad_Ali_vs._Floyd_Patterson_%282nd_meeting%29.

14 "Former Champ, Muhammad Ali to Fight in South Africa," *Boxing News* (October, 1972), http://www.boxingforum24.com/showthread.php?t=291665 and Grant Farred, *What's My Name? Black Vernacular Intellectuals* (Minneapolis: University of Minnesota Press, 2003), p. 78.

15 Farred, *What's My Name?*

16 Hauser, *Muhammad Ali: His Life and Times*, p. 249.

17 "Muhammad Ali vs Bob Foster," *BoxRec Encyclopedia*, http://boxrec.com/media/index.php/Muhammad_Ali_vs._Bob_Foster.

18 This memorandum from Bob Arum to Theodore Friedman is cited in Hauser, *Muhammad Ali: His Life and Times*, p. 244.

19 Tom Gray, "Best I've Faced: Joe Bugner," http://ringtv.craveonline.com/news/330445-best-ive-faced-joe-bugner.

20 See Richard Goldstein, "Ken Norton, A Championship Fighter Who Broke Ali's Jaw, is Dead at 70," *New York Times* (September 18, 2013), http://www.nytimes.com/2013/09/19/sports/ken-norton-a-championship-fighter-who-broke-alis-jaw-is-dead-at-70.html; Jonathan Snowden, "One Punch: How Ken Norton Became a Boxing Legend in a Single Night,"

Bleacher Report (September 13, 2013), http://bleacherreport.com/articles/1779469-one-punch-how-ken-norton-became-a-boxing-legend-in-a-single-night.

21 Goldstein, "Ken Norton, A Championship Fighter Who Broke Ali's Jaw, is Dead at 70." Also, "Ali Plans an Annihilation," *Evening Independent* (March 31, 1973); "Ali Norton in TV Bout," *Milwaukee Sentinel* (March 31, 1973); "Hypnotist Aided Norton," *Toledo Blade* (April 2, 1973).

22 See "Muhammad Ali vs Ken Norton (1st meeting)," *BoxRec Boxing Encyclopedia*, http://boxrec.com/media/index.php/Muhammad_Ali_vs._Ken_Norton_%281st_meeting%2.

23 Frank Lotierzo, "Interview with Ken Norton: Norton Speaks on Fights with Ali," *The Sweet Science*, http://www.thesweetscience.com/article-archives/1072-interview-with-ken-norton-norton-speaks-on-fights-with-ali.

24 "X-Ray of Muhammad Ali's Jaw from Split Decision," *X-Rays of Famous People*, http://www.two-views.com/X-RAY/muhammad_ali.html.

25 Hauser, *Muhammad Ali: His Life and Times*, p. 256.

26 Tom Gray, "Ferdie Pacheco recalls Muhammad Ali vs Joe Frazier II-40 Years Later," *The Ring*, http://ringtv.craveonline.com/news/315299-ferdie-pacheco-recalls-muhammad-ali-vs-joe-frazier-ii-40-years-later.

CHAPTER 7

THE RUMBLE, THE THRILLA, AND THE END OF A CAREER

Muhammad Ali's last fifteen fights, comprising one-quarter of his total ring appearances, took place between October of 1974 and his retirement in December of 1981. He did not pursue victory in the ring at the frenetic pace of his early career, but his effort to retain his title was no less intense than in his first quest for the World Heavyweight Championship in 1964. He regained the title he coveted against George Foreman and held it through a series of fights against the best heavyweights of his day and lesser-known boxers. As opposition to the war in Vietnam entered the mainstream of public opinion, Ali's views began to seem less radical and garnered respect and even wider popularity as he earned the world heavyweight title for a second and then a third time. Throughout this period, Ali continued to speak in the voice of a champion and of a black hero who spoke to and, to an extent, for, his people.

After defeating Joe Frazier in New York in January of 1974, Ali was ready to take on George Foreman, the world heavyweight champion. By late summer, the nation was reeling from the aftermath of the Watergate break-in and cover-up that had culminated in Richard Nixon's resignation. The former champ rhymed, "If you think the world was surprised when Nixon resigned, wait 'til I kick Foreman's behind!"[1] Like Ali, Foreman was an Olympic gold medalist, having won in the heavyweight division in Mexico City in 1968. Nicknamed "Big George," Foreman brought a professional record of forty wins, thirty-seven by knockout, and no losses to the confrontation and claimed, "My opponents don't worry about losing. They worry about getting hurt." By most accounts, Ali, who was seven years Foreman's senior, did not stand a chance. *New York Times* columnist Dave Anderson even suggested that Ali could be counted out in the first round.[2] Ali, however, stuck to his prediction that he would prevail. He spent much of his training time watching film of Foreman's fights and speculated that the champion did not have the stamina to last more than a few rounds because he was so accustomed to besting his opponents in the early rounds. This observation proved to be the critical element in Ali's strategy that enabled him to win the fight.

In addition to bringing together two of the greatest fighters of the decade, the fight was a tour de force for promoter Don King. King had first made his living in the numbers racket in Cleveland and served four years in prison for non-negligent homicide. He was new to the fight game, and he saw an opportunity in a potential Ali–Foreman confrontation. Race played a significant role in arranging this fight: King was able to outwit Bob Arum to gain the trust of both Ali and Foreman, convincing them that he should promote the fight because he was black. However, the new promoter proved to be unable to book the fight in the United States despite the fame of both fighters because, he said, "nobody wanted to work with me in America." Instead, he sought and gained financial backing from the dictator of Zaire, Mobutu Sese Seko. This was also a battle for recognition, as Foreman was defending both the World Boxing Association and World Boxing Council titles for the third time.

The bout itself presented a number of images to fight fans—a championship fight in a black African nation; a black promoter who was as outspoken and outlandish as Ali himself; a corrupt and dictatorial regime that brutalized its citizens with a dictator who had seized power by murdering his predecessor; and a battle between two boxing titans with different styles, both in and out of the ring. The fight's African promoter was a dictator who, according to David Zirin, had seized power

> and then looted a quarter of the country's wealth–secured the fight arm in arm with a social parasite named Don King. Together they dressed up the fight in the colors of Black nationalism.[3]

Ali appreciated the idea of a championship fight in Africa, but there were more skeptical voices that asked, "Why Zaire?" Columnist Jim Murray of the *Los Angeles Times* quipped, "They're holding the world heavyweight championship fight in the Congo. I guess the top of Mount Everest was busy."[4]

A fight of this magnitude generated enthusiasm in the public and the press. Ali, a master at generating his own hype, was the perfect contender. The championship fight, the first ever fought in Africa, needed a descriptive phrase that would capture the public's imagination. At first, King created the slogan, "From the slave ship to the championship," but the Zairian dictator, who had promised each fighter $5,000,000, understandably took offense. Ali called the fight "The Rumble in the Jungle," and the name stuck.

Locating the fight in Zaire was more than just a question of logistics and financial backing for Don King. To Ali, it represented a return to African roots for America's black citizens. Residing in the president's palace at N-Sele, forty miles from the capital, he was insulated from poverty or governmental repression and had nothing but praise for the country, saying:

> I wish all black people in America could see this. In America, we've been led to believe we can't do without the white man, and all we know about Africa is jungles . . . We never get shown African cars and African boats and African jet planes. They never tell us about African TV stations. And everything here is black.[5]

Everywhere he went, Ali was recognized and treated as a conquering hero. The hype preceding the fight included a music festival that featured some of the major black performers of the day, including James Brown, Bill Withers, The Spinners and Miriam Mekeba. Eventually, Ali would tire of Zaire and the long training regimen in the intense Central African heat, but to the public, he offered effusive praise for the black African nation.

Postponed for a month because Foreman suffered a cut over his eye in a sparring session, the fight was held on October 30, 1974 at the outdoor Stade du 20 Mai in Kinshasa. Before the fight, Foreman kept to himself and made no effort to excite crowds of supporters. In contrast, Ali reveled in shouts—"Ali Bomaye" ("Ali, kill him!")—that greeted him wherever he went. Where Foreman tended to be sullen with reporters, Ali took every opportunity to speak, calling Foreman "The Mummy" whose only talent was knocking out his opponents.

Sixty thousand people witnessed the upset in which Ali knocked out Foreman in the eighth round. They also witnessed a demonstration of Ali's soon-to-be-famous "rope-a-dope" technique in which he backed into the ropes in a defensive posture that forced Forman to throw so many punches that he was exhausted by the sixth round. Ali's realization that he had the stamina to outlast "Big George" was the key to his victory. By the eighth round, he enjoyed taunting Foreman: "Come on, sucker, show me something. I can't feel it. You ain't nothing but a chump. You done run out of gas, now I'm gonna kick your ass."[6] Ali then connected with a left hook and a right, sending Foreman to the canvas. Columnist Dave Anderson described the fight in the *New York Times*:

> Under an African moon a few hours before dawn, the 32-year-old Ali sent his 25-year-old rival crashing to the floor with a left and a chopping right. It was a bee harassing a bear, stinging incessantly until his arm-weary adversary succumbed to sheer persistence . . . Ali, disdaining his usual butterfly tactics, took Foreman's most powerful punches without flinching and without wobbling except for a brief moment in the second round. Suddenly, with Foreman

stumbling on weary legs near the end of the eighth, Ali exploded a left-right combination. Spinning backward, Foreman flopped onto the canvas. Ali had predicted that "after the 10th round, Foreman will fall on his face from exhaustion." As it developed, in the eighth Foreman toppled onto his rump from exhaustion. Groping to his feet, he was counted out by Zack Clayton, the referee, at 2 minutes 58 seconds of the round.[7]

The press was enthusiastic about Ali's victory. Some writers recognized that Ali could have been even more brutal as he took down Foreman. According to sports journalist Tim Dahlberg:

> The fight was over, but it could have been worse. As Foreman was going down, Ali had the perfect chance to hit him with another right hand, but didn't. "He started to do it, then put the gun back in the holster." Foreman said "He had mercy on me. Would I have done the same for him at that time? No."

"He whupped me," said Foreman years later. "Don't tell anybody, but he really got me."[8]

In a post-fight interview with British writer Hugh McIlvanney, Ali crowed that he had beaten not only his rival in the ring but the writers and pundits who predicted his demise:

> "I kicked a lot of asses – not only George's," he said. "All those writers who said I was washed up, all those people who thought I had nothin' left to offer but my mouth, all them that been against me from the start and waitin' for me to get the biggest beatin' of all times. They thought big bad George Foreman, the baddest man alive, could do it for them but they know better now."

He also reflected on the personal importance of his victory:

> "Muhammad Ali stops George Foreman," he muttered with his eyes closed. "Man, that is a hell of a upset. It will be weeks before I realize the impact of this. I don't feel like I'm champion again yet. I can't wait to see all them magazines. They got to say I'm the greatest now, the greatest of all times. I fooled them all."[9]

In 1975, Ali fought three times before facing Joe Frazier for the third time. First, he fought Chuck Wepner for nearly a full fifteen rounds in a defense of his newly earned WBA and WBC titles at the Richfield Coliseum near Cleveland, Ohio before winning by technical knockout. Wepner, who was nicknamed the "Bayonne Bleeder," had made his name as a light heavyweight. The challenger knew he was fighting both Ali and his personal reputation as a "bum," a fighter who persisted in the fight game in spite of never earning enough to give up his regular job. Wepner's face carried the scars of numerous battles, yet he was proud of his record and was unwilling to give up boxing because he loved the ring. On the eve of his fight with Ali, Wepner told Mark Kram of *Sports Illustrated*:

> I don't know why people have been so unkind. I've worked for this shot. Ali wanted to fight somebody white who was ranked. What's he going to do? Fight Jerry Quarry again? Hell, Quarry wasn't even competitive against Ali. In my mind, Ali is the greatest heavyweight that ever lived, but he may be through. He better be ready. And if he leans on those ropes, I'm going to pick him up and throw him out of the ring.[10]

Ali was far from through. Wepner hoped to upset the new champion, but Ali was in control for the first eight rounds. The challenger was able to keep Ali off the ropes and even knocked the champ down in the ninth round. But when Ali got to his feet, he took charge again and battered his opponent so severely that the referee stopped the fight in the fifteenth round. Ali's titles remained in place, and Wepner's gritty performance earned him a purse of $100,000 to Ali's $1.6 million. The fight inspired Sylvester Stallone's first "*Rocky*" film.

Six weeks after his victory over Wepner, Ali took on Ron Lyle in Las Vegas on May 16, 1976. Lyle, like Sonny Liston, had learned to box while serving a prison sentence for murder. While serving time in Colorado for his participation in a gang fight, he was stabbed and pronounced dead on the operating table. Lyle recovered and eventually caught the attention of the prison's athletic director, who encouraged him to box. A promising record in prison and as an amateur after his parole in 1969 led Lyle to the ranks of the heavyweight professionals. He lost to Jerry Quarry but defeated Jimmy Ellis, Buster Mathis, and Oscar Bonavena before taking on Ali at the age of thirty-four. According to Lyle's obituary in 2011 in the *Guardian*:

> The big punching Lyle had been ahead on all three judges' cards against a lethargic looking Ali before the champion unleashed a terrific right hand to the head and landed around 30 more unanswered blows to prompt the referee to call the fight off.

Although Ali was clearly getting the best of him, Lyle felt that the fight should have continued. He said he "felt robbed of the greatest honor in all sport." Nevertheless, he gained respect for having taken Ali into the eleventh round.[11] For Ali, this was another defense of his WBA and WBC titles. Lyle had the advantage in points, but Ali's powerful punches gave him the fight.

Ali then traveled to Kuala Lampur, Malaysia to defend his titles against Joe Bugner in front of an audience of 22,000. It promised to be a relatively bland affair that cried out for a gimmick. John Condon, Director of Publicity for Madison Square Garden who had refined the phrase "rope-a-dope" to describe Ali's trick of leaning against the ropes to force his opponent to punch to the point of exhaustion, suggested that Ali announce that the Bugner fight would be his last. The ruse lasted for only a few minutes during a meeting with the press, until Ali realized that retirement would mean that he would not fight Joe Frazier again. The retirement proposal was instantly off the table. Biographer Thomas Hauser put this incident into perspective, focusing on Ali's all-consuming need for the limelight when he wrote that the champ was "like a child raised in a circus trunk. Boxing was the world he knew. It was where he'd been born and raised. And like most performers, he was compelled to go where the light shone brightest."[12] That light did not shine in the ring with Joe Bugner, but the champ took home $2,000,000 in a close but unanimous decision in fifteen rounds. It was time to take on Joe Frazier for the third time.

Ali often claimed that his tirades against other fighters were part of an act in which he played the part of the fool or the clown and cast his opponents in the role of an animal (Sonny Liston was a "big old bear" and Floyd Patterson was a "rabbit") or an Uncle Tom or a fake black hero. He claimed to be friendly with the men he beat in the ring, and this was often true. Frequently, he and his opponents were able to overcome the animus that resulted from Ali's verbal excesses, and occasionally, as in the case of Jimmy Ellis, he fought one of his own sparring partners and childhood friends. In the case of Joe Frazier, there was no friendship, no rapprochement after a bitter battle, no love for an opponent as a man. Joe Frazier went to his grave hating and disparaging Muhammad Ali, as he refused to accept Ali's assertion that his insults were just part of the publicity game.

The two men had once been friends. Frazier befriended Ali during his exile from professional boxing and supported his efforts to regain his license to fight in New York. When their first bout, dubbed the "Fight of the Century," was imminent, Frazier even shared in the anticipation of a large purse from their proposed fight. He wrote that, after Ali beat Jimmy Ellis, he drove with Ali from his home in Philadelphia to New York:

> We talked about how much we were going to make out of our fight. We were laughin' and havin' fun. We were friends, we were great friends. I said, "Why not? Come on, man, let's do it." He was a brother. He called me Joe: "Hey Smokin' Joe!" In New York we were gonna put on this commotion.

But, as he often did, Ali caused a "commotion" to his advantage. On the same trip, Frazier stopped at a shoe store, and Ali found his promotional opening. He announced Frazier's presence and went on to shout, "He's got my title! I want my title! He ain't the champ, he's the chump. I'm the people's champ."[13]

For Ali, this incident might have been nothing more than a bit of pre-fight banter, but Frazier took Ali's comments as an insult. As the fight approached,

Ali no longer pretended that the fight was part of a friendly rivalry. He characterized Frazier as "too dumb" and "too ugly" to be the heavyweight champion and, of course, he claimed that he would re-capture the crown. He went so far as to declare that, "Anybody black who thinks Frazier can whup me is an Uncle Tom." These remarks did more than sell tickets and raise the temperature of the Ali–Frazier rivalry; they deeply hurt the champ, who felt that he and Ali had been friends. Frazier asked, "What's wrong with this guy? Has he gone crazy? He called me an Uncle Tom."

> For a guy who did as much for him as I did, that was cruel. I grew up like the black man—he didn't. I cooked the liquor. I cut the wood. I worked the farm.
>
> I lived in the ghetto. Yes, I tommed; when he asked me to help him get a license,
>
> I tommed for him. For him! He betrayed my friendship. He called me stupid. He said I was so ugly that my mother ran and hid when she gave birth to me. I was shocked. I sat down and said to myself, "I'm gonna kill him . . . Simple as that. I'm gonna kill him."[14]

That is precisely what happened. Frazier won the fight in a dramatic fifteen rounds in a battle that left both men battered. At the time, Ali appeared to give credit to Frazier's skill by recognizing that he had been beaten. He said he was satisfied with the fight, even though he lost. He said, "I know I lost to a great champion." When the two men met again in New York in January of 1974, Ali won easily in twelve rounds. Frazier still carried the sting of Ali's earlier taunts and insults, saying:

> Maybe I don't rap as good as he do. Rapping ain't my bag. I believe in doing a job of work, not talking about it. I don't think a man has to go around shouting and play-acting to prove he is something. And a real man don't go around putting other guys down, trampling their feelings in the dirt, making out they're nothing. People say Clay's words don't mean a thing and that I should ignore them. I know all them insults are nonsense but he's saying them and that means something. Why should any man talk to me the way he talks?[15]

As soon as Ali unseated George Foreman to regain the world heavyweight title, he set his sights on Frazier once again. This was the fight that Ali named with a return to his rhyming ways. Pulling a small rubber gorilla doll out of his pocket, he again challenged Frazier, "Come on, gorilla! We're in Manila! Come on, gorilla, this is a thrilla." Ali–Frazier III came to be known as the "Thrilla in Manila." Ali won the attention of reporters and audiences for his vituperative remarks directed at Frazier:

> Joe Frazier should give his face to the Wildlife Fund. He's so ugly, blind men go the other way. Ugly! Ugly! Ugly! He not only looks bad, you can smell him in

another country. What will the people of Manila think? That black brothers are animals. Ignorant. Stupid. Ugly and smelly.

Ali's verbal abuse of Frazier was all too typical of the manner in which he baited his opponents outside the ring. His verbal quickness often led him to abusive verbal cruelty that also characterized his performances in the ring. He called "the Bear" Sonny Liston a chump after beating him and taunted Ernie Terrell with cries of "What's my name?" as he pummeled him.

In a fight promoted by Don King in the Araneta Coliseum in Quezon City near Manila, the elder statesmen of the ring fought for huge guaranteed purses—$4.5 million to go to Ali and $2 million to Frazier, in addition to a percentage of the proceeds. The fight was held at 10:45 in the morning to accommodate viewers in 380 closed-circuit locations in the United States, along with broadcasts in sixty-eight other countries. From all the proceeds, Ali earned nearly $9 million, while Frazier saw about $5 million. They fought for money, for the championship, and for the opportunity to hurt each other.[16]

The "Thrilla in Manila," held on October 1, 1975, was brutal. William Nack wrote that, "Those who were there witnessed prizefighting in its grandest manner, the final epic in a running blood feud between two men, each fighting to own the heart of the other. The fight called upon all their will and courage as they pitched from one ring post to another emitting fearful grunts and squeals." Ali began with a barrage of punches, and Frazier demonstrated that he could take the punches and throw his own volley of left hooks. In the middle rounds, Frazier was able to overpower Ali and negate the effectiveness of the rope-a-dope technique with a flurry of punches. He had the advantage in the middle rounds. Nack described Ali at the end of the tenth round as looking like "a half-drowned man who had just been pulled from Manila Bay." But Frazier began to lose his stamina, and Ali grabbed the advantage in the tenth round. He mounted an attack that continued into the thirteenth round, when he hit Frazier so hard that his mouthpiece flew from his mouth into the crowd. An undisclosed cataract clouded Frazier's vision in his left eye, and Ali's punches had nearly closed his right eye, rendering Frazier effectively blind in the fourteenth round. He continued to fight hard and refused to believe his trainer, Eddie Futch, when he declared the fight over. Frazier insisted that he wanted to continue, but Futch told him, "It's all over. No one will forget what you did here today." Both fighters were exhausted from their ordeal. Ali told reporters that the fight was "as close to dying" as any experience he had ever had.[17]

In spite of the hype, the "Thrilla in Manilla" was not a classic moment in the ring. Some boxing writers have even suggested that this was not among Ali's more impressive victories, arguing that Frazier had failed to disclose his eye problem or a sore shoulder and that neither fighter was in his prime. Mike Silver called the fight "damaged goods from the outset." It was a battle that no one but Ali seemed to want, as he launched his personal media campaign to "whup" Joe Frazier one more time, perhaps to prove something about his own physical prowess. The first battle between the two men had been impressive, and the second was a disappointment that many people, including Frazier, insisted had been "stolen" to give Ali a victory. A third fight could be nothing but disappointing. Comparing it to the 1971 "Fight of the Century," Silver asked, "Why dishonor the memory of that first magnificent classic with another fight staged four and a half years later between two over-the-hill legends? There was nothing left to prove." Frazier fought hard but was clearly in bad shape. Writing in *Sports Illustrated* on the occasion of Frazier's death, Richard Hoffer wrote that, by the fifteenth round, "there wasn't anything left in either man." He called the fight "victory, but by attrition." Silver noted that, "Beating up a tired old version of Joe Frazier was not the great accomplishment it's made out to be by Ali's army of frenzied sycophants."[18] Even in victory, Ali could not hide the fact that he had taken a significant beating, including 440 hard blows from his opponent. William Nack described the outcome:

> Two of Ali's greatest virtues as a fighter, the depth of his bravery and the strength of his chin, worked their wickedness on him in the end. He took some terrible punishment, and that bravery and that chin kept him standing there, lolling wearily on the ropes, long after the rest of him had vanished.[19]

Before and during the fight, Ali presented a *persona* that reminded many of his "I am the greatest" days as a young fighter with a lot to prove. He bragged, he baited Frazier, and he behaved like an arrogant, petulant child as he insulted every aspect of Frazier's life and career, from his intelligence to his boxing style. His antics with a toy gorilla at a pre-fight press conference lent an air of over-the-top hostility to the proceedings. But after the fight, Ali was more mature in his assessment of the outcome. He told reporters, "I'll tell the world right now, he brings out the best in me. I'm gonna tell ya, that's one helluva man, God bless him . . . Joe Frazier is the greatest fighter in the world, next to me."[20]

Ali's apparent magnanimity in victory did not cool the hostility between the two fighters. After the fight, Ali made an attempt to apologize to Frazier, telling his son, "Tell your dad the things I said I didn't really mean." But Frazier did not accept the apology, telling his son, "He should have come to me, son. He should say it to my face." Frazier remained convinced that he had won all three of his fights with Ali and that a bit of the spotlight that he deserved had been taken away from him. He rebuffed Ali's attempts to make amends and even wrote in his autobiography:

> Truth is, I'd like to rumble with that sucker again—beat him up piece by piece and mail him back to Jesus . . . Now people ask me if I feel bad for him, now that things aren't going so well for him. Nope. I don't. Fact is, I don't give a damn. They want me to love him, but I'll open up the graveyard and bury his ass when the Lord chooses to take him.[21]

Joe Frazier died of liver cancer on November 7, 2011. He was sixty-seven years old.

After the Thrilla, sportswriters and fans began to observe that the champ was not the same. He and Frazier had both taken brutal beatings. Writing in 1984, *New York Times* columnist Dave Anderson noted that, in Ali's final fourteen fights in the six years following his victory in Manila, Ali fought a total of 176 rounds, an average of 12.6 rounds per fight. Gone were the days of the first-round knockout or the four or five rounds spent dancing in the ring to keep his opponent at bay prior to a devastating blow that would end the fight with Ali suffering barely a scratch. After the struggle in Manila, Ali was described as "worn and weary" when he faced reporters. Anderson wrote, "For once, he had little to say, even as the victor in what will be remembered as perhaps his noblest hour as a gladiator." But, based on the punishment he took and Ali's subsequent decline, Anderson asked a key question, "For Ali, what was the eventual price of the Thrilla in Manila?"[22] That price was revealed gradually in what doctors later called "Parkinson's Syndrome." This collection of physical symptoms that includes tremors and a general slowing of reflexes is not confined to boxers, but taking punches over many years contributed to Ali's ailments. The champ would not become aware of his physical decline for several years.

Ali successfully defended his World Heavyweight Championship six times after his victory over Frazier before losing the title to Leon Spinks on February 15, 1978 in Las Vegas. First, he faced the "Lion of Belgium," Jean-Pierre Coopman, on February 20, 1976 in San Juan, Puerto Rico. The two fighters were pictured on the cover of *Sports Illustrated*. Under the headline, "Ali's Road Show Rolls On" was the sub headline "The Champ Tames His Lion." Fight fans, including many from Belgium, flocked to the Roberto Clemente Stadium. It's difficult to imagine that they came to see the fight, which ended when Ali knocked Coopman out in the fifth round in what Mark Kram called "the worst mismatch in heavyweight championship history" and also "the most overpriced," with ringside seats costing $200. Instead, they came to see the celebrity, Muhammad Ali. Hinting that the animus of the Frazier fight was behind the champ and that he fought less for glory than for money to finance his generosity and philanthropy, Kram described Ali as a phenomenon unto himself, in and outside the ring, observing that boxing

> is only a small part of the Muhammad Ali picture; interest in ring esthetics did not generate the millions of dollars involved in this fight, nor does it move the multitudes that shadow his every step wherever he chooses to fight. It is the man that counts.[23]

Ali spoke about his reasons for fighting every few months as he lay in wait for the chance to fight Ken Norton. Clearly, he was not under pressure to defend his title so frequently, but he had other reasons for entering the ring:

> I'm doin' a lot of things for charity. I'm buildin' a school. I'm buildin' a hospital. I need money. I got a million for this fight, but look what's left. Taxes cut it to $600,000 here, and my expenses and taxes at home knock it down to $350,000. Then out comes my manager's end. I can't go on forever, but I'm gonna raise some hell while I can.

There was a hint of Ali's youthful playfulness in the pre-fight banter with little of the vitriol of the Frazier fight. He clearly saw this fight as an opportunity to "rest" after having taken a real beating at the hands of Frazier. In response to Ali's usual antics, Coopman's manager opined that, "Ali can't psyche him because he can't understand a word Ali says."[24]

Against the advice of his manager Herbert Muhammad, the champ played the clown early in the fight. When, in the fourth round, Muhammad threatened to walk out of the arena if Ali did not get down to the business of winning, the champ went to work. Later, Coopman described the moment: "I was not hit hard. I was not unconscious, but I could not get up. It felt like a 500-pound bag had me pinned down." In spite of his loss, Coopman earned a place in boxing history as one of Ali's opponents who eventually earned honors as the European heavyweight champion, although he held that title for only two months. Kram noted that, after his defeat, Coopman returned to his home in Ingelmunster, in Flanders,

> back to a $4.50 an hour job chiseling stones for the restoration of medieval cathedrals. He can be content with the knowledge that there will not be one more poppy in Flanders' fields and that no man who climbs into a ring with Muhammad Ali can ever be a nonentity again.[25]

Jean-Pierre Coopman retired from boxing in 1980 and devoted his energies to painting portraits of famous fighters, including Muhammad Ali.

Ali had thought of the Coopman fight as a "rest" that he did not need to take seriously. He approached his next bout against Philadelphia slugger

Jimmy Young with a similar lack of intensity, and it nearly cost him his title. Young, who had trained at Joe Frazier's Philadelphia gym, was a dock worker by trade whose meager earnings from boxing kept him working on the Delaware River waterfront. It seemed unlikely that he would even get a chance to challenge Ali for the World Heavyweight Championship, but the two fought on April 30, 1976 in Landover, Maryland. Ali's lack of serious training showed, as he weighed in at 230 pounds, his heaviest weight to date in the ring. He carried twenty-one pounds more than Young. Ali was far more experienced than his challenger, who was described by Mark Kram as "a fighter of slight craft and a few cute moves. On the attack, his jab is a trifle, his punching of no account. On defense, caution marks his every move, his eyes are always on the exit doors." Ali was favored because of his reputation and experience and the fact that, as Kram noted, "A challenger is not given a champion's title. He must take that title."[26]

In spite of his Philadelphia lineage—Philadelphia fighters were known at the time as hard-punching aggressive fighters—Young showed a tendency to avoid contact rather than take control of the action in the ring. Six times during the fight when Ali confronted him Young stuck his head outside the ropes, forcing a stoppage of the clock and giving Young a brief rest. Kram described the move:

> Young was a passive figure against Ali. On six occasions he ducked outside the ropes and stayed there like a man looking outside a window. It was not acciden-
> tal . . . It was unconscionable behavior for a man who wants the heavyweight championship of the world.[27]

Ali's lack of serious presence in the fight earned him boos from the crowd, but Young's obvious avoidance move earned him fewer points from the judges. Although the Associated Press scored the fight 69–66 for Young, the three judges were unanimous in awarding the decision, and the retention of his title, to Ali. After the fight, Young confessed that the reason he had ducked through the ropes was "to take the pressure off me." At the same time, Ali was aware that he had not adequately prepared for the fight. He told reporters, "I weigh 230 pounds, just what I weigh when I'm in terrible shape. I'm 34 and I'm telling you what I did was a miracle, going 15 rounds and beating that young man. I've been eating too much pie, too much ice cream." Sports writers were less kind. Mark Kram called the fight's fifteen rounds "some of the worst and most numbing in heavyweight history."[28]

In spite of the controversy surrounding the fight, with some in the crowd and the sporting press even declaring that Ali had been beaten, Young had not made an affirmative case that he deserved the heavyweight crown. Mark Kram called Ali "a champion who was not prepared to fight the way he could and should . . . When he steps into the ring for $1.6 million, he owes it to himself and to his position to be worth every cent of it."[29] Although the fight was a fifteen-round win by decision, a successful title defense, and a generous payday for the champion, it was an embarrassment.

The champ's next title defense took pace in Munich, Germany on May 24, a mere three weeks after the misadventure in Landover. Ali's opponent was Richard Dunn, a fighter who was three years younger than Ali from Bradford, England. Dunn had earned and successfully defended his British and Commonwealth Heavyweight Championship, but he was no match for Ali, who had lost ten pounds and trained hard for the fight. He knocked Dunn out in 2:05 minutes in the fifth round. This fight was notable less for its ring appeal than for the lack of interest shown by the American public in Ali's title defense. In contrast, the British press covered the fight as a battle of a national hero against the established champion. Indeed, Dunn's reputation in his home country was based in large part on the fact that, although Ali knocked him down a total of five times, he was able to get up and continue fighting. London's *Telegraph* summarized Dunn's career:

> Dunn's career blossomed late after he joined the veteran manager George Biddles, who took him to a £100,000 payday against Muhammad Ali for the world title in Munich in 1976. Dunn, a southpaw with a down-to-earth approach, gave everything he had but was rescued, after several knockdowns, in round five. Unlike Joe Bugner, who was pilloried for a negative performance against Ali the previous year, Dunn was considered a hero.[30]

As the date of the fight approached with ticket sales languishing, Ali agreed to accept a smaller purse in return for 2,000 tickets, which he distributed to American soldiers in Germany. In spite of his position against the Vietnam War, Ali had long insisted that he had no animus against American military personnel. At the time of the Dunn fight, Ali said, "If I was a soldier, I'd want to see me; and I got nothing against them for going in the Army. I didn't go because of my religion, but them soldiers are just doing their job."[31] Ali defended his title again, albeit in a lackluster battle. But the military personnel had a special evening to remember, thanks of the generosity of Muhammad Ali. Interestingly, this fight did not attract a lot of media attention in the United States.

Ali's next fight was neither a title defense nor even a boxing match. In an outrageous move with the promise of a very large payday, Ali agreed to battle Antonio Inoki, a professional wrestler, for the "martial arts championship of the world," in Tokyo, Japan on June 26, 1976. In an era prior to the emergence of mixed martial arts as an official sport, professional wrestling was a popular form of entertainment that many fans cheered as if the matches were spontaneous rather than staged battles between heroes and villains. The "sport" was popular throughout the world, and Inoki was a star in Japan. The battle between the two men was to be governed by a unique set of rules. According to the *Guardian*:

> Ali would wear four-ounce gloves, and would be able to tag out of any grapple by touching the ropes. Inoki would be bare-handed. There would be no kneeing, kicking, or hitting below the belt. Anyone thrown out of the ring would have 20 seconds to get back in.

The pre-fight publicity demonstrated that Inoki was as big a self-promoter as his American opponent. Ali named his opponent "The Pelican" because of his prominent chin. Inoki replied through a Japanese translator that Ali should take care that he does not damage his fist, should it happen to connect with that chin. He also said, "I don't know how seriously Muhammad Ali is taking the fight, but if he doesn't take it seriously, he could suffer damage."[32]

Ali accepted an offer of $6 million to participate in a match shown in the United States by wrestling promoter Vince McMahon, Sr., who projected the fight on closed-circuit television at New York's Shea Stadium. To add to the circus atmosphere in New York, McMahon added a live contest between boxer Chuck Wepner and wrestler Andre the Giant. In Tokyo, the fight promoters planned that Ali would throw a punch that would accidentally hit the referee toward the end of the fight. As the referee lay on the canvas, Ali would lean over him, showing concern for his welfare and contrition over the misdirected punch. Then, Inoki would sneak up on Ali and kick him in the head, knocking him out. At that point, the referee would regain consciousness and count the American out. Inoki would win the match in his home country, Ali would have a spot on the moral high ground because of his solicitous behavior toward the referee, the audience would have a show, and the ref would go home with a headache. When Ali learned of this plan, he balked. As the *Guardian* reported, the fight's organizers were left "with a fixed fight that no one was prepared to throw."

The actual fight was almost as surreal as the plan to stage the spectacle. Inoki developed a strategy that would prevent him from taking a punch from Ali: he would stay on the canvas and kick his way through the bout. Ali threw only six punches in fifteen rounds, only two of which hit their mark, as Inoki kicked him, tripped him, and flipped him on to the canvas a number of times. The final score was a draw. Originally, Inoki scored more points but was docked because of fouls, so the final score was even, leaving neither fighter satisfied, the crowd yelling "Money back!" and throwing garbage, and the groundskeepers at Tokyo's Budokan arena busy cleaning up for days after the fight.[33]

Ali suffered more than a bruised ego. He never received his promised $6 million because of irregularities in the financing of the event. In addition, he suffered two dangerous blood clots as a result of the numerous kicks Inoki delivered to his legs. Ali's doctor, Ferdie Pacheco, implored the champ to skip an exhibition fight in Korea and the opening of a shopping mall in Manila, but Ali met these commitments and suffered some serious physical consequences. Pacheco remembered that Ali ignored his advice because

> half the entourage had home remedies to get him in shape. Bundini told him to put heat on his legs. Someone else brought in a Turkish masseuse to massage the leg, like you need to massage a broken blood vessel that's pumping. And the upshot of it was that, by the time Ali got back to the United States, he had to be hospitalized for blood clots and muscle damage.[34]

A passion for notoriety, and no small amount of hubris, had pushed Ali to jeopardize his health and his boxing career. He was headed for a third fight with Ken Norton, the tough fighter who had broken his jaw in 1973 and whom he saw as a serious contender. He would have to be more serious about his training and his approach to fighting to prevail as heavyweight champion.

Ali waited only three months before going into the ring against Norton at Yankee Stadium on September 28, 1976. Throughout his career, Ali had fought some "easy" opponents, misjudged the skill or motivation of others who made him work hard for a win, and even stepped into a wrestling ring in a fight with unfamiliar rules and severe physical consequences. But he trained hard in Arizona and then at the Concord Hotel in the Catskill Mountains to get ready for Norton. Bob Arum was his promoter this time, and even Arum's traditional approach could not insure a "normal" boxing event. With an advance sale of 30,000, the event promised to be a major crowd event that New York handles well because of its highly skilled police force. The problem was that the New York Police Department had gone on strike. Only 19,000 people came to Yankee Stadium to see the third meeting between Norton and Ali. Some of those in attendance were pickpockets and purse snatchers. With police officers demonstrating outside the stadium, pandemonium reigned inside. The fight in the ring was only part of the story that evening.

As with some of Ali's previous fights, his third battle with Ken Norton was a battle of attrition. Norton, who was only a year and a half younger than Ali, was strong and in good shape, while Ali had struggled to train hard after his encounter with Inoki's kicks. Norton dominated in the early rounds, after which Ali won five of six rounds. The winner would be determined by the judges' scoring of the fifteenth and final round. Over the course of fifteen rounds, Norton jabbed more times than Ali (94 to the champ's 71), of which more hit their mark (33 percent to Ali's 21 percent), while Ali threw more power punches (364) but landed only 35 percent to Norton's 346 power punches, of which 55 percent landed. Boxing referee Arthur Mercante offered his perspective on how Ali won the final round and the fight:

> Before the round, I went to both corners like I always do. Angelo Dundee was telling Ali, "You've got three more minutes. Fight like hell; we need this round." And then, in Norton's corner, I heard his manager, Bob Biron, tell him, "Be careful; stay away from him. Don't take chances, because you have the fight won." And I said to myself, "Gee, that's not such good advice, to tell Norton to coast. This fight is close." But Norton did coast. He gave away the first two-and-a-half minutes of the last round to Ali. And even though he came on strong in the last thirty seconds, it wasn't enough. Ali won the round.[35]

Norton felt bitter and cheated. He had followed the advice of his handlers, and Ali had made a last-minute push for the victory. Although he respected Ali, he remained convinced, like Joe Frazier before him, that he had beaten the champ. Ali's skills were on the wane, but he had enough left to win once again.

Ali waited nearly eight months before entering the ring again, this time against the Spaniard, Alfredo Evangelista. Evangelista was barely a contender, in spite of the WBC rankings that placed him in the top ten. The fight was held in Landover, Maryland. The champ was nearly twelve years older and twelve pounds heavier than his challenger. The fight ran fifteen rounds, with Ali declared the winner in a dull contest. Broadcaster Howard Cosell knew that this evening had not seen Ali at his best: "Evangelista couldn't fight a lick, and by then Ali wasn't fighting much either. The fact that the bout went fifteen rounds told you Ali was shot." Ali recognized the diminution of his skills when he said after the fight, "I'm 35-years-old and I danced fifteen rounds. It's a miracle."[36] Perhaps he should have retired from the ring, but Ali felt the pressure of paying alimony, child support, taxes, and salaries and expenses for his entourage, and support for various charitable ventures. He could not retire, so he prepared to take on yet another contender, Earnie Shavers.

In the 1970s, Shavers was widely regarded as one of boxing's hardest hitters. In the decades since the fight, which took place in Madison Square Garden on September 29, 1977, boxing writers have wondered why he was not able to beat Ali. The champ, in his usual style, played with Shavers in prefight interviews, calling the challenger "The Acorn" because of his shaved head. Shavers took the joke in stride, and after their fight, he noted that, in spite of his victory, the champ "found out that night that The Acorn is a tough nut to crack."[37] During the early rounds, Ali was playful and Shavers hit hard. Jim Amato, who called this fight "one of the best," described the early action:

> The relaxed and confident Ali easily outboxed Earnie in round one and was doing the same in round two. Then out of nowhere a crackling Shavers right hand stunned Ali and sent him wobbling backwards. Hurt and glassy eyed, Ali waved Earnie in again. Again Shavers landed with dynamic force staggering Ali. Only Muhammad's tremendous heart, chin and cunning enabled him to survive the round.

Energy and cunning prevailed throughout the fight. Ali led the scoring for the first eleven rounds, but Shavers fought mightily and effectively in the following three rounds. According to Amato, the fifteenth round

> saw two desperate warriors engaging in a thrilling toe to toe slugfest. Ali seemed revived and Earnie was letting it all hang out in a last ditch effort to win the crown. Earnie edged Ali during the first two minutes of the round and then he finally tired. Ali came on and hurt Earnie for the first time in the bout. Showing a remarkable will to survive Shavers refused to fall although he was beaten around the ring. At last the final bell sounded saving Earnie and putting his fate in the scorecards.

Once again, the crowd saw the scoring one way and the judges another. Ali was the victor, now having defended his WBA and WBC titles for the tenth time.[38]

Shavers was generous in his assessment of the outcome, but he also recognized that Ali was not the fighter he had once been. He said that, after he hit Ali in the second round, the champ

> wobbled, and then he wobbled some more. But Ali was so good at conning, I thought he was playing possum with me. I didn't realize how bad off he was. Later, when I watched the tape, I saw it, but at the time I was fooled. He could do that; that's why he was Ali. And he beat me. When the fight was over, I thought I'd won. But looking at the tape over and over, it was close but I can see how the judges voted for him.

Shavers was a hard-hitting boxer with surprisingly few knockouts who never earned a heavyweight title. With his usual over-the-top yet generous spirit, Ali declared after the fight that "Earnie hit me so hard, he shook my kinfolk back in Africa."[39]

Ali knew his skills were declining, but he made every effort to hide this fact behind his usual banter. At the time, he was filming television commercials between fights, and audiences could detect a slight slur in the champ's speech as well as an obvious slowing of his reflexes. The day after Ali's win over Shavers, Teddy Brenner, who was in charge of arranging boxing matches for the Garden, implored the champ to consider retiring. He reminded Ali that boxing is an unkind game, especially for a thirty-five-year-old whose recent victories had been based on his ability to take punches rather than his lightning speed and devastating right hand. Brenner then announced at Ali's press conference that he would not arrange any more fights for the champion at the Garden. He told Ali and the audience that "The trick in boxing is to get out at the right time, and the fifteenth round last night was the right time for Ali."[40] The champ paid little attention to Brenner's exhortation. It would take another four years and four grueling fights for him to decide to retire, but it was clear that Ali's reign as heavyweight champion was approaching its end.

The torch was about to pass to a younger generation of fighters. Just as the twenty-four-year-old Cassius Clay couldn't wait to unseat Sonny Liston, "the Big Ugly Bear," the thirty-six-year-old Muhammad Ali was vulnerable to younger fighters. Leon Spinks was twenty-five years old with only seven professional fights behind him when he faced Ali for the first time. Promoter Bob Arum signed the fighters to battle for the WBA and WBC titles in Las Vegas on February 5, 1978. The fight did not immediately inspire much public interest, and the WBC had to arrange for Spinks to fight the Italian heavyweight Alfi Righetti so that he could qualify as a contender. At first glance, the Ali–Spinks battle did not look like a particularly interesting contest with an aging champion facing a nearly unknown and inexperienced challenger. Before the fight, Ali refrained from his usual histrionics, claiming that he would look stupid if he carried on in his usual style against an opponent he did not take seriously. Ali also failed to take his training seriously, and no one in his large entourage was willing to criticize the champion. He had always been a fighter who paid little attention to suggestions or criticism, and this time his stubbornness hurt him. Spinks was in good enough shape to give Ali a genuine challenge. Even with a right hand injured in training, Spinks proved to be a formidable opponent, and a late-round rally never materialized for Ali. The scoring was remarkably close, with the Associated Press giving Ali 143 points to 142 for the challenger, but the only score cards that mattered belonged to the judges. Based in part on Spinks's domination in the last three rounds, he won the fight. Ali had lost his title in the ring for the first time. He told reporters after the fight, "I let him rob my house while I was out to lunch."[41]

After losing to Spinks, Ali was once again tempted to fight in South Africa. Bob Arum proposed that he fight a white challenger at the Sun City resort in the segregated country. Despite pleas from black athletes and political leaders that he not give favorable publicity to the South African government, Ali was tempted by the potential $14 million purse. The negotiations did not go far because of complications in the two countries' tax laws, and Ali eventually expressed his own reservations about the project:

> What worries me is getting whupped by a white man in South Africa . . .
>
> That's what the world needs . . . me getting whupped by a white man in South Africa. [But] if I beat him too bad and then leave the country, they might beat up some of the brothers.

The champ concluded that the fight was "too touchy." Recognizing his own symbolic role outside the ring, he concluded, "It's more than a sport when I get involved."[42]

The second fight between Ali and Spinks attracted significant public attention. Fans wanted to see if Ali could be the only heavyweight to win the championship for a third time. Spinks was defending his WBA title, but he had lost his WBC crown for giving Ali a re-match rather than allowing Ken Norton a chance to fight Spinks for that title. Ali was twenty pounds heavier than Spinks for the fight, which took place before 63,350 fans in the New Orleans Super Dome. The television audience on ABC was about ninety million viewers. These fans witnessed a different and aggressive Ali, who took control of the fight from the early rounds and scored a unanimous and undisputed victory in a fight that went the full fifteen rounds. *Sports Illustrated* journalist Pat Putnam described Ali's "demonstration by an old master educating an inexperienced youngster in the fine points of the craft."

> Ali assuredly did not go to the ropes, as he had done while losing his beloved championship to Leon in their fight in Las Vegas in February. Gone was the infamous rope-a-dope, by means of which Ali had coasted for long periods during his last few fights. This was the first time in recent memory that Ali stayed in the center of the ring, circling, jabbing and throwing occasional, if not very accurate, combinations, the first time in years he had not engaged in any extraneous foolishness. And when in doubt, he would seize Spinks in a mighty bear hug. At 221 pounds against 201, it was no contest.[43]

Ali had won the fight and the WBA crown. He was the heavyweight champion once again. He told *New York Magazine* writer Vic Ziegel:

> Do you know if I beat him the first time I wouldn't of got no credit for it. He only had seven fights . . . the kid was nothing . . . So I'm glad he won. It's a perfect scene. You couldn't write a better movie than this. This is it. Just what I need. Competition. Fighting odds. Can the old champ regain his title for a third time? Think of it. A third time. Do or die. And you know what makes me laugh? He's the same guy. Only difference is he got eight fights now.[44]

But time was running out on Muhammad Ali's professional boxing career. On June 26, 1979, he announced his retirement. There is some controversy as to whether or not Ali received a $300,000 payment from Bob Arum to step out of the ring so that the promoter could arrange another fight. Arum insists that he paid the money, Ali says he never received it, and manager Herbert Muhammad says he does not remember the transaction, even though Arum was said to have paid the bonus to him.

After a "farewell tour" of Europe, Ali fought twice more before his ring career was finally over. His loss to Larry Holmes by a technical knockout in the eleventh round in a failed attempt to re-capture the WBC heavyweight crown took place in Las Vegas on October 2, 1980. Holmes brought a record of 35–0 to the ring and was defending his WBC title for the eighth time. Somehow, neither Ali nor his fans seems to have believed that his retirement a year and a half prior to the bout was, or at least should have been, serious. The cover of *Sports Illustrated* before the fight showed a picture of a combative Ali with a familiar-sounding rant:

> He's no Liston. He's no Frazier. He's only Larry Holmes, and he's nothing. I can see it now. Pop! Pop! Bam! Holmes is down. Eight . . . nine . . . ten! For the world-record-setting, never-to-be broken fourth time, Muhammad Ali is the heavyweight champion of the world!

Commentary on the real action in the ring was quite different:

> In an absolutely disgusting bout, the 31 year old champion dismantled the 38 year old legend in 10 rounds of a scheduled 15 round bout. There were no knockdowns, but Holmes dominated the fight and was given every round by all three judges. Finally, Ali's corner stopped the fight after the tenth round.[45]

By the late 1970s, questions about Ali's physical condition began to overshadow commentary on his boxing ability. Prior to the Holmes fight, the Nevada State Athletic Commission had ordered Ali to submit to a neurological examination. The Mayo Clinic doctors reported that, "Muhammad Ali was a little off when he tried to touch his finger to his nose. He had trouble coordinating his speech, and the fight legend couldn't hop on one foot well." These difficulties were not sufficient to prevent the Commission from allowing the fight, and it is interesting to speculate that publicity and large paydays were more influential than the state of a fighter's health, especially when that fighter had the reputation and cachet of Muhammad Ali. Crowds would turn out even to see him defeated. Ali's emerging physical difficulties were a well-known secret that no one in his entourage wanted to acknowledge, especially when there was money to be made in the ring. Even as the loser, Ali was promised a purse of $8 million. Ali himself blamed the Las Vegas heat and sensitivity to his thyroid medication for his weak state during the fight. He promised to fight again, against very clear indications that this would be a bad idea because of the physical impairments that were starting to show themselves.[46]

Called the "Drama in Bahama," Ali's last fight was a loss in the eleventh round to a twenty-seven-year-old Jamaican fighter, Trevor Berbick. When asked before the fight why he was willing to take physical punishment in the ring once again, in spite of the obvious disadvantages of fighting once more, Ali said, "Not because I'm bored. Not because I miss the limelight. Not because anybody makes me. It's just the idea. Four times a champ. I remember when Floyd Patterson regained his championship." The idea of regaining his title clearly dominated Ali's thinking. He was also consumed with the idea of his own popularity. He told reporters, "Everybody knows me. Not just in the West, but in China, in Russia, in Morocco, in Libya. They know me all over the world."[47] As to the issue of the damage he had sustained as a result of his long career in the ring, he dismissed the idea, suggesting that he was just tired and that everyone over the age of forty would be rooting for him. Perhaps that was true, but Ali was clearly blind to his physical impairments.

Ali outweighed his opponent by eighteen pounds, but the extra weight was no advantage in this battle. Ali held his own for seven rounds, mainly because Berbick missed his mark on a number of punches. In the end, Berbick dominated the fight because Ali was even less able to connect with his punches. He lost in a unanimous decision and told the assembled reporters, "Father Time caught up with me. In my younger days, I wouldn't have had any trouble. But I just couldn't do what I wanted to do."[48] The real question was why Ali had stayed in the ring so long when logic and common sense should have forced his retirement after he defeated Joe Frazier in Manila. Like many a tragic hero, Ali was afflicted by hubris and tempted by flattery and money. According to Australian sports writer Matthew Syed, "His vast entourage wanted him to box on, as did his religious mentors. Indeed, the wider world, still traumatised by Watergate and Vietnam, yearned for the escapism provided by Ali's global roadshow, with its glorious pre-bout vaudeville." Ali's personal physician, Ferdie Pacheco, who left Ali's entourage in frustration after the "wrestling" match in Tokyo and Ali's refusal to take care of his injuries, said:

> His tragedy was that he loved his life so much that he wanted to prolong it in the spotlight. The tragedy became that a man who could have been a tremendous leader for his people became muted by an illness caused by boxing. And that is when the Muhammad Ali I knew came to an end.[49]

Finally, Ali's ring career was over, but his life remains a subject of great interest. He had spoken to the world in the voice of a heavyweight champion, a member of the Nation of Islam, a political activist, and a phoenix in the ring. Even though his voice is nearly silent today, Muhammad Ali's life outside the ring has proven to be as varied and exciting as his boxing career.

NOTES

1 Margena A. Christian, "Muhammad Ali vs George Foreman: Rumble in the Jungle 40 Years Later," *Ebony* (May, 2014), p. 130.

2 Thomas Hauser, *Muhammad Ali: His Life and Times* (New York: Simon & Schuster, 1991), p. 260.

3 David Zirin, "The Hidden History of Muhammad Ali," *International Socialist Review* Issue 33 (January–February, 2004), http://www.isreview.org/issues/33/muhammadali.shtml.

4 Hauser, *Muhammad Ali: His Life and Times*, p. 265.

5 Ibid.

6 "The World Was His Canvas," *Newsweek* (October 25, 1999), http://www.newsweek.com/world-was-his-canvas-167950.

7 Dave Anderson, "Ali Regains Title, Flooring Foreman," *New York Times* (October 30, 1974), http://www.nytimes.com/books/98/10/25/specials/ali-foreman.html.

8 Tim Dahlberg, "Foreman Finally at Peace with Loss to Ali," *Bleacher Report* (October 28, 2009), http://bleacherreport.com/articles/280207-foreman-finally-at-peace-with-loss-to-ali; Kevin Mitchell, "We're Still in Awe of Muhammad Ali and George Foreman, 34 Years On," *Guardian* (October 30, 2009), http://www.theguardian.com/sport/blog/2009/oct/30/muhammad-ali-george-foreman.

9 Hugh McIlvanney, "The Greatest Again," http://www.kilmarnockacademy.co.uk/famoushmcilvanneygreatestagain.htm.

10 Mark Kram, "They Have Kept Him in Stitches," *Sports Illustrated* (March 24, 1975), http://www.si.com/vault/1975/03/24/576616/they-have-kept-him-in-stitches.

11 John Rawling, "Ron Lyle Obituary," *Guardian* (November 27, 2011), http://www.theguardian.com/sport/2011/nov/27/ron-lyle.

12 Hauser, *Muhammad Ali: His Life and Times*, p. 304.

13 William Nack, "The Fight's Over, Joe," *Sports Illustrated* (September 30, 1996), http://www.si.com/vault/1996/09/30/208924/the-fights-over-joe-more-than-two-decades-after-they-last-met-in-the-ring-joe-frazier-is-still-taking-shots-at-muhammad-ali-but-this-time-its-a-war-of-words.

14 Ibid.

15 Simon Burnton, "Muhammad Ali on Joe Frazier: That's One Helluva Man and God Bless Him," *Guardian* (November 8, 2011), http://www.theguardian.com/sport/2011/nov/08/muhammad-ali-joe-frazier.

16 Nack, "The Fight's Over, Joe"; Burnton, "Muhammad Ali on Joe Frazier"; "Muhammad Ali vs Joe Frazier (3rd meeting)," *BoxRec Encyclopedia*, http://boxrec.com/media/index.php/Muhammad_Ali_vs._Joe_Frazier_(3rd_meeting).

17 Nack, "The Fight's Over, Joe" and "Muhammad Ali vs Joe Frazier (3rd meeting)."

18 Richard Hoffer, "Joe Frazier 1944–2011," *Sports Illustrated*, http://www.si.com/vault/2011/11/21/106132910/joe-frazier-1944--2011; Mike Silver, "The Myth of 'The Thrilla in Manila,'" *Boxing.com* (September 30, 2012), http://www.boxing.com/the_myth_of_the_thrilla_in_manilla.html.

19 William Nack, "Muhammad Ali," *Sports Illustrated* (September 19, 1994), http://www.si.com/vault/1994/09/19/132063/1-muhammad-ali.

20 "Muhammad Ali vs Joe Frazier (3rd meeting)."

21 Nack, "The Fight's Over, Joe."

22 Dave Anderson, "For Ali, What Price the Thrilla in Manila," *New York Times* (September 23, 1984), http://www.nytimes.com/books/98/10/25/specials/ali-price.html.

23 Mark Kram, "One-Nighter in San Juan," *Sports Illustrated* (March 1, 1976), http://www.si.com/vault/1976/03/01/559159/one-nighter-in-san-juan.

24 "Muhammad Ali vs Jean-Pierre Coopman," *BoxRec Encyclopedia*, http://boxrec.com/media/index.php/Muhammad_Ali_vs._Jean-Pierre_Coopman.

25 Kram, "One-Nighter in San Juan"; "Muhammad Ali vs Jean-Pierre Coopman."

26 Mark Kram, "The Champ Looked Like a Chump," *Sports Illustrated* (May 10, 1976), http://www.si.com/vault/1976/05/10/616347/the-champ-looked-like-a-chump.

27 Ibid.

28 "Muhammad Ali vs Jimmy Young," *BoxRec Encyclopedia*, http://boxrec.com/media/index.php/Muhammad_Ali_vs._Jimmy_Young.

29 Kram, "The Champ Looked Like a Chump."

30 Bob Mee, "Fight Night in Great Tradition," *Telegraph* (December 8, 2005), http://www.telegraph.co.uk/sport/othersports/boxing/2369432/Fight-night-in-great-tradition.html.

31 Hauser, *Muhammad Ali: His Life and Times*, p. 333.

32 "The Forgotten Story of Muhammad Ali v Antonio Inoki," *Guardian* (November 11, 2009), http://www.theguardian.com/sport/blog/2009/nov/11/the-forgotten-story-of-ali-inoki.

33 Ibid.

34 Ibid.; Hauser, *Muhammad Ali: His Life and Times*, p. 338.

35 These statistics are cited in "Ali-Norton III: Who Really Won?" *The Wall Street Journal* (September 19, 2013), http://online.wsj.com/news/articles/SB10001424127887323380204579085120768490880. Arthur Mercante, in Hauser, *Muhammad Ali: His Life and Times*, pp. 339–40.

36 Howard Cosell in Hauser, *Muhammad Ali: His Life and Times*, p. 341 and "Muhammad Ali vs Alfredo Evangelista," *BoxRec Encyclopedia*, http://boxrec.com/media/index.php/Muhammad_Ali_vs._Alfredo_Evangelista.

37 Thomas Hauser, *The Lost Legacy of Muhammad Ali* (Toronto: Sports Classic Books, 2005), p. 168.

38 Jim Amato, "The Ali vs Shavers Bout: One of the Best," *Boxing News* (August 21, 2010), http://www.boxingnews24.com/2010/08/the-ali-vs-shavers-bout-one-of-the-best/.

39 Hauser, *Muhammad Ali: His Life and Times*, p. 347; "Muhammad Ali vs Earnie Shavers," *BoxRec Encyclopedia*, http://boxrec.com/media/index.php/Muhammad_Ali_vs._Earnie_Shavers.

40 Hauser, *Muhammad Ali: His Life and Times*, pp. 348–9.

41 Hauser, *Muhammad Ali: His Life and Times*, pp. 352–3 and "Muhammad Ali vs Leon Spinks (1st meeting)," *BoxRec Encyclopedia*, http://boxrec.com/media/index.php?title=Fight:365.

42 Mike Marqusee, *Redemption Song: Muhammad Ali and the Spirit of the Sixties* (New York: Verso, 1999), pp. 287–8.

43 Pat Putnam, "One More Time to the Top," *Sports Illustrated* (September 25, 1978), http://archive.today/fUFK7#selection-451.53–454.0.

44 Vic Ziegel, "Ali, Spinks, and the Battle of New Orleans," *New York Magazine* (October 2, 1978), http://nymag.com/news/sports/48897/.

45 "Muhammad Ali vs Larry Holmes: The Last Hurrah Was Anything But," Fightsaga.com, http://www.fightsaga.com/news/item/2613-Muhammad-Ali-vs-Larry-Holmes-The-Last-Hurrah-Was-Anything-But.

46 Ibid.; "Larry Holmes vs Muhammad Ali," *BoxRec Encyclopedia*, http://boxrec.com/media/index.php/Larry_Holmes_vs._Muhammad_Ali.

47 George Vecsey, "At 39, Ali Has More Points to Prove," *New York Times* (November 29, 1981), http://www.nytimes.com/1981/11/29/sports/at-39-ali-has-more-points-to-prove.htm.

48 "Trevor Berbick vs Muhammad Ali," *BoxRec Encyclopedia*, http://boxrec.com/media/index.php/Trevor_Berbick_vs._Muhammad_Ali.

49 Matthew Syed, "Don't Ignore the Dark Side of the Greatest," *The Australian* (January 17, 2007).

Epilogue

"I Won't Miss Boxing, Boxing Will Miss Me"

Boxing has not forgotten Muhammad Ali, but others have taken the spotlight since his retirement. He was deemed the Greatest of All Time by fans and boxing writers, and since his retirement he has received numerous honors from boxing organizations and presidents, but the sport has continued without him. Champions such as Sugar Ray Leonard, Marvin Hagler, Mike Tyson, a seemingly ageless George Foreman, and many others have entertained fans and earned huge purses for their prowess in the ring. Some are colorful personalities, but none has approached Ali's larger-than-life political and social impact. For his brave political stand against induction during the Vietnam War, for his role as a spokesperson for the independence of the black man in America, and for his generosity and grace as an aging and ailing warrior, Ali is respected as an American who demonstrated his patriotism by taking the right to free association (as a Muslim) and freedom of religion and speech (as a draft resister) seriously. He occupies an exalted status as an American hero far beyond his accomplishments in the ring.

Ali experienced two careers. In the first, prior to his suspension from boxing in 1967, he appeared unstoppable, as a fighter, as a Muslim, and as a young black man in a changing world. He energized boxing by talking trash and creating a new style in the ring that relied on speed and energy more than the proverbial knockout punch. By taking a stand against the draft that could have sent him to prison but instead cost him three and a half years of a career, Ali had to create a new image and style. The more mature post-suspension Ali was no less creative in the ring, but he was hardly the same fighter he had been in the 1960s. Joyce Carol Oates described the new Ali:

> He'd lost his legs, thus his primary line of defense. Like the maturing writer who learns to replace the incandescent head-on energies of youth with what is called

technique, Ali would have to descend into his physical being and experience for the first time the punishment ("the nearest thing to death") that is the lot of the great boxer willing to put himself to the test.

"The secret of Ali's mature success, and the secret of his tragedy," Oates continued, was that "*he could take a punch*."[1] The consequence of Ali's willingness to take punches has been, since his retirement from the ring, a decades-long struggle with the symptoms of Parkinson's Syndrome. The symptoms, including a tremor and slurred speech, can be attributed to years of damage to the brain from sports like boxing. Dr. Dennis Cope, Ali's physician in the 1980s, differentiated the champ's condition from brain injuries that lead to mental deterioration, noting that,

> From the tests that we've done we have established that it's not punch-drunk syndrome—there's no evidence of deterioration of his ability to think. Although Ali moves slowly today and is virtually unable to speak, he is, by his own account, at peace with his life and the choices he made over the years.[2]

When asked in 1988 if he had regrets about having pursued boxing, a sport that very likely contributed to his disease, he told *New York Times* writer Peter Tauber:

> Over two million people have it. They weren't all boxers. If you told me I could go back in my life and start over healthy and that with boxing this would happen—stay Cassius Clay and it wouldn't—I'd take this route. It was worth it.[3]

Throughout his life, Ali made choices and was never shy about telling the world what he was doing and why. That he expressed no regrets about those choices speaks to their sincerity, whatever the price.

Parkinson's Syndrome generally affects people over the age of sixty, making Ali's diagnosis all the more dramatic because he was still a relatively young man and his startling accomplishments in his twenties were still fresh in the public's mind. The disease causes symptoms such as tremors, stiffness, and a loss of balance.[4] In Ali's case, his loss of the ability to speak clearly and with sufficient volume to be heard from more than a few inches away is a particularly tragic irony. The "Louisville Lip" is now barely able to communicate, except through gestures and writing.

Boxing in the twenty-first century has considerably less of the luster of the Ali years, when fans hung on his every word as well as every punch. Boxing is still a sport, but the athletic and entertainment niche it once occupied has been contested by new sports such as mixed martial arts and the resurgence of professional wrestling. The WWF, the "World Wrestling Federation" whose name sounded almost like a sports league, has been transformed into the WWE, the "World Wrestling Entertainment," a glitzy conglomerate that promises drama, heroes, villains, and controlled outcomes without the stigma of the "fix." Ali had learned the craft of hype from professional wrestler Gorgeous George, and today's wrestling entertainers have taken that craft to a heightened level of absurdity that has made the WWE a lucrative entertainment powerhouse.

Throughout his career, Ali focused almost to the point of obsession on earning significant amounts of money in the ring. He cited family obligations, alimony payments, and contributions to charity as reasons for demanding lucrative paydays, and he also supported a sizeable entourage of hangers-on whose bills he paid at his training camp and wherever he traveled. From Bundini Brown to members of the Nation of Islam who traveled with him, to attorney Spiros Anthony who is said to have absconded with more than $3,000,000, people took unfair advantage of Ali's generous spirit. Associate Gene Dibble told Thomas Hauser:

> It didn't take a genius to hustle Ali. In the ring, he might have been the smartest man ever. But when it came to money and knowing who to trust, his decisions weren't very smart. I've never seen a man who made so much money, tried to make so much money, and at the same time had such tremendous disregard for money. I've just never met anyone like that. I hated the way people stole from him. I'd say, "Ali, if you don't care about yourself, think about your children. These people are stealing from your kids." But it went on and on forever.[5]

One of the most dramatic examples of the exploitation of Ali and his good name occurred in early 1981. Ross Fields, alias Harold Smith, created Muhammad Ali Amateur Sports (MAAS) and Muhammad Ali Professional Sports (MAPS) to promote boxing at both the amateur and professional levels. In return for the use of his name, Ali was promised both fees for his appearances and 25 percent of the net profits from the events sponsored by the two organizations. Smith promoted events and paid fighters, but he also manipulated the bank accounts associated with the Ali organizations, stealing $21,305,000 from the Wells Fargo Bank of California. Ali was cleared of involvement in the bank scandal, but Smith was happy to share blame for the embezzlement:

> The people in the bank felt that by getting involved with Ali through me that Ali could do something for them later. I could never have gotten that money from the bank without Muhammad Ali's name. And if you think what I did was wrong; well, I'm not going to tell you that I wasn't guilty of something, but look at all the savings and loan institutions. They've been ripped off for billions of dollars—not millions, billions—and none of them white guys is gonna do one day in jail. My situation was the same sort of thing, but I'm a nigger and I got caught being involved with the wrong people.[6]

It soon became clear that Smith had used Ali and his name. When the scandal broke, Ali commented that, "A guy used my name to embezzle $21,000,000. Ain't many names that can steal that much."[7] He was innocent, if gullible, and Smith went to jail for five years for his crime.

Many people used Ali's image and his voice for profit. They were not always called to account for these exploitive actions, and Dave Kindred, an expert on the relationship between Ali and Howard Cosell, one of the champ's few supporters among media reporters and commenters, observed:

> Nobody steps up and says, "Yeah, I hustled Ali." Nobody admits they exploited him and screwed him over. But that's what happens. They act like Ali has an infinite number of lives and skins, and anyone can take what they want and it won't matter. But it does matter. It takes a toll, and it's a tragedy.[8]

Ali chose toward the end of his career to use his image to sell a variety of commercial products. He exercised some control over that image, just as he had controlled the hype of his younger days. In 1978, the now-defunct Gino's hamburger restaurant chain founded by football players Gino Marchetti, Johnny Unitas, and Ordell Braase hired Ali to tape a commercial announcing the return of the "Gino's Giant" burger. In the 1970s, Gino's was the original outlet for Kentucky Fried Chicken, and the chain was the first to feature the triple-decker hamburger that Ali pitched. Eventually, the chain was absorbed by Roy Rogers, part of the Marriott food empire, but Ali was in the company of personalities like Soupy Sales and Dom Delouise as a Gino's spokesperson.[9] Later, a national Pizza Hut commercial featured trainer Angelo Dundee trying to give advice to a young (white) fighter who demanded, "What do you know about boxing?" The trainer and his fighter leave the ring for a local Pizza Hut, where a delicious pizza appears out of nowhere, courtesy of a smiling Muhammad Ali at a neighboring table. Corny or inspiring, the scene of the commercial, with its old-fashioned ring in black and white, was a throwback to images of boxing's golden age.[10]

In 1980, fight fans and the general public saw Ali in a television commercial for D-Con, a product used to kill roaches and mice in homes. The print ad that accompanied the commercial in many magazines featured Ali's portrait and signature over the slogan "d-con four/gone. Knocks out bugs in a whole room." On television, the champ hit the heavy bag with enthusiasm and then shouted to the camera, "I don't want you livin' wit' roaches." His image also appeared on the product label on the box of roach traps.[11] This was a popular commercial that capitalized on Ali's reputation as a hard-hitting fighter and fast-talking sports figure. But fans could detect a slurring and slight lack of clarity in the champ's speech. Nevertheless, the commercial entertained audiences for two seasons.

Footage of Ali in his prime shouting "I am the greatest!" appears in a 2014 commercial for Dr. Pepper. The theme of the ad, which was featured around Memorial Day as a tribute to the American people, is the idea that Americans are "one of a kind," just like the soda.[12] The champ also appeared in a British commercial for Unigate milk products and a 1976 commercial for a Muhammad Ali toy that could easily beat up its rivals. Early footage of a young Ali shadowboxing appears in an Apple computer commercial, "Think Different," and the retired slugger also sang the praises of Motocraft car replacement parts, among other products. Even as a retired boxer, Ali remained in the public eye, if only during commercial breaks. In 1993, the Associated Press reported that Ali was tied with Babe Ruth as the most recognized athlete, out of over 800 dead or living athletes, in America. The study conducted by Nye Lavalle's Sports Marketing Group found that over 97 percent of Americans, over twelve years of age, identified both Ali and Ruth.[13]

In an incident that took place in the late 1970s, Ali became a public figure against his will, and he responded by going to court to protect his privacy. According to Ali's complaint in the Southern District of New York, *Playgirl* magazine had published

> an impressionistic caricature of a nude African-American man seated on a stool in the corner of a boxing ring with both hands taped and outstretched resting on the ropes on either side.

The former champ asked for an injunction against distribution of the issue of the magazine on the grounds that his common law right of publicity had been infringed upon and also that the publication had violated New York State's privacy law. He sought monetary damages because of the harm to his reputation and the resulting economic losses. Ali maintained that this incident was particularly damaging because he had worked hard to establish a "commercially valuable propriety interest in his likeness and reputation." Ali felt he was entitled to legal remedy because Section 51 of New York State's Civil Rights Law provided that any person

> whose name, portrait or picture is used within this state for ... the purposes of trade without the written consent [of that person] may maintain an equitable action ... against the person, firm or corporation so using his name, portrait or picture, to prevent and restrain the use thereof; and may also sue and recover damages for any injury sustained by reason of such use.[14]

The court found that the image resembled Ali, even though it was captioned "Mystery Man" and that the poem that accompanied the picture referred to the fighter as "The Greatest" and was written in Ali's now-famous doggerel style. The court further held that the image was art rather than news and that the former heavyweight champion had the right to protect his likeness and unique "poetic" style. In response to the suit, *Playgirl* argued that Ali was a public figure who actively sought to remain in the public eye. In his opinion, Judge Joseph Gagliardi observed that:

> Even a cursory inspection of the picture which is the subject of this action strongly suggests that the facial characteristics of the black male portrayed are those of Muhammad Ali. The cheekbones, broad nose and wideset brown eyes, together with the distinctive smile and close cropped black hair are recognizable as the features of the plaintiff, one of the most widely known athletes of our time. In addition, the figure depicted is seated on a stool in the corner of a boxing ring with both hands taped and outstretched resting on the ropes on either side. Although the picture is captioned "Mystery Man," the identification of the individual as Ali is further implied by an accompanying verse which refers to the figure as "the Greatest". This court may take judicial notice that plaintiff Ali has regularly claimed that appellation for himself and that his efforts to identify himself in the public mind as "the Greatest" have been so successful that he is regularly identified as such in the news media.[15]

The court ruled in Ali's favor. This ruling transcended Ali's particular complaint in that it helped to expand the definition of identity to include physical characteristics that may qualify for legal protection.[16]

Even before his final retirement from the ring, Ali began to exhibit the effects of having taken too many punches. In early 1980, the champ was contemplating a return to the ring to fight John Tate for the WBA heavyweight title for the purpose of earning the heavyweight crown for a record fourth time and earning a purse of $6,000,000. But in a moment of caution about his health and the damage he might suffer from another fight, he told a Las Vegas audience, "I don't want to end up like Joe Louis." Louis, who happened to be in the audience to hear this remark, had suffered a stroke and was earning a meager livelihood serving as a greeter at a local casino. Ferdie Pacheco, Ali's former doctor, shared his caution, having urged the champ to hang up his gloves as early as 1976. He told *Sports Illustrated*, "Ali should never, never fight again. If he keeps putting new endings on his story, one of them is going to be tragic."[17]

Ali did not fight John Tate in 1980. Instead, he lost a WBC title fight to Larry Holmes on October 2 and his last fight to Trevor Berbick on December 11, 1981. Throughout the early 1980s, his speech continued to slur, and his voice grew raspier. In 1984, Ali was diagnosed with Parkinson's Syndrome. He was only forty-two years old. Ali's struggle with the deterioration of his body reflects the struggles of his second career. Joyce Carol Oates has even described him in Shakespearean terms:

> Where in his feckless youth Ali was a dazzling figure combining, say, the brashness of Hotspur and the insouciance of Lear's Fool, he became in these dark, brooding, increasingly willed fights the closest analogue boxing contains to Lear himself; or, rather, since there is no great fight without two great boxers, the title matches Ali–Frazier I (which Frazier won by a decision) and Ali-Frazier III (which Ali won, just barely, when Frazier virtually collapsed after the fourteenth round) are boxing's analogues to *King Lear*—ordeals of unfathomable human courage and resilience raised to the level of classic tragedy. These somber and terrifying boxing matches make us weep for their very futility; we seem to be in the presence of human experience too profound to be named— beyond the strategies and diminishments of language. The mystic's dark night of the soul, transmogrified as a brutal meditation of the body.[18]

Perhaps because of his illness and the strength he exhibits today as a public figure, perhaps because his stand against the Vietnam War and the military draft falls clearly within the mainstream of public opinion today, and perhaps because many people have chosen to ignore or forget his affiliation with the Nation of Islam and its separatist ideology, Ali today is characterized as a true man of the people. His boxing victories long past but captured on film and video, Ali today is frequently praised for his humanitarian work and his courage in the face of his disease. For example, heavyweight boxer turned minister Earnie Shavers praised Ali's faith and his positive influence on many people when he observed that he and Ali

> are of different religions. I'm a born-again Christian. But both of us believe in God, and we both have peace in our hearts. I preach all over the world these days. People know me on every continent because I fought Muhammad Ali. They open their hearts to me because of him. And that's why I say, most of what I am today I owe to God, but I also owe a lot to Ali. I'll never forget his kindness to me. The man has such a big heart. He just wants to help everybody. And seeing how he is today, his health, it kind of hurts me. But wherever I go, wherever I speak, I ask people to pray for Ali.[19]

Other boxers also credited their experience of fighting Ali as formative in their careers, even when they lost. Both George Chuvalo and Jean-Pierre Coopman gained fame and respect in Canada and Belgium respectively because they had competed in the ring with Ali.[20]

Twenty-first-century writing about Muhammad Ali that focuses on him as a courageous humanitarian paints a picture, not of the young braggart whose immaturity nearly obscured his boxing prowess, but of an elder statesman of sports who now devoted his remaining energy to helping others.

Writing in 2002 as Ali turned sixty, Jack Newfield observed that Ali's status as an elder statesman, not just of the sport of boxing but of the world has, in fact, been enhanced by the public's realization of his infirmity:

> The once-reviled Cassius Clay has come to be perceived as America's Buddha, our Dalai Lama, who personified peace and harmony. Ali at 60 is the most famous face on the planet, and probably the most loved person, if a democratic election were held that included Africa, the Islamic world, America and Vietnam. His trembling hands and muted speech from Parkinson's disease only make him seem more revered, vulnerable, and heroic; he is not afraid to display his impairment to the world. He has a serenity that allows him not to hide.[21]

One reason that Ali's image has softened, so to speak, in his old age is that writers now focus less on his Nation of Islam affiliation than in previous decades when black separatism and Black Muslims were terms that conjured up images of danger and violence. Since 1975, Ali has practiced a more inclusive version of Sunni Islam. He prays daily and maintains Islam's dietary practices but, like everything else about Ali, his religious identity is very much his own, and he is at peace with his religious choices. Even in the prime of his career, Ali's relationship to Islam, according to Jack Newfield, was never a matter of strict observance:

> He never obeyed all its practices. He was promiscuous with women. He kept the White Angelo Dundee as his trainer, Ferdie Pacheco as his doctor and Bundini Brown as his camp cheerleader, even though Bundini was a black Jew who chased white women. Ali never displayed any hostility toward white people. He dumped Don King as his promoter in 1976 for Bob Arum, a Jew from Brooklyn. It is possible that his religious conversion was initially more of a social awakening, his way of asserting black pride and solidarity.

Indeed, in a moment of humor and candor, Ali told Newfield that he became a devout Muslim only in the 1980s, "when my career was over, and miniskirts went out of style."[22]

The Muhammad Ali Center, a museum and cultural center that includes exhibits on the champ's life and serves as a home for public programs in the Louisville community, opened to much fanfare in 2005. Located on North 6th Street in Louisville's "Museum Row," the Center promotes Ali's Six "Core Principles": Confidence (belief in oneself, one's abilities, and one's future); Conviction (a firm belief that gives one the courage to stand behind that belief, despite pressure to do otherwise); Dedication (the act of devoting all of one's energy, effort, and abilities to a certain task); Giving (to present voluntarily without expecting something in return); Respect (esteem for, or a sense of the worth or excellence of, oneself and others); and Spirituality (a sense of awe, reverence, and inner peace inspired by a connection to all of creation and/or that which is greater than oneself).[23] The Center serves as a source of information about Ali's life and career and as a venue for a variety of community activities. Ali and his wife, Lonnie, have brought his instinct to help others back home to Louisville.

Another sign that Ali's reputation has transcended boxing is the presence of the Muhammad Ali Institute for Peace and Justice at the University of Louisville. The Institute sponsors student and faculty research as well as initiatives that

> support human dignity, foster responsible citizenship, further peace and justice and address the impact of violence in local, state, national and international arenas. The Ali Institute has a special concern for young people living with violence in urban areas; therefore, we seek to equip the young and those working with them to be agents of peace and justice in their communities.[24]

The Institute supports an educational media campaign related to issues of violence in urban areas; a two-year Ali Scholars Program for University of Louisville undergraduates; programming on campus; service initiatives; and a faculty-in-residence program for visiting scholars.

Ali's recent reputation centers on his humanitarian efforts, his ecumenical approach to race and ethnicity, and his life as a Parkinson's Syndrome survivor. Three examples help to illustrate the range of Ali's activities in recent decades. In 1997, Ali traveled to the Ivory Coast (Cote d'Ivoire) in response to a request from Sister Sponsa Beltran, who was caring for more than one hundred Liberian refugee children who had been driven from their country by a seven-year civil war. To the nun's surprise, Ali arrived with toys, food, and gifts for the children. Although his voice was muted, he shook hands and spoke quietly with the children. His presence provided cheer in a cheerless situation.[25]

The champ's relationship with his trainer, Angelo Dundee, who was born Angelo Mirena, was the stuff of legend. The trainer, twenty years Ali's senior, was one of the few people who knew how to "handle" the champ, and he usually did so by leaving him alone, with only a few suggestions as to how to approach an opponent. Their long relationship inspired the National Italian American Foundation to present both Ali and Dundee with the "One America" award in support of the Foundation's efforts on behalf of racial and ethnic cooperation.

In 1996, Ali visited Cuba with the Foundation for Education and Disarmament, bringing medicine for sufferers of Parkinson's disease. Although this was just a small gesture, it was Ali's hope that his donation would help to pave the way for greater understanding and cooperation between the United States and Cuba. These examples are only a few illustrations of Ali's inclination to help others, especially children, with his presence as well as his money. Throughout his career, Ali performed numerous acts of kindness that he asked the press not to report. Even as recently as 2014, Ali was lauded in his hometown newspaper, the Louisville *Courier-Journal*, for the inspiration he provided to a young woman dying of cancer:

> When dying cancer patient Jill Brzezinski-Conley met Muhammad Ali this week, they embraced tearfully, held hands, and shared the unspoken bond of two fighters —both betrayed by their bodies but strong in spirit. It didn't matter that the 72-year-old boxing great, largely silenced by Parkinson's disease, never said a word. "Even without saying anything, looking in my eyes he said everything . . . He jumped right in my heart and my soul," said Jill Conley, whose journey with incurable breast cancer is being chronicled by *The Courier-Journal* and USA TODAY. "It was one of the greatest moments of my life and one I will never forget."[26]

Ali's silence and his gentle demeanor speak to his current status as a humanitarian rather than as the Greatest of All Time in the ring.

As the twentieth century drew to a close, most Americans had lost sight of Muhammad Ali, but he re-appeared at the Summer Olympic Games in Atlanta.

On July 19, 1996, 11,000 Olympic athletes from 197 countries gathered for the lighting of the cauldron with the torch that had traveled 15,000 miles throughout the world in anticipation of the opening of the Games. Olympic gold medalist and then-heavyweight champion Evander Holyfield took the Olympic torch and began a lap around the stadium. He was joined by Greek hurdler Voula Patoulidou a former gold medal winner in the 100-meter event. They then handed the torch to American swimmer Janet Evans. The crowd was completely surprised to see Evans hand the torch to Muhammad Ali, the gold medal winner from 1960. Ali kindled a fuse that lit a fire that was pulled above the cauldron to light the flame that officially opened the Olympics. Ali appeared frail, and his hands shook, but he was definitely the main attraction at the 1996 opening ceremonies. Mychal Denzel Smith described the impact of his appearance: "His trembling hands and muted speech from Parkinson's disease only make him seem more revered, vulnerable and heroic; he is not afraid to display his impairment to the world. He has a serenity that allows him not to hide."[27]

The image of a frail man regarded by many as the "Greatest of All Time" inspired Congress to consider the absence of safety precautions in professional boxing. Unlike many other professional sports, boxing does not have a centralized regulatory body or even standard rules that apply throughout the country. For reasons of tradition or vanity, for example, boxers in the professional ring do not wear the protective head gear that is required of Golden

Gloves and Olympic boxers. With the Professional Boxing Safety Act of 1996, Congress provided minimum safety precautions such as a required physical examination for all boxers and the presence of an ambulance at all fighting venues. Inspired by Ali's physical deterioration that was clearly a result of his profession and the common exploitation of fighters by unscrupulous promoters, the rigging of matches, and the creation of false ratings, the 106th Congress passed the Muhammad Ali Boxing Reform Act on May 26, 2000 as an amendment to the 1996 legislation. The purpose of the law was to promote safety and protect the contractual rights of boxers and to regulate an industry that had no league structure or other oversight beyond state boxing commissions. Nevertheless, effective regulation of boxing still relied on the active oversight of state boxing commissions. Writing in the *New York Law Journal* ten years after the enactment of the Ali Act, Bruce J. Zabarauskas observed that the law provides

> some degree of uniformity of boxing laws across the nation by addressing the most perceived abuses of boxers, who unlike other athletes do not have a bargaining organization to address their interests. However, the Ali Act recognizes the need for local regulation of boxing as well. Thus, the Ali Act relies upon the athletic and boxing commissions of each state to address the specific details relating to each professional boxing match.[28]

Although the Muhammad Ali Boxing Reform Act was a step toward greater safety and protections for fighters from coercive or illegal practices, it suffered from a lack of genuine enforcement mechanisms at the federal level, leaving enforcement to the states. Nevertheless, the law is considered a tribute to Ali and part of his legacy. The law was even invoked by supporters of the new sport of mixed martial arts as potentially helpful in establishing greater organization and protection for fighters in a violent and minimally regulated commercial fighting enterprise.[29]

Throughout his long career, Muhammad Ai engaged in a constantly evolving process of reinvention. He created his personal image, his Muslim identity, his conviction that he would not go to war because he "had no quarrel with them Viet Cong," and his revered status as a humanitarian and stoic Parkinson's survivor, and, of course, his unorthodox style in the ring. Ali was aware of his influence on others, especially with regard to his position on the Vietnam War. He told *Black Scholar* magazine in 1970:

> When I didn't go to Vietnam, I was by myself, almost. Now everybody is against it. Right? I wasn't wrong then. I used to always say: "I'm pretty." "I'm beautiful." And now all the black folk have signs saying "black is beautiful." They're just getting around to seeing it.[30]

Ali energized the fight game, brought excitement to boxing, and gave fans a good reason to see him in person or on closed-circuit television. In 1989, Gary Smith asked in *Sports Illustrated*:

> Who else elevated an audience . . .? When Joe Frazier beat Ali in 1971, the thousands of closed-circuit viewers around me applauded or jeered for a few moments and then went their separate ways. But each time Ali won, people laughed and hugged, there was a communion.

And Smith offered a summary of his view of Ali's career: "No other athlete has so commanded our attention. And the careers of few have been so varied, so complex and so little tainted by hypocrisy."[31]

Today, Muhammad Ali lives quietly in Arizona, with his fourth wife, Lonnie. The image on the cover of the June, 2014 issue of the *AARP Bulletin* shows the champ with his eyes closed in his wife's embrace. The article inside focuses on his battle with a debilitating illness and the daily care he requires. Readers gained insight into the daily life of a man who once moved with lightning speed but now lives in a body that can best be described as "frozen." Lonnie Ali described this struggle in familiar language that was used to describe the earlier struggles in his life:

> This is the beauty of Muhammad. He has made this illness, as horrible as it is, as much as it has taken away from him, serve him in some way. If there was ever anyone who always lands on his feet, and comes out smelling like a rose, it is Muhammad. It is his remarkable attitude toward life. He has never let anything stand in his way.[32]

The life of Muhammad Ali, a man who reinvented himself as his world and the circumstances in which he found himself required, is best summarized by Jack Newfield:

> The moral of his imperfect life remains: redemption through suffering, emancipation through courage, vindication through adherence to principle. Whenever he got knocked down, he got up, which is the best any of us can do.[33]

There was never a fighter who did it better than Muhammad Ali, the Greatest of All Time. Whether armed with a bombastic pre-fight speech, a crisp right cross, or the deep conviction of his beliefs, he spoke his mind. And he truly was the greatest.

Notes

1 Joyce Carol Oates, "The Cruelest Sport," *The New York Review of Books* (February 13, 1992), http://www.nybooks.com/articles/archives/1992/feb/13/the-cruelest-sport/?page=2.

2 Peter Tauber, "Ali: Still Magic," *New York Times* (July 17, 1988), http://www.nytimes.com/books/98/10/25/specials/ali-magic.html.

3 Ibid.

4 According to Dr. Howard Hurtig, an expert on Parkinson's disease at the University of Pennsylvania, "Does he [Ali] have 'traumatic parkinsonism' (my term) from repeated blows to the head during his boxing career or does he have coincidental, regular PD, like millions of others? No one knows. There is a syndrome known as 'dementia pugilistica' that has been known for decades to afflict boxers, producing a clinical picture of Alzheimer's disease with Parkinson features. My guess is that many of the damaged professional football players emerging from the shadows will have parkinsonian features. There is a growing body of medical literature on the neuropathological changes in the brains of traumatized ball players and boxers—quite similar to what is seen in Alzheimer brains."

5 Thomas Hauser, *Muhammad Ali: His Life and Times* (New York: Simon & Schuster, 1991), pp. 372–3.

6 Ibid., p. 424.

7 *Parade* Magazine (April 5, 1981) in ibid., pp. 424–5.

8 Ibid, p. 439.

9 "Gino's Burgers are Making a Comeback," *Baltimore Sun* (January 2, 2010), http://weblogs.baltimoresun.com/entertainment/dining/reviews/blog/2010/01/ginos_burgers_are_making_a_com.html; "A History of Gino's Hamburgers," http://ginoshamburgers.homestead.com/GinosHamburgersHistory.htm.

10 http://boxing-ring.blogspot.com/2012/02/muhammad-ali-angelo-dundee-pizza-hut.html.

11 "Muhammad Ali in Iconic d-Con Roach Commercial, 1980," http://www.fightsaga.com/tidbits/Bizarre/item/3531-Muhammad-Ali-in-iconic-d-CON-Roach-commercial-1980-(Video).

12 http://adland.tv/commercials/dr-pepper-one-3178-million-1-americans-2014-30-usa.

13 "Muhammad Ali," http://ossports.homestead.com/MuhammadAli/MuhammadAli.html.

14 *ALI v. PLAYGIRL, INC.*, NO. 78 CIV. 445.447 F.Supp. 723 (1978) and Andres F. Quintana, "Muhammad Ali: The Greatest in Court," *Marquette Sports Law Review* Vol. 18, Issue 1 (Fall, 2007), p. 199.

15 *ALI v. PLAYGIRL, INC.* 447 F. Supp. 723 (1978), http://www.leagle.com/decision/19781170447FSupp723_11068.xml/ALI%20v.%20PLAYGIRL,%20INC.

16 Quintana, "Muhammad Ali: The Greatest in Court," pp. 200–1.

17 Jerry Kirshenbaum, ed., "Scorecard," *Sports Illustrated* (March 10, 1980), http://www.si.com/vault/1980/03/10/824446/scorecard.

18 Oates, "The Cruelest Sport."

19 Hauser, *Muhammad Ali: His Life and Times*, pp. 347–8.

20 John C. Walter, "Muhammad Ali, Exemplar to the World," http://www.americansc.org.uk/online/Ali.htm, p. 7.

21 Jack Newfield, "The Meaning of Muhammad," *The Nation* (February 4, 2002), http://www.thenation.com/article/meaning-muhammad.

22 Ibid.

23 Muhammad Ali Center, http://www.alicenter.org/muhammad-ali#Six_Core_Principles.

24 The Muhammad Ali Institute for Peace and Justice, http://louisville.edu/aliinstitute/about-us.

25 "Muhammad Delivers Aid to Liberian Refugees," *Associated Press* (August 20, 1997), http://www.apnewsarchive.com/1997/Muhammad-Ali-delivers-aid-to-Liberian-refugees/id-8b230c6b31cefd5851ab22645be0f62c.

26 "Cancer Patient Jill Conley meets Muhammad Ali," *USA Today* (October 30, 2014), http://www.usatoday.com/story/sports/boxing/2014/10/30/breast-cancer-patient-meets-muhammad-ali/18187847/.

27 Rick Weinberg, "Ali Lights the Flame at the 1996 Olympics," ESPN, http://sports.espn.go.com/espn/espn25/story?page=moments/8; Mychal Denzel Smith, "The Meaning of Muhammad," *The Nation* (January 17, 2002).

28 Bruce J. Zabarauskas, "The Regulation of Professional Boxing in New York," New *York Law Journal* Vol. 243, No. 23 (February 4, 2010), http://www.tklaw.com/files/Publication/ff079023-6589-4533-bfaa-a328ce9c2883/Presentation/PublicationAttachment/0a687b59-bc8a-45cf-901e-b126643155d6/The-Regulation-of-Professional-Boxing-in-New-York.pdf.

29 "1996 Professional Boxing Safety Act," https://www.ncdps.gov/index2.cfm?a=000003,000005, 000009,000132,000133; Trent Cooke, "How the Muhammad Ali Boxing Reform Act Changed Professional Boxing," *FightMatch* (March 17, 2013), http://fitz101.com/how-the-muhammad-ali-boxing-reform-act-changed-professional-fighting/; "Muhammad Ali Boxing Reform Act," https://www.govtrack.us/congress/bills/106/hr1832/text; "Fighting for Respect: MMA's Struggle for Acceptance and How the Muhammad Ali Act Would Give it a Sporting Chance," *West Virginia Law Review* Vol. 112 (2009), pp. 287–95.

30 "*The Black Scholar* Interviews Muhammad Ali," *The Black Scholar* Vol. 1, No. 8 (June 1970), http://www.jstor.org/discover/10.2307/41206252?uid=3739832&uid=2129&uid=2&uid=70&uid=4&uid=3739256&sid=21104775927487.

31 Gary Smith, "A Celebration of Muhammad Ali," *Sports Illustrated* (November 15, 1989).

32 Jon Saraceno, "Caring for The Champ," *AARP Bulletin* Vol. 55, No. 5 (June, 2014), pp. 10–14.

33 Newfield, "The Meaning of Muhammad."

PART **II**

DOCUMENTS

WRITERS (AND ALI) ON MUHAMMAD ALI

Throughout his long career in and out of the ring, Muhammad Ali has had a lot to say. Interestingly, many writers focused on Ali's words as well as his prowess as a boxer. We can follow the trajectory of his career as a young fighter, a world champion, a member of the Nation of Islam, a draft resister, and a retired survivor of a debilitating disease through the words of others and, of course, Ali himself.

––––––––––––

Dick Schaap on the young Cassius Clay in 1960: On a ride uptown in Manhattan a few days before the Rome Olympics, "Cassius monopolized the conversation. I forget his exact words, but I remember the message: 'I'm great, I'm beautiful, I'm going to Rome and I'm gonna whip all those cats and then I'm coming back and turning pro and becoming the champion of the world.' I'd never heard an athlete like him; he had no doubts, no fears, no second thoughts, not an ounce of false humility . . . He was, even then, an original, so outrageously bold he was funny. We all laughed at him, and he didn't mind the laughter, but rode with it, using it to feed his ego, to nourish his self-image."

Dick Schaap, "From Louisville to the Nation of Islam: My Ups and Downs with Ali," *Sport Magazine* (1971) reprinted in http://thestacks.deadspin.com/ from-louisville-to-the-nation-of-islam-my-ups-and-down-1428081378.

***Sports Illustrated* writer Huston Horn commented on Cassius Clay's first string of professional fights in 1960 and 1961:** "Cassius has, in fact, fought only eight times professionally, and in every case his opponents were chosen not because they would draw a big crowd but because it could be reasonably concluded in advance that they would either keel over or succumb to the blind staggers after a few rounds with the boy wonder. So far the has-beens or never-weres he has fought have accommodated Clay's matchmakers."

Huston Horn, "'Who Made Me—is Me!'" *Sports Illustrated* (September 25, 1961).

TIME magazine in a sarcastic comment in 1963 on Clay's "greatness": "Cassius Clay is Hercules, struggling through the twelve labors. He is Jason, chasing the Golden Fleece. He is Galahad, Cyrano, D'Artagnan. When he scowls, strong men shudder, when he smiles, women swoon. The mysteries of the universe are his Tinker Toys. He rattles thunder and looses the lightning." "Sport: The Dream," *TIME* magazine (March 22, 1963).

Many observers felt that Clay was an immature young man whose main motive for agreeing to fight Sonny Liston was the money he would make: "Ruing the day, the many from Cassius Clay's Louisville Sponsoring Group chewed his lip while the boxer with the florid signature and the rococo personality signed on the dotted line. 'We did not want this fight so soon,' the man said, 'but Cassius insisted and we had to give in. After all, wise or unwise, it's his decision and his career.' Far removed from such morbidity, the irrepressible Clay slapped down the pen in a Denver hotel last week after agreeing to fight Sony Liston for the world heavyweight championship next February. 'Somebody pinch me,' he exulted while visions of dollar signs danced before his big brown eyes. 'If I'm not asleep, this is a dream come true.' . . . Clay may be wise to go ahead with the fight now. His acute business instinct tells him that his name has been in decline since his bout with Henry Cooper last June. And his image has become like emery paper: it sparkles a little and grates a lot."

Huston Horn, "A Rueful Dream Come True," *Sports Illustrated* (November 18, 1963).

A month before Clay announced his membership in the Nation of Islam, Dick Schaap broke the story of the young contender's affiliation: "The brash young boxer, who celebrated his 22d birthday last week, may not be a card-carrying Muslim. But, unquestionably, he sympathizes with Muslim aims and, by his presence at their meetings, lends them prestige. He is the first nationally famous Negro to take an active part in the Muslim movement . . . Clay's romance with the Muslims may be a fleeting thing, and it is unlikely to have any damaging effect on his career. It might even be beneficial for the gate of his Feb. 25 fight with Liston. Some spectators may be attracted by the hope of seeing Clay defeated, and Sonny Liston, of all people, will be cast in the strange role of hero."

Dick Schaap, "The Challenger and the Muslims," *Herald Tribune* (February 23, 1964).

Cassius Clay defended his religious conversion shortly after announcing his membership in the Nation of Islam: "I go to a Black Muslim meeting and what do I see? I see that there's no smoking and no drinking and their women wear dresses down to the floor. And then I come out on the street and you tell me I shouldn't go in there. Well, there must be something in there if you don't want me to go in there."

Robert Lipsyte, "Clay Discusses in Future, Liston and Black Muslims," *New York Times* (February 27, 1964).

Floyd Patterson on Ali's relationship with the Nation of Islam: "Clay is so young and has been so misled by the wrong people that he doesn't appreciate how far we have come and how much harm he has done by joining the Black Muslims. He might as well have joined the Ku Klux Klan." Floyd Patterson (with Milton Gross), "I Want to Destroy Clay," *Sports Illustrated* (October 19, 1964).

***Amsterdam News* columnist James L. Hicks on why Muhammad Ali was an "uppity Negro":** "Cassius's crowning insult to white people was to come when he started acting intelligent and letting white people know he had a mind of his own. That was simply too much and they began looking around for ways to 'get 'im.' Suddenly, there it was, The Army. What better vehicle to use to put an uppity Negro back in his place than the United States Army?"

James L. Hicks, "The 'Uppity' Negro," *Amsterdam News* (March 26, 1966).

***TIME* magazine commented on Ali's fall from boxing grace in 1966:** "There must be times when Cassius Clay wonders what in the name of Allah has happened to him. Just yesterday, he was 'the Greatest,' a carefree teenager who chatted amusingly about winning the heavyweight-championship of the world, condemned by Congressmen. He is the 'champion of the world,' but it is a smallish world of eleven states, the United Kingdom, Europe, Africa, and the Brotherhood of Black Muslims."

"Prizefighting: Speaking of Indignities," *TIME* magazine (April 8, 1966).

Ferde Pacheco (Ali's physician) expressed his views on the meaning of Ali's anti-draft stand in 1966: "We're getting back to the Korean War status, where the guy who goes into the Army is no longer a jerk but a man who's doing his duty and is to be applauded. Now comes Cassius saying he ain't got nothing against no Viet Congs. Had he come out a year ago with that, many people might have said, 'Well, another Clay witticism.' Now he says it and he sounds like a traitor. And then he compounds the problem by saying it's a white man's war when there's a lot of colored people over there dying."

Jack Olsen, "A Case of Conscience," *Sports Illustrated* (April 11, 1966).

Joe Louis said he would have "clobbered" Cassius Clay: "Cassius Clay's got lots of ability, but he's not The Greatest. He's a guy with a million dollars worth of confidence and a dime's worth of courage. In all honesty, I feel it in my bones. Clay can be clobbered, and if you'll pardon an old-timer talking, I am certain I know how . . .

Trouble with Clay, he thinks he knows it all. Fights with his mouth. He won't listen. Me, the first thing I learned in the fight game was to keep my trap shut and my ears wide open, especially when my wise old trainer, Chappie Blackburn, was telling me things for my own good."

Joe Louis, "How I Would Have Clobbered Clay, Part I," *Ring Magazine* (February, 1967).

Basketball star Bill Russell voiced his respect for Ali's stand against the draft: "I envy Muhammad Ali. He faces a possible five years in jail and he has been stripped of his heavyweight championship, but I still envy him. He has something I have never been able to attain and something very few people I know possess. He possesses an absolute and sincere faith."

Bill Russell with Tex Maule, "I Am not Worried About Ali," *Sports Illustrated* (June 19, 1967).

Trainer Angelo Dundee on the pressures Ali faced because of his stand on the draft: "After the Patterson fight [which Ali won by a technical knock-out in twelve rounds on November 22, 1965] the world changed for Ali. The pressures were bigger and the problems were bigger and it wasn't as easy for him to be relaxed and happy-go-lucky. His draft status and his beliefs and his stubborn refusal to compromise with anyone or anything cost him, although he wasn't alone in any of these things."

Angelo Dundee with Tex Maule, "He Could Go to Jail and Still be Champ," *Sports Illustrated* (August 28, 1967).

Muhammad Ali on his punishment for draft resistance as a test of his faith: "The Koran says you must be tested . . . God will try you. He tried Job and He tried Abraham and He tried Elijah Muhammad too. Elijah spent three years in prison during the war [for draft evasion] studying. If I was in jail tomorrow, I'd study and preach to the other prisoners. The loneliness and the confinement and the food, that would be a test. But a man who believes in a Supreme Being does not fear."

Tex Maule, "For Ali, A Time to Preach," *Sports Illustrated* (February 19, 1968).

Muhammad Ali to an audience of 750 students at New Jersey's Fairleigh Dickinson University during his suspension from boxing: "What if everyone went to Canada like the white boys? . . . I'm only following the law. I'm going to be a man and do it the legal way. If I lose I'll go to jail."

"Muhammad Ali at Fairleigh Dickinson," *Amsterdam News* (April 20, 1968).

TIME **magazine on the first Ali/Frazier "Fight of the Century":** "Whether it deserves that title, of course, will depend on what actually takes place in the ring. But at a time when public interest in boxing as a sport has fallen off, the Ali-Frazier match is unquestionably the fight of this year, if not the past ten. Certainly it has accumulated a record number of firsts and mosts. Never before have two undefeated professional heavyweight champions met: Frazier has 23 knockouts in 26 consecutive victories, Ali 25 KOs in 31 straight wins. Never before has the public been willing to spend so much to see two men whack away at each other in the ring."

"Sport: Bull v Butterfly: A Clash of Champions," *TIME* magazine (March 8, 1971).

Ali reflecting on his loss to Joe Frazier in the "Fight of the Century": "Fighting is more of a business now than the glory of who won. After all, when all the praise is over . . . when all the fanfare is done, all that counts is what you have to show for it. All the bleeding; the world still turns. I was so tired. I lost it. But I didn't shed one tear. I got to keep living. I'm not ashamed."

George Plimpton, "No Requiem for a Heavyweight," *Sports Illustrated* (April 5, 1971).

TIME **magazine on Ali's Loss to Leon Spinks in 1978:** "Through everything, Ali was a fighter. In his youth, when he psyched himself into manic pretentions and took the title from Sonny Liston, he was a dazzling, dancing fighter. In midcareer, when he willed his body through three epic bouts with Joe Frazier, he was a courageous fighter. Toward the end, when he paced his guttering resources to turn away muscular challengers like Ken Norton, he was a thinking fighter. Last week, he was an old fighter. He had to match the craft of his past against an opponent who seemed to have little more than youth, stamina—and courage—on his side."

"The Greatest is Gone," *TIME* magazine (February 27, 1978).

Writer Rick Telander on Ali in 1991: "Ali was the heavyweight champion of the world during some of the world's most turbulent times, and he stood onstage and spoke his mind. But he was not, as some people now claim, a leader or a role model or even a martyr. He was a man of incredible boxing skills and determination, blessed with verve and an intuitive understanding of life's unfairness. As a black man he spoke for minorities. As a war-hater, he spoke for many. But the public wouldn't have cared about him at all had he not been able to do one barbaric thing—knock men out."

Rick Telander, "Facing Facts About Ali: He Was Not the Greatest at Knowing When to Quit, Nor Were the Fans Who Blithely Cheered Him On," *Sports Illustrated* (July 1, 1991).

Richard Hoffer, writing ten years later: "Ali was something much more interesting, at least as far as history ought to be concerned. He was original, all self-invention. His rhymes, his rope-a-dope, his ability to transform turmoil into a carnival act—these were riffs on top of the bass line of his time. A fantastic jazz. They were of a piece: the verbal hijinks, the right hand to George Foreman's jaw, his induction stance, the one not more important than the other. That was his genius, and the historians who insist upon significance miss the point, Ali wasn't some social artifact; he was much rarer than that. Just one of a kind is all."

Richard Hoffer, "The Eternal Muhammad," *Sports Illustrated* (December 24, 2001).

Muhammad Ali's Draft Notice

Like many young men in the 1960s, Ali received a notice to appear for induction from his local Louisville, Kentucky draft board. The notice required him to appear for induction in Houston, Texas.

ORDER FOR TRANSFERRED MAN TO REPORT FOR INDUCTION

FROM: The President of the United States
TO: Mr. Cassius Marcellus Clay, Jr.
AKA Muhammad Ali
5962 Ardmore Street
Houston, Texas 77021

Greetings:

Having heretofore been ordered to report for induction by Local Board No. 47. State of Kentucky, Louisville, Kentucky, which is your Local Board of origin, and having been transferred upon your own request to Local Board No. 61, State of Texas, Houston, Texas, which is your Local Board of Transfer for delivery to an induction station, you will therefore report to the last named Local Board at 3rd Floor, 701 San Jacinto St., Houston, Texas 77022 on April 28, 1967, at 8:30 A.M.

Source

National Constitution Center.

"THE PASSION OF MUHAMMAD ALI," COVER OF *ESQUIRE* MAGAZINE, APRIL 1968

For the April, 1968 issue of *Esquire* magazine, designer George Lois wanted to pose Muhammad Ali as the martyred St. Sebastian. At first, Ali refused because St. Sebastian was a Roman soldier was was killed for having converted to Christianity. After much discussion, Lois was able to get the consent of Hon. Elijah Muhammad and Ali posed for the cover, which depicted him as a stoic martyr against the US government, which had convicted him of draft evasion. The cover was a huge success, and Ali won his case in the Supreme Court in 1971.

SOURCE

Courtesy of George Lois.

SUPREME COURT OPINION IN *CASSIUS CLAY ALSO KNOWN AS MUHAMMAD ALI V. UNITED STATES* (1971)

Ali appealed his conviction for draft evasion to the United States Supreme Court, which ruled in his favor on June 28, 1971.

Cassius Marsellus CLAY, Jr. also known as Muhammad Ali, Petitioner, v. UNITED STATES.

403 U.S. 698 (91 S.Ct. 2068, 29 L.Ed.2d 810)
Cassius Marsellus CLAY, Jr. also known as Muhammad Ali, Petitioner, v. UNITED STATES. No. 783.
Argued: April 19, 1971.
Decided: June 28, 1971.

- per_curiam
- concurrence, DOUGLAS
- concurrence, HARLAN

Chauncey Eskridge, Chicago, Ill., for petitioner.
Solicitor Gen. Erwin N. Griswold for respondent.

PER CURIAM.

The petitioner was convicted for willful refusal to submit to induction into the Armed Forces. 62 Stat. 622, as amended, 50 U.S.C. App. § 462(a). (1964 ed., Supp. V). The judgment of conviction was affirmed by the Court of

Appeals for the Fifth Circuit. 1 We granted certiorari, 400 U.S. 990, 91 S. Ct. 457, 27 L.Ed.2d 438 to consider whether the induction notice was invalid because grounded upon an erroneous denial of the petitioner's claim to be classified as a conscientious objector.

* The petitioner's application for classification as a conscientious objector was turned down by his local draft board, and he took an administrative appeal. The State Appeal Board tentatively classified him I—A (eligible for unrestricted military service) and referred his file to the Department of Justice for an advisory recommendation, in accordance with then-applicable procedures. 50 U.S.C.A. App. § 456(j) (1964 ed., Supp. V). The FBI then conducted an 'inquiry' as required by the statute, interviewing some 35 persons, including members of the petitioner's family and many of his friends, neighbors, and business and religious associates.

There followed a hearing on 'the character and good faith of the (petitioner's objections' before a hearing officer appointed by the Department. The hearing officer, a retired judge of many years' experience, 2 heard testimony from the petitioner's mother and father, from one of his attorneys, from a minister of his religion, and from the petitioner himself. He also had the benefit of a full report from the FBI. On the basis of this record the hearing officer concluded that the registrant was sincere in his objection on religious grounds to participation in war in any form, and he recommended that the conscientious objector claim be sustained. 3

Notwithstanding this recommendation, the Department of Justice wrote a letter to the Appeal Board, advising it that the petitioner's conscientious objector claim should be denied. Upon receipt of this letter of advice, the Board denied the petitioner's claim without a statement of reasons. After various further proceedings which it is not necessary to recount here, the petitioner was ordered to report for induction. He refused to take the traditional step forward, and this prosecution and conviction followed.

II

In order to qualify for classification as a conscientious objector, a registrant must satisfy three basic tests. He must show that he is conscientiously opposed to war in any form. Gillette v. United States, 401 U.S. 437, 91 S. Ct. 828, 28 L. Ed.2d 168. He must show that this opposition is based upon religious training and belief, as the term has been construed in our decisions. United States v. Seeger, 380 U.S. 163, 85 S. Ct. 850, 13 L.Ed.2d 733; Welsh v. United States, 398 U.S. 333, 90 S. Ct. 1792, 26 L.Ed.2d 308. And he must show that this objection is sincere. Witmer v. United States, 348 U.S. 375, 75 S. Ct. 392, 99 L. Ed. 428. In applying these tests, the Selective Service System must be concerned with the registrant as an individual, not with its own interpretation of the dogma of the religious sect, if any, to which he may belong. United States v. Seeger, supra; Gillette v. United States, supra; Williams v. United States, 5 Cir., 216 F.2d 350, 352.

In asking us to affirm the judgment of conviction, the Government argues that there was a 'basis in fact,' cf. Estep v. United States, 327 U.S. 114, 66 S. Ct. 423, 90 L. Ed. 567, for holding that the petitioner is not opposed to 'war in any form,' but is only selectively opposed to certain wars. See Gillette v. United States, supra. Counsel for the petitioner, needless to say, takes the opposite position. The issue is one that need not be resolved in this case. For we have concluded that even if the Government's position on this question is correct, the conviction before us must still be set aside for another quite independent reason.

III

The petitioner's criminal conviction stemmed from the Selective Service System's denial of his appeal seeking conscientious objector status. That denial, for which no reasons were ever given, was, as we have said, based on a recommendation of the Department of Justice, overruling its hearing officer and advising the Appeal Board that it 'finds that the registrant's conscientious-objector claim is not sustained and recommends to your Board that he be not (so) classified.' This finding was contained in a long letter of explanation, from which it is evident that Selective Service officials were led to believe that the Department had found that the petitioner had failed to satisfy each of the three basic tests for qualification as a conscientious objector.

As to the requirement that a registrant must be opposed to war in any form, the Department letter said that the petitioner's expressed beliefs 'do not appear to preclude military service in any form, but rather are limited to military service in the Armed Forces of the United States. * * * These constitute only objections to certain types of war in certain circumstances, rather than a general scruple against participation in war in any form. However, only a general scruple against participation in war in any form can support an exemption as a conscientious objector under the Act. United States v. Kauten, 2 Cir., 133 F.2d 703.'

As to the requirement that a registrant's opposition must be based upon religious training and belief, the Department letter said: 'It seems clear that the teachings of the Nation of Islam preclude fighting for the United States not because of objections to participation in war in any form but rather because of political and racial objections to policies of the United States as interpreted by Elijah Muhammad. * * * It is therefore our conclusion that registrant's claimed objections to participation in war insofar as they are based upon the teachings of the Nation of Islam, rest on grounds which primarily are political and racial.'

As to the requirement that a registrant's opposition to war must be sincere, that part of the letter began by stating that 'the registrant has not consistently manifested his conscientious-objector claim. Such a course of overt manifestations is requisite to establishing a subjective state of mind and belief.' There followed several paragraphs reciting the timing and circumstances of the petitioner's conscientious objector claim, and a concluding paragraph seeming to state a rule of law—that 'a registrant has not shown overt manifestations sufficient to establish his subjective belief where, as here, his conscientious-objector claim was not asserted until military service became imminent. Campbell v. United States, 4 Cir., 221 F.2d 454. United States v. Corliss, 280 F.2d 808, cert. denied, 364 U.S. 884, 81 S. Ct. 167, 5 L.Ed.2d 105.'

In this Court the Government has now fully conceded that the petitioner's beliefs are based upon 'religious training and belief,' as defined in United States v. Seeger, supra: 'There is no dispute that petitioner's professed beliefs were founded on basic tenets of the Muslim religion, as he understood them, and derived in substantial part from his devotion to Allah as the Supreme Being. Thus, under this Court's decision in United States v. Seeger, 380 U.S. 163, 85 S. Ct. 850, 13 L.Ed.2d 733, his claim unquestionably was within the 'religious training and belief' clause of the exemption provision.' 4 This concession is clearly correct. For the record shows that the petitioner's beliefs are founded on tenets of the Muslim religion as he understands them. They are surely no less religiously based than those of the three registrants before this Court in Seeger. See also Welsh v. United States, 398 U.S. 333, 90 S. Ct. 1792, 26 L.Ed.2d 308.

The Government in this Court has also made clear that it no longer questions the sincerity of the petitioner's beliefs. 5 This concession is also correct. The Department hearing officer—the only person at the administrative appeal level who carefully examined the petitioner and other witnesses in person and who had the benefit of the full FBI file—found 'that the registrant is sincere in his objection.' The Department of Justice was wrong in advising the Board in terms of a purported rule of law that it should disregard this finding simply because of the circumstances and timing of the petitioner's claim. See Ehlert v. United States, 402 U.S. 99, 103–104, 91 S. Ct. 1319, 1322–1323, 28 L. Ed. 625; United States ex rel. Lehman v. Laird, 4 Cir., 430 F.2d 96, 99; United States v. Abbott, 8 Cir., 425 F.2d 910, 915; United States ex rel. Tobias v. Laird, 4 Cir., 413 F.2d 936, 939–940; Cohen v. Laird, D.C., 315 F.Supp. 1265, 1277–1278.

Since the Appeal Board gave no reasons for its denial of the petitioner's claim, there is absolutely no way of knowing upon which of the three grounds offered in the Department's letter it relied. Yet the Government now acknowledges that two of those grounds were not valid. And, the Government's concession aside, it is indisputably clear, for the reasons stated, that the Department was simply wrong as a matter of law in advising that the petitioner's beliefs were not religiously based and were not sincerely held.

This case, therefore, falls squarely within the four coners of this Court's decision in Sicurella v. United States, 348 U.S. 385, 75 S. Ct. 403, 99 L. Ed. 436. There as here the Court was asked to hold that an error in an advice letter prepared by the Department of Justice did not require reversal of a criminal conviction because there was a ground on which the Appeal Board might properly have denied a conscientious objector classification. This Court refused to consider the proffered alternative ground:

'(W)e feel that this error of law by the Department, to which the Appeal Board might naturally look for guidance on such questions, must vitiate the entire proceedings at least where it is not clear that the Board relied on some legitimate ground. Here, where it is impossible to determine on exactly which grounds the Appeal Board decided, the integrity of the Selective Service System demands, at least, that the Government not recommend illegal grounds. There is an impressive body of lower court cases taking this position and we believe that they state the correct rule.' Di., at 392, 75 S. Ct., at 406.

The doctrine thus articulated 16 years ago in Sicurella was hardly new. It was long ago established as essential to the administration of criminal justice. Stromberg v. California, 283 U.S. 359, 51 S. Ct. 532, 75 L. Ed. 1117. In Stromberg the Court reversed a conviction for violation of a California statute containing three separate clauses, finding one of the three clauses constitutionally invalid. As Chief Justice Hughes put the matter, '(I)t is impossible to say under which clause of the statute the conviction was obtained.' Thus, 'if any of the clauses in question is invalid under the Federal Constitution, the conviction cannot be upheld.' Id., at 368, 51 S. Ct., at 535.

The application of this doctrine in the area of Selective Service law goes back at least to 1945, and Judge Learned Hand's opinion for the Second Circuit in United States ex rel. Levy v. Cain, 149 F.2d 338. It is a doctrine that has been consistently and repeatedly followed by the federal courts in dealing with the criminal sanctions of the selective service laws. See, e.g., United States v. Lemmens, 430 F.2d 619, 623–624 (CA7 1970); United States v. Broyles, 423 F.2d 1299, 1303–1304 (CA4 1970); United States v. Haughton, 413 F.2d 736 (CA9 1969); United States v. Jakobson, 325 F.2d 409, 416–417 (CA2 1963), aff'd sub nom. United States v. Seeger, 380 U.S. 163, 85 S.Ct. 850, 13 L.Ed.2d 733; Kretchet v. United States, 284 F.2d 561, 565–566 (CA9 1960); Ypparila v. United States, 219 F.2d 465, 469 (CA10 1954); United States v. Englander, 271 F. Supp. 182 (SDNY 1967); United States v. Erikson, 149 F. Supp. 576, 578–579 (SDNY 1957). In every one of the above cases the defendant was acquitted or the conviction set aside under the Sicurella application of the Stromberg doctrine.

The long established rule of law embodied in these settled precedents thus clearly requires that the judgment before us be reversed.

It is so ordered

Judgment reversed.

Mr. Justice MARSHALL took no part in the consideration or decision of this case.

Mr. Justice DOUGLAS, concurring.

I would reverse this judgment of conviction and set the petitioner free.

In Sicurella v. United States, 348 U.S. 385, 75 S. Ct. 403, 99 L. Ed. 436, 1 the wars that the applicant would fight were not 'carnal' but those 'in defense of Kingdom interest.' Id., at 389, 75 S.Ct., at 405. Since it was impossible to determine on exactly which ground the Appeal Board had based its decision, we reversed the decision sustaining the judgment of conviction. We said: 'It is difficult for us to believe that the Congress had in mind this type of activity when it said the thrust of conscientious objection must go to 'participation in war in any form.' Id., at 390, 75 S. Ct., at 405.

In the present case there is no line between 'carnal' was and 'spiritual' or symbolic wars.

Those who know the history of the Mediterranean littoral know that the jihad of the Moslem was a bloody war.

This case is very close in its essentials to Negre v. Larsen, 401 U.S. 437, 91 S.Ct. 828, decided March 8, 1971. The church to which that registrant belonged favored 'just' wars and provided guidelines to define them. The church did not oppose the war in Vietnam but the registrant refused to comply with an order to go to Vietnam because participating in that conflict would violate his conscience. The Court refused to grant him relief as a conscientious objector, overruling his constitutional claim.

The case of Clay is somewhat different, though analogous. While there are some bits of evidence showing conscientious objection to the Vietnam conflict, the basic objection was based on the teachings of his religion. He testified that he was 'sincere in every bit of what the Holy Qur'an and the teachings of the Honorable Elijah Muhammad tell us and it is that we are not to participate in wars on the side of nobody who—on the side of non believers, and this is a Christian country and this is not a Muslim country, and the Government and the history and the facts shows that every more toward the Honorable Elijah Muhammad is made to distort and is made to ridicule him and is made to condemn him and the Government has admitted that the police of Los Angeles were wrong about attacking and killing our brothers and sisters and they were wrong in Newark, New Jersey, and they were wrong in Louisiana, and the outright, every day oppressors and enemies are the people as a whole, the whites of this nation. So, we are not, according to the Holy Qur'an, to even as much as aid in passing a cup of water to the—even a wounded. I mean, this is in the Holy Qur'an, and as I said earlier, this is not me talking to get the draft board—or to dodge nothing. This is there before I was borned and it will be there when I'm dead but we believe in not only that part of it, but all of it.'

At another point he testified: (T)he Holy Qur'an do teach us that we do not take part of—in any part of war unless declared by Allah himself, or unless it's an Islamic World War, or a Holy War, and it goes as far—the Holy Qur'an is talking still, and saying we are not to even as much as aid the infidels or the nonbelievers in Islam, even to as much as handing them a cup of water during battle.'

'So, this is the teachings of the Holy Qur'an before I was born, and the Qur'an, we follow not only that part of it, but every part.' The Koran defines jihad as an injunction to the believers to war against non-believers: 2

'O ye who believe! Shall I guide you to a gainful trade which will save you from painful punishment? Believe in Allah and His Apostle and carry on warfare (jihad) in the path of Allah with your possessions and your persons. That is better for you. If ye have knowledge, He will forgive your sins, and will place you in the Gardens beneath which the streams flow, and in fine houses in the Gardens of Eden: that is the great gain.' M. Khadduri, War and Peace in the Law of Islam 55–56 (1955).

The Sale edition of the Koran, which first appeared in England in 1734, gives the following translation at 410–411 (9th ed. 1923):

'Thus God propoundeth unto men their examples. When ye encounter the unbelievers, strike off their heads, until ye have made a great slaughter among them; and bind them in bonds; and either give them a free dismission afterwards, or exact a ransom; until the war shall have laid down its arms. This shall ye do. Verily if God pleased he could take vengeance on them, without your assistance; but he commandeth you to fight his battles, that he may prove the one of you by the other. And as to those who fight in defence of God's true religion, God will not suffer their works to perish: he will guide them, and will dispose their heart aright; and he will lead them into paradise, of which he hath told them. O true believers, if ye assist God, by fighting for his religion, he will assist you against your enemies; and will set your feet fast. * * *'

War is not the exclusive type of jihad; there is action by the believer's heart, by his tongue, by his hands, as well as by the sword. War and Peace in the Law of Islam 56. As respects the military aspects it is written:

'The jihad, in other words, is a sanction against polytheism and must be suffered by all non-Muslims who reject Islam, or, in the case of the dhimmis (Scripturaries), refuse to pay the poll tax. The jihad, therefore, may be defined as the litigation between Islam and polytheism; it is also a form of punishment to be inflicted upon Islam's enemies and the renegades from the faith. Thus in Islam, as in Western Christendom, the jihad is the bellum justum.' Id., 59.

The jihad in the Moslem's counterpart of the 'just' war as it has been known in the West. 3 Neither Clay nor Negre should be subject to punishment because he will not renounce the 'truth' of the teaching of his respective church that wars indeed may exist which are just wars in which a Moslem or Catholic has a respective duty to participate.

What Clay's testimony adds up to is that he believes only in war as sanctioned by the Koran, that is to say, a religious war against nonbelievers. All other wars are unjust.

That is a matter of belief, of conscience, of religious principle. Both Clay and Negre were 'by reason of religious training and belief' conscientiously opposed to participation in war of the character proscribed by their respective religions. That belief is a matter of conscience protected by the First Amendment which Congress has no power to qualify or dilute as it did in § 6(j) of the Military Selective Service Act of 1967, 50 U.S.C. App. § 456(j) (1964 ed., Supp. V) when it restricted the exemption to those 'conscientiously opposed to participation in war in any form.' For the reasons I stated in Negre and in Gillette v. United States, 401 U.S. 437, 463 and 470, 91 S. Ct. 828, 843 and 846, 28 L.Ed.2d 168, that construction puts Clay in a class honored by the First Amendment, even though those schooled in a different conception of 'just' wars may find it quite irrational.

I would reverse the judgment below.

Mr. Justice HARLAN, concurring in the result.

I concur in the result on the following ground. The Department of Justice advice letter was at least susceptible of the reading that petitioner's proof of sincerity was insufficient as a matter of law because his conscientious objector claim had not been timely asserted. This would have been erroneous advice had the Department's letter been so read. Since the Appeals Board might have acted on such an interpretation of the letter, reversal is required under Sicurella v. United States, 348 U.S. 385, 75 S.Ct. 403, 99 L.Ed. 436 (1955).

1 The original judgment of affirmance, 397 F.2d 901, was set aside by this Court on a ground wholly unrelated to the issues now before us, sub nom. Giordano v. United States, 394 U.S. 310, 89 S. Ct. 1163, 22 L.Ed.2d 297. Upon remand, the Court of Appeals again affirmed the conviction. 430 F.2d 165.

2 The hearing officer was Judge Lawrence Grauman, who had served on a Kentucky circuit court for some 25 years.

3 Applicable regulations, 32 CFR § 1626.25 (1967 ed.), did not require that the hearing officer's report be transmitted to the Appeal Board, and the Government declined to disclose it to the petitioner. The statements in text are taken from the description of that report in the letter of advice from the Department of Justice, recommending denial of the petitioner's claim.

4 Brief for the United States 12.

5 'We do not here seek to support the denial of petitioner's claim on the ground of insincerity * * *.' Id., at 33. United States, 33.

1 As to the Court's analysis of Sicurella v. United States, 348 U.S. 385, 75 S. Ct. 403, 99 L. Ed. 436, and its application of Stromberg v. California, 283 U.S. 359, 51 S. Ct. 532, 75 L. Ed. 1117, little need be said. The Court is, of course, quite accurate if opposition to 'war in any form' as explained in Gillette v. United States, and Negre v. Larsen, 401 U.S. 437, 91 S. Ct. 828, 28 L.Ed.2d 168, is the law. But in my view the ruling in Gillette and Negre was unconstitutional. Hence of the three possible grounds on which the Board denied conscientious objector status, none was valid.

2 Koran 61:10–13 'War, then, is here an integral part of the legal system; for in accordance with the doctrine of the jihad, which is recognized as 'the peak of religion,' the Islamic commonwealth must be expanding, relentlessly, like a caravan continuously on the move, until it becomes coterminous with humanity, at which time war will have been transposed into universal peace.' A. Bozeman, The Future of Law in a Multicultural World 81–82 (1971).

3 The last attempt to use the jihad as a significant force was made in 1914 by the Ottoman sultan; but it failed and the jihad has fallen into disuse. See 1 A. Toynbee, Survey of International Affairs, 1925, p. 43 et seq. (1927); 8 Encyclopedia of the Social Sciences 401–403 (1932).

Source

Legal Information Institute,
www.law.cornell.edu/supremecourt/text/403/698.

BIBLIOGRAPHY

"50 Stunning Olympic Moments, No. 17: Cassius Clay Wins Gold in 1960," http://www.theguardian.com/sport/london-2013-olympics-blog/2012.

Ali, Muhammad with Richard Durham, *The Greatest: My Own Story*. New York: Random House, 1975.

Ali v. Division of State Athletic Commission, 308 F. Supp. 11 12 (S.D.N.Y. 1969).

ALI v. PLAYGIRL, INC. NO. 78 CIV. 445.447 F.Supp. 723 (1978).

Anderson, Dave. "Ali Regains Title, Flooring Foreman," *New York Times* (October 30, 1974), http://www.nytimes.com/books/98/10/25/specials/ali-foreman.html.

Anderson, Dave. "For Ali, What Price the Thrilla in Manila," *New York Times* (September 23, 1984), http://www.nytimes.com/books/98/10/25/specials/ali-price.html.

Berkow, Ira. Obituary, "Joe Elsby Martin, 80, Muhammad Ali's First Boxing Teacher," *New York Times* (September 17, 1996).

"*The Black Scholar* Interviews Muhammad Ali" *The Black Scholar* (June, 1970).

"Boxing was Allah's Way of Getting Me Fame to Do Something Bigger," *Emirates 24/7* (September 18, 2009).

Brennan, Michael. "Ali and His Educators," *Sports Illustrated* (September 22, 1980), http://sportsillustrated.cnn.com/vault/article/magazine/MAG1148116/index.htm.

"Bush Presents Ali with Presidential Medal of Freedom," *Associated Press* (November 14, 2005), http://sports.espn.go.com/sports/boxing/news/story?id=2219166.

Carlson, Peter. "Gorgeous George Tutors Cassius Clay," *American History* Vol. 46, Issue 5 (December, 2011).

Carpenter, Frank G. "A Kentucky Gladiator: General Cassius M. Clay Talks of His Duels and Fights," *St. Louis Globe-Democrat*, published in the Sacramento *Record-Union* (November 14, 1891), http://bowieknifefightsfighters.blogspot.com/2011/11/03cassius-marcellus-clay.

Cassius Marcellus Clay also known as Muhammad Ali, Petitioner v. United States 403 U.S. 698 (1971).

Chafe, William H. *Civilities and Civil Rights: Greensboro, North Carolina and the Black Struggle for Freedom*. New York: Oxford University Press, 1980.

Christian, Margena A. "Muhammad Ali vs George Foreman: Rumble in the Jungle 40 Years Later," *Ebony* (May, 2014), p. 130.

Cleaver, Eldridge. *Soul on Ice*. New York: Dell, 1968.

Coy, Daniel Bennett. "Imagining Dissent: Muhammad Ali, Daily Newspapers, and the State, 1966–1971," Master's Thesis, University of Tennessee, 2004.

Daniels, Nick. "A Legend in the Making: Cassius Clay's Madison Bouts," *The Badger Herald* (April 24, 2014).

de Tocqueville, Alexis. *Journal Entry* from his visit to Ohio (December 2, 1831), http://www.tocqueville.org/oh.htm.

"Declassified NSA Files Show Agency Spied on Muhammad Ali and MLK," *Guardian* (September 26, 2013), http://www.theguardian.com/world/2013/sep/26/nsa-surveillance-anti-vietnam- muhammad-ali-mlk.

"Disreputable if Not Outright Illegal: National Security Agency versus Martin Luther King, Muhammad Ali, Art Buchwald, Frank Church et al.," *National Security Archive* (November 14, 2008), http://www2.gwu.edu/~nsarchiv/NSAEBB/NSAEBB441/.

Dundee, Angelo with Bert Randolph Sugar. *My View from the Corner: A Life in Boxing* (New York: McGraw-Hill, 2008).

Eastman, Dick. "Muhammad Ali's Irish Heritage," http://www.irishculturalsociety.com/essaysandmisc/muhammadali.html.

Edwards, Harry. *The Revolt of the Black Athlete*. Berkeley: University of California Press, 1969.

Eisen, Lou. "The Redemption of Muhammad Ali," *Fight Network* (June 25, 2013), http://fightnetwork.com/news/39470:the-redemption-of-muhammad-ali/.

Eyes on the Prize II Interviews: Angelo Dundee (March 28, 1989), http://digital.wustl.edu/e/eii/eiiweb/dun5427.0117.040angelodundee.html.

Eyes on the Prize II Interviews: Edwin Pope (June 19, 1989), http://digital.wustl.edu/e/eii/eiiweb/pop5427.0310.131edwinpope.html.

Eyes on the Prize Interviews: Herbert Muhammad (June 4, 1989), http://digital.wustl.edu/e/eii/eiiweb/muh5427.0439.116marc_record_interviewee_process.html.

Ezra, Michael. "Muhammad Ali's Main Bout: African American Economic Power and the World Heavyweight Title," avery.cofc.edu/wpcontent/uploads/2012/08/Charleston-Ali.pdf.

Farred, Grant. *What's My Name? Black Vernacular Intellectuals*. Minneapolis: University of Minnesota Press, 2003.

"Fighting for Respect: MMA's Struggle for Acceptance and How the Muhammad Ali Act Would Give it a Sporting Chance," *West Virginia Law Review* Vol. 112 (2009).

Gilmore, Mikal. "How Muhammad Ali Conquered Fear and Changed the World" *Men's Journal* (November, 2011), http://www.mensjournal.com/magazine/how-muhammad-ali-conquered-fear-and-changed-the-world-20130205.

Golden Gloves of America Official Website, http://goldengloves.com.welcome.

Gorn, Elliott J., ed. *Muhammad Ali: The People's Champ*. Urbana and Chicago: University of Illinois Press, 1997.

Gorsevski, Ellen W. and Michael L. Butterworth. "Muhammad Ali's Fighting Words: The Paradox of Violence in Nonviolent Rhetoric," *Quarterly Journal of Speech* Vol. 97, No. 1 (February, 2011).

Gray, Tom. "Ferdie Pacheco recalls Muhammad Ali vs Joe Frazier II-40 Years Later," *The Ring*, http://ringtv.craveonline.com/news/315299-ferdie-pacheco-recalls-muhammad-ali-vs-joe-frazier-ii-40-years-later.

Haley, Alex. Interview with Cassius Clay, *Playboy* (October, 1964), http://www.alex-haley.com/alex_haley_cassius_clay_interview.htm.

Hauser, Thomas. *The Lost Legacy of Muhammad Ali*. Toronto: Sport Classic Books, 2005.

Hauser, Thomas. *Muhammad Ali: His Life and Times*. New York: Simon & Schuster, 1991.

"Henry Cooper vs Cassius Clay: The Punch that (Almost) Changed the World," *Daily Mail* (London), http://www.dailymail.co.uk/sport/othersports/article1382819/Henry-Cooper-v-Cassius-Clay-The-punch-changed-world.html.

Hoffer, Richard. "Joe Frazier 1944–2011," *Sports Illustrated* (November 11, 2011), http://sportsillustrated.cnn.com/vault/topic/article/Joe_Frazier/1900–01–01/2100–12–31/dd/index.htm.

Horn, Huston. "The 400,000 Bellyache," *Sports Illustrated* (November 23, 1964), http://www.si.com/vault/article/magazine/MAG1076631/index.htm.

Horn, Huston. "The Eleven Men Behind Cassius Clay," *Sports Illustrated* (March 11, 1963), http://si.com/vault/article/magazine/MAG1074600/index.htm.

Horn, Huston. "Fast Talk and a Slow Fight," *Sports Illustrated* (July 31, 1961), http://sportsillustrated.cnn.com/vault/article/magazine/MAG1072828/2/index.htm.

Horn, Huston. "Who Made Me—is Me," *Sports Illustrated* (September 25, 1961), http://www.cnnsi.com/vault/article/magazine/MAG1073035/2/index.htm.

Howard, Gregory Allen, "The Power of Dreams . . . In Louisville," http://www.gregoryallenhoward.com/powerofdreams.html.

Jenkins, Sally. "The Mouth that Roared," *Smithsonian* Vol. 44, Issue 10 (February, 2014).

Kane, Martin. "A Muslim Ministers to a Southpaw," *Sports Illustrated* (September 19, 1966), http://sportsillustrated.cnn.com/vault/article/magazine/MAG1079034/index.htm.

Kiger, Patrick. "Muhammad Ali's Speech at Howard University 1967," http://blogs.weta.org/boundarystones/2014/04/14/muhammad-alis-speech- howard-university-1967.

Kindred, Dave. *Sound and Fury.* New York: Free Press, 2006.

King, Jr., Martin Luther. "Beyond Vietnam: A Time to Break Silence," Speech to Clergy and Laity Concerned delivered at Riverside Church (April 4, 1967), http://www.hartford-hwp.com/archives/45a/058.html.

Kram, Mark. "After Muhammad, A Graveyard," *Sports Illustrated* (April 3, 1967), http://sportsillustrated.cnn.com/vault/article/magazine/MAG1079695/2/index.htm.

Kram, Mark. "The Champ Looked Like a Chump," *Sports Illustrated* (May 10, 1976), http://www.si.com/vault/1976/05/10/616347/the-champ-looked-like-a-chump.

Kram, Mark. "One Nighter in San Juan," *Sports Illustrated* (March 1, 1976), http://www.si.com/vault/1976/03/01/559159/one-nighter-in-san-juan.

Kram, Mark. "They Have Kept Him in Stitches," *Sports Illustrated* (March 24, 1975), http://www.si.com/vault/1975/03/24/576616/they-have-kept-him-in-stitches.

Lipsyte, Robert. "Clay Refuses Army Oath: Stripped of Boxing Crown," *New York Times* (April 28, 1967), http://www.nytimes.com/books/98/10/25/specials/ali- army.html.

Lipsyte, Robert. "Clay Wins Title in Seventh-Round Upset As Liston is Halted by Shoulder Injury," *New York Times* (February 26, 1964), http://www.nytimes.com/books/98/10/25/specials/ali-upset.html.

Lipsyte, Robert. "Politics Wins in the Ring," *New York Times* (April 28, 1967), http://www.nytimes.com/packages/html/sports/year_in_sports/04.28.html.

Lipsyte, Robert. "Winner by a Decision," *Smithsonian* (February, 2004).

McIlvanney, Hugh. "When the Mountain Came to Muhammad," *Guardian* (March 9, 1971), http://www.theguardian.com/sport/2011/nov/08/joe-frazier-muhammad-ali-1971.

Malcolm X (with Alex Haley). *The Autobiography of Malcolm X.* New York: Ballantine Books, 1964.

Mano, D. Keith. "Still the Greatest," *National Review* Vol. 50, Issue 21 (November 9, 1998).

Marable, Manning. *Malcolm X: A Life of Reinvention.* New York: Viking, 2011.

Maraniss, David. *Rome 1960: The Olympics that Changed the World.* New York: Simon & Schuster, 2008.

Marqusee, Mike. *Redemption Song: Muhammad Ali and the Spirit of the Sixties.* London and New York: Verso, 2005.

Matthews, Les. "The 'Greatest One' Pays a Visit to the Amsterdam News," *Amsterdam News* (March 7, 1964).

Maule, Tex. "A Quick, Hard Right and a Needless Storm of Protest," *Sports Illustrated* (June 7, 1965), http://sportsillustrated.cnn.com/vault/article/magazine/MAG1077300/index.htm.

Maule, Tex. "The Baddest of All Looks Over the Universe," *Sports Illustrated* (February 15, 1965), http://sportsillustrated.cnn.com/vault/article/magazine/MAG1076902/index.htm.

Maule, Tex. "Cruel Ali With All the Skills," *Sports Illustrated* (February 13, 1967), http://si.com/vault/article/magazine/MAG1079523/1/index.htm.

Maule, Tex. "End of a Beautiful Friendship," *Sports Illustrated* (August 2, 1971), http://www.si.com/vault/1971/08/02/611673/end-of-a-beautiful-friendship.

Maule, Tex. "Got to Look Good to Allah," *Sports Illustrated* (November 29, 1971), http://www.si.com/vault/1971/11/29/613926/got-to-look-good-to-allah.

Maule, Tex. "Liston's Edge: A Lethal Left," *Sports Illustrated* (February 24, 1964), http://sports illustrated.ca/vault/article/magazine/MAG1075666/index.htm

Maule, Tex. "The Sting of the Louisville Lip," *Sports Illustrated* (February 17, 1964), http://sports illustrated.cnn.com/vault/article/magazine/MAG1075646/3/index.htm.

Mee, Bob. "Fight Night in Great Tradition," *Telegraph* (December 8, 2005), http://www.telegraph.co.uk/sport/othersports/boxing/2369432/Fight-night-in-great-tradition.html.

Meltsner, Michael. "Me and Muhammad," *Marquette Sports Law Review* Vol. 12, Issue 2 (Spring, 2002).

Memorandum, Federal Bureau of Investigation, "Nation of Islam," www.columbia.edu/cu/. . ./071659hthp-transcript.pdf.

Mitchell, Kevin. "We're Still in Awe of Muhammad Ali and George Foreman, 34 Years On," *Guardian* (October 30, 2009), http://www.theguardian.com/sport/blog/2009/oct/30/muhammad-ali-george- foreman.

"Muhammad Ali Boxing Reform Act," https://www.govtrack.us/congress/bills/106/hr1832/text.

"Muhammad Ali was Great, but not the Greatest," *New York Amsterdam News* (December 19, 2002).

Muhammad Ali v. Connally, 266 Supp. 345: United States District Court S.D. Texas, Houston Division.

Muhammad Ali v. Division of State Athletic Commission of New York, No 69 Civ. 4867, 316 F. Supp. 1246 (1970).

Murray, Jim. "Ascent of a King," *Sports Illustrated* (June 7, 1965), http://sportsillustrated.cnn.com/vault/article/magazine/MAG1155947/index.htm.

Nack, William. "Muhammad Ali," *Sports Illustrated* (September 19, 1994), http://www.si.com/vault/1994/09/19/132063/1-muhammad-ali.

Newfield, Jack. "The Meaning of Muhammad," *The Nation* (February 4, 2002), http://www.thenation.com/article/meaning-muhammad.

Oates, Joyce Carol. "The Cruelest Sport," *The New York Review of Books* (February 13, 1992), http://www.nybooks.com/articles/archives/1992/feb/13/the-cruelest-sport/?page=2.

Oates, Joyce Carol. "Muhammad Ali: The Greatest," ESPN, *Sports Century*. New York: Hyperion, 1999. http://www.usfca.edu/jco/muhammadali/.

Olsen, Jack. "A Case of Conscience," *Sports Illustrated* (April 11, 1966), http://sportsillustrated.cnn.com/vault/article/magazine/MAG1078395/3/index.htm.

Olsen, Jack. "All Alone With the Future," *Sports Illustrated* (May 9, 1966), http://sportsillustrated.cnn.com/vault/article/magazine/MAG1078513/4/index.htm.

Olsen, Jack. *Black is Best*. New York: Putnam, 1967.

Olsen, Jack. "The Fight's Over, Joe," *Sports Illustrated* (September 30, 1996), http://www.si.com/vault/1996/09/30/208924/the-fights-over-joe-more-than-two-decades-after-they-last-met-in-the-ring-joe-frazier-is-still-taking-shots-at-muhammad-ali-but-this-time-its-a-war-of-words.

Olsen, Jack. "Growing Up Scared in Louisville," *Sports Illustrated* (April 18, 1966), http://sports illustrated.cnn.com/vault/article/magazine/MAG1078435/1/index.htm.

Olsen, Jack. "Learning Elijah's Advanced Lesson in Hate," *Sports Illustrated* (May 2, 1966) http://cnnsi.com/vault/article/magazine/MAG1078487/index.htm.

Quintana, Andres F. "Muhammad Ali: The Greatest in Court," *Marquette Sports Law Review* Vol. 18, Issue 1 (Fall, 2007).

PBS, "The American Experience," The Murder of Emmett Till, http://www.pbs.org/wgbh/amex/till/timeline/timeline2.html

Patterson, Floyd and Jack Mahon. "Cassius Clay Must be Beaten," *Sports Illustrated* (October 11, 1965), http://cnnsi.com/vault/article/magazine/MAG1077772/index.htm.

Plimpton, George. "No Requiem for a Heavyweight," *Sports Illustrated* (April 5, 1971), http://cnnsi.printthis.clickability.com/pt/cpt?expire=&title=The+filght.

Poinsett, Alex. "A Look at Cassius Clay: Biggest Mouth in Boxing," *Ebony* Vol. 188, No. 5 (March, 1963).

"Prizefighting: Feats of Clay" *TIME* (August 12, 1966), http://content.time.com/time/magazine/article/0,9171,842624,00.html.

Putnam, Pat. "One More Time to the Top," *Sports Illustrated* (September 25, 1978), http://archive.today/fUFK7#selection-451.53–454.0.

Remnick, David. *King of the World*. New York: Vintage, 1998.

Rhoden, William C. "In Ali's Voice from the Past, a Stand for the Ages," *New York Times* (June 20, 2013), http://www.nytimes.com/2013/06/21/sports/in-alis-voice-from-the-past-a-stand-for-the-ages.html?_r=0.

Rogin, Gilbert. "Campaign's End for an Ancient Warrior," *Sports Illustrated* (November 26, 1962), http://sportsillustrated.cnn.com/vault/article/magazine/MAG1074343/index.htm.

Rogin, Gilbert. "Cautious Comes of Age," *Sports Illustrated* (October 16, 1961), http://sportsillustrated.cnn.com/vault/article/magazine/MAG1073086/1/index.htm.

Rogin, Gilbert. "Champion as Long as He Wants," *Sports Illustrated* (November 29, 1965), http://sportsillustrated.cnn.com/vault/article/magazine/MAG1077948/index.htm.

Rogin, Gilbert. "The Facts About the Big Fight," *Sports Illustrated* (October 8, 1962), http://sportsillustrated.cnn.com/vault/article/magazine/MAG1147918/2/index.htm.

Rogin, Gilbert. "Not a Great Fight, But it Was a Real One," *Sports Illustrated* (December 6, 1965), http://sportsillustrated.cnn.com/vault/article/magazine/MAG1077979/1/index.htm.

Saeed, Amir. "What's in a Name? Muhammad Ali and the Politics of Cultural Identity," *Culture, Sport, and Society* Vol. 5, Issue 3 (Autumn, 2003).

Saraceno, Jon. "Caring for The Champ," *AARP Bulletin* Vol. 55, No. 5 (June, 2014), pp. 10–14.

Samuelson, Robert J. "LBJ Signs Draft Law Cutting Graduate 2-S," *The Harvard Crimson* (July 3, 1967), http://www.thecrimson.com/article/1967/7/3/lbj-signs-draft-law-cutting-graduate/.

Schaap, Dick. "Cassius Clay Almost Says He's a Muslim," *Amsterdam News* (January 25, 1964).

Schaap, Dick. "The Challenger & the Muslim," *New York Herald Tribute* (January 23, 1964), http://thestacks.deadspin.com/the-challenger-and-the-muslims- 1428091998.

Schaap, Dick. "From Louisville to the Nation of Islam: My Ups and Downs With Ali," *Sport Magazine* (1971), http://thestacks.deadspin.com/from-louisville-to-the-nation-of-islam-my-ups-and-down-1428081378.

Schreiner, Bruce. "Muhammad Ali's Childhood Friends Reflect On His Early Days," *Huffington Post* (January 10, 2012).

Shapiro, Peter. "Freshman Deferments End as Nixon Signs New Draft Legislation," *The Harvard Crimson* (September 29, 1971), http://www.thecrimson.com/article/1971/9/29/freshman-deferments-end-as-nixon-signs/.

Silver, Michael. "Where Were You on March 8, 1971?" *ESPN Classic* (November 19, 2003), http://espn.go.com/classic/s/silver_ali_frazier.html.

Smith, Gary. "A Celebration of Muhammad Ali," *Sports Illustrated* (November 15, 1989).

Smith, Maureen. "*Muhammad Speaks* and Muhammad Ali: Intersections of the Nation of Islam and Sport in the 1960s," *International Sports Studies* Vol. 21, No. 1 (2001).

"Sonny Liston-From the Big House to the Big Time," http://sports.jrank.org/pages/2863/Liston-Sonny-From-Big-House-Big-Time.html.

Tauber, Peter. "Ali: Still Magic," *New York Times* (July 17, 1988), http://www.nytimes.com/books/98/10/25/specials/ali-magic.html.

Tosches, Nick. *The Devil and Sonny Liston* (Boston: Little, Brown, 2000).

Vecsey, George. "At 39, Ali Has More Points to Prove," *New York Times* (November 29, 1981), http://www.nytimes.com/1981/11/29/sports/at-39-ali-has-more-points-to-prove.htm.

Ward, Nathan. "A Total Eclipse of the Sonny," *American Heritage* Vol. 57, Issue 5 (October, 2006).

Wilkes, David. "Welcome Back to Ireland, Muhammad O'Ali: Boxing Legend Thrills 10,000 With Visit to Home of his Irish Great Grandfather," *Mail Online* (September 2, 2009), http://www.dailymail.co.uk/news/article-1210524/Muhammad-Ali-freeman-ancestral-home-Ireland.html.

Wright, Branson. "Remembering Cleveland's Muhammad Ali Summit, 45 Years Later," *Cleveland Plain Dealer* (June 3, 2012), http://www.cleveland.com/sports/index.ssf/2012/06/gathering_of_stars.html.

Zabarauskas, Bruce J. "The Regulation of Professional Boxing in New York," New *York Law Journal* Vol. 243, No. 23 (February 4, 2010),http://www.tklaw.com/files/Publication/ff079023–6589–4533-bfaa-a328ce9c2883/Presentation/PublicationAttachment/0a687b59-bc8a-45cf-901e-b126643155d6/The-Regulation-of-Professional-Boxing-in-New-York.pdf.

Ziegel, Vic. "Ali, Spinks, and the Battle of New Orleans," *New York Magazine* (October 2, 1978), http://nymag.com/news/sports/48897/.

Zirin, David. "The Hidden History of Muhammad Ali," *International Socialist Review* Issue 33 (January–February, 2004), http://www.isreview.org/issues/33/muhammadali.shtml.

Zirin, David. "Knocked the Hell out by 'The Trials of Muhammad Ali," *The Nation.com* (August 17, 2013), http://www.thenation.com/blog/175804/knocked-hell-out- trials-muhammad-ali.

Zirin, David. "The Revolt of the Black Athlete: The Hidden History of Muhammad Ali," *International Socialist Review* Issue 33 (January–February, 2004), http://www.isreview.org/issues/33/muhammadali.shtml.

Zirin, David. "Rumble, Young Man, Rumble: Muhammad Ali and the 1960s," http://daily-struggles.tumblr.com/post/16010802743/rumble-young-man-rumble- muhammad-ali-and-the-1960s.

Zirin, David. *What's My Name, Fool? Sports and Resistance in the United States*. Chicago: Haymarket Books, 2005.

INDEX